News Media in the Arab World

ITJOUR
1300
0023

News Media in the Arab World

A study of 10 Arab and Muslim countries

**EDITED BY
BARRIE GUNTER
AND ROGER DICKINSON**

B L O O M S B U R Y

NEW YORK · LONDON · NEW DELHI · SYDNEY

Bloomsbury Academic

An imprint of Bloomsbury Publishing Plc

1385 Broadway	50 Bedford Square
New York	London
NY 10018	WC1B 3DP
USA	UK

www.bloomsbury.com

First published 2013

Library of Congress Cataloging-in-Publication Data
News media in the Arab world: a study of 10 Arab and
Muslim countries / edited by Barrie Gunter and Roger Dickinson.
pages cm
Includes bibliographical references and index.
ISBN 978-1-4411-1407-5 (hardcover: alk. paper) –
ISBN 978-1-4411-7466-6 (pbk.: alk. paper)   1. Journalism –
Arab countries.   2. Press – Arab countries.   3. Television broadcasting of news –
Arab countries.   4. Broadcast journalism – Arab countries.
5. Reporters and reporting – Arab countries.   6. Journalism – Objectivity –
Arab countries.   7. Mass media – Arabic countries.   I. Gunter,
Barrie editor of compilation.   II. Dickinson, Roger 1956 – editor of compilation.
PN5359.N49 2013
073.927–dc23
2012050838

ISBN: HB: 978-1-4411-1407-5
PB: 978-1-4411-7466-6
e-PDF: 978-1-4411-0239-3
e-Pub: 978-1-4411-4488-1

Typeset by Newgen Imaging Systems Pvt Ltd, Chennai, India
Printed and bound in the United States of America

Contents

About the contributors

The contributors comprise academic members of staff at the Department of Media and Communication, University of Leicester and a number of Arab authors who are current (Al-Shaikh,) or recent (Al-Jaber, Al-Rawi, Elareshi, Mohammed, Nussibeh) students at the department. Three of the latter (Al-Shaikh, Elareshi, Mohammed) are academics in their own countries where they teach about media and communication, and the other two (Al-Jaber, Nuseibeh) are journalists. The writing team therefore embraces experienced academic authors and members with specialist knowledge of media in the Arab world.

Khalid Al-Jaber is the research director of *The Peninsula*, an Arabic daily newspaper in Qatar. Al-Jaber's interest and expertise are in communication research spanning a wide range of areas from global media organizations to international communication, mass media in Middle East and Arab Gulf region, and public diplomacy. He studied for his PhD at the Department of Media and Communication, University of Leicester between 2009 and 2012.

Ebrahim Abdulrahman Al-Shaikh is a PhD student of Media in the Department of Media and Communication, University of Leicester. He has also been employed as a journalist by *Akbhar Al-Kaleej*, an Arabic daily newspaper in Bahrain. He is interested in political and cultural communication issues in the Middle East, particularly in the Arab Gulf region.

Vincent Campbell is a lecturer in the Department of Media and Communication. He is the author of *Information Age Journalism: Journalism Studies in International Context* (Arnold, 2004) and has written journal articles, books chapters and other publications on journalism and political communication. Among his specialist areas of interest are international political communication and the relationship between journalism, new media and politics.

Roger Dickinson is a Senior Lecturer in the Department of Media and Communication at the University of Leicester. His research interests include the sociology of journalists and journalism, the study of media audiences and the media and health. His most recent work on journalists and journalism has appeared in *Journalism Studies, Cultural Sociology, Journalism, Theory, Practice and Criticism* and *The Routledge Companion to Journalism Studies* (edited by Stuart Allan).

Mokhtar Elareshi obtained his PhD at the Department of Media and Communication, University of Leicester in 2012. His thesis was based on research on the impact of international satellite TV news services on the consumption of indigenous news services in Libya. He has taught at the University of Libya, Tripoli.

Barrie Gunter is a Professor of Mass Communication, Department of Media and Communication. He is an author of 50 books and more than 250 journal articles, book chapters and other publications on media, marketing and management issues. Among his specialist areas of interest are media audiences, new media developments and the impact of news.

Julian Matthews is a Lecturer in the Department of Media and Communication at the University of Leicester. He is the Communication and Media Section Editor for the international journal *Sociology Compass* and is a Convenor of the British Sociological Association Media Study Group. His research interests include the production of news, journalism and its representations of health, the environment and other social issues. He has published work in a range of academic journals.

Hamza Mohammed obtained his PhD from the Department of Media and Communication, University of Leicester in 2008. He has worked as a journalist and in public relations in the Middle East and currently teaches at the University of Sharjah. His research interests centre on news and agenda-setting.

Zaki Hasan Nuseibeh is a Palestinian journalist, teacher and writer. He has worked in the Palestinian news industry since 1974. He holds a BA degree in Arabic Language and Literature from the Hebrew University in Jerusalem and an MA in Mass Communications from the University of Leicester.

1

The Changing Nature of News and the Arab World

Barrie Gunter and Roger Dickinson

News markets are evolving dramatically in the Middle East and across North Africa. The emergence of the internet and of satellite television (TV) news channels has changed the media landscape in these countries and provided new media experiences for the indigenous populations. New media have been embraced in particular by younger people in the Arab world. These changes have implications for the way news businesses are run and regulated in the region. They have created greater competition for audiences and placed some established news providers under threat. These initial tasters have whetted public news appetites across the Arab world and created a hunger for less parochial news coverage. Whether this is seen as good or not varies between countries. The news is important to Arab populations, but the question of what now constitutes valued news has become more open as wider choices of news have been made available.

Even though the media landscape in Arab world has changed dramatically since the end of the twentieth century, characterized in particular by the emergence of TV satellite channels and penetration of the Internet, there is still a disjunction between the promises carried by these technology developments and the realities of Arab politics and societies (Amin, 2001). One media typology has distinguished between the mobilized press controlled by government, loyalist press that is privately owned yet loyal to the current government and therefore succumbs to direct or indirect government censorship, and a diverse press that can operate with relative freedom (Rugh, 1979). Until the 1990s, the Arab press tended mostly to fall into the category of a mobilized press although some news operations could be conceived as loyalist (Hafez, 2001). Thus, the mass media have remained under the tight control of Arab governments. In general, in this region, the media have been little more than extensions of government information ministries (Rugh, 2004). It remains to be seen how far this will change in those Arab countries that experienced political revolutions in 2011. These actions were driven often by young people who utilized digital technologies to organize protests and publicize them to the outside world. When their governments closed down even more tightly on media news operations, individual activists created their own news channels via blogging, microblogging and social media sites on the internet (see Diamond, 2012).

There are disparities within Arab countries in respect of the availability or accessibility of media among their citizens. Digital divides exist based on hierarchical social and economic structures that distinguish sub-groups of Arab societies. Income status is also linked to educational level and literacy which, in turn, can create further media divides. These societal divisions run deeper in some Arab countries than in others. Wherever they exist, however, they exert critical influences over the use of different media – both traditional and new. They can also contribute to knowledge gaps between different social factions within Arab societies (Rugh, 2004).

Despite these digital divides, for some observers the emergence of new news providers on satellite TV platforms and the speed with which they have been embraced by Arab peoples are posing serious threats to the authoritarian control of their governments (El-Nawawy and Iskander, 2002; Mernissi, 2007). For the first time, news media in this region have begun to represent a type of 'fourth estate' – an alternative source of political opinion from incumbent administrations (Hafez, 2006).

Early developments in Arab media

The earliest Arab press has been traced back to the early nineteenth century with *Al-Waqa'i al-Misreya* in 1828. Other publications followed including *Al-Mubashir* in 1848 (Algeria), *Al-Anba'* in 1858 (Lebanon), *Al-Ra'id* in 1860 (Tunisia), *Tarabulus al-Gharb* in 1864 (Libya), *Al-Zawra'* in 1869 (Iraq) and *San'a* in 1879 (Yemen). During the earliest years of the press, the Arab world experienced a number of occupations including Ottoman, French, British and Italian. Newspapers were largely propaganda instruments during these spells that represented the opinion of the ruling authorities. Even so, national press publications surfaced to represent the views and interests of the indigenous populations and as such played a significant part in the cultivation and establishment of Arab nationalism (Bakr et al., 1985).

During the twentieth century, the Arab press continued to play an important role in representing Arab political and cultural values. One significant characteristic of Arab newspapers and magazines is that they have tended to be privately owned and operated, although aligned with political factions or influential business figures with close government links. Government owned newspapers have also sat alongside those in private ownership in some Arab countries such as Algeria, Egypt, Iraq and Libya.

While government owned newspapers have been financially sheltered by the public purse, private publications have often struggled in the face of low circulation figures and high production costs. The choice of political allegiances could also make a difference to the prospects of newspapers in terms of public patronage and favourable treatment by governments (Bakr et al., 1985). The critical delimiting factor with regard to the influence of the printed press, however, has always been the widespread illiteracy rates in Arab countries.

Broadcasting was founded in the Arab world with the launch of the first radio stations in Algeria in 1925, Egypt in 1926 and Tunisia in 1935. Some of these initial services were privately owned and run on commercial models, although many were government owned and non-profit making. Some Arab countries depended upon Western governments to build their initial transmission networks which then operated under the control of outside broadcasting authorities. This arrangement occurred in Tunisia which received help from France in the construction of its radio transmission system. Despite the early appearance of commercial radio stations, the general preference in most Arab nations, as radio services were rolled out between the mid-1930s and early 1970s, was to avoid an advertising-funded model. Government authorities took control over radio networks, providing full funding support and in return expected to exert political control over content.

The potential power of radio was realized during the Egyptian revolution of the early 1950s when it emerged as the primary medium to reach the masses. It was not restricted in its influence by the illiteracy rates of the population and provided news on latest developments more quickly than newspapers could manage. As more Arab states gained their independence from Western occupiers, radio was increasingly acknowledged by Arab governments as an important extension of the political public sphere (Bakr et al., 1985).

TV broadcasting in the Arab world began in the mid-1950s with government operated services in Morocco in 1954, Algeria, Iraq and Lebanon in 1956 and in other Arab countries over the next two decades. As with radio, the first TV stations were commercial, though subsequently most Arab states opted for a government controlled model (Boyd, 1999). Following the very first station launches, there were just a small number of experiments with commercial TV in Iraq, Morocco and Lebanon (Boyd, 1991; Boulos, 1996; Kraidy, 1998a,b). Hybrid stations were not unusual that were government controlled but also carried some advertising to raise additional revenue (Bakr et al., 1985). The only Arab territory to sustain commercial TV across the pre-satellite TV era was the Emirate of Dubai.

Broadcasters were subservient to government information ministries and news broadcasts were limited in terms of the types of news stories they reported and the formats adopted within the broadcasts themselves. Most news reporting comprised little more than talking heads against a simple studio set reporting positively on government policies and performance and events attended by heads of state and other leading officials (Sakr, 2000). At this time, TV was conceived as a national resource that could be utilized for the betterment of the nation. Most TV services were funded entirely by governments and were in consequence seen as an extension of them. The models for this type of broadcasting system derived from Britain and France where public service broadcasting operations were regarded as resources designed for the informational, educational and cultural enrichment of society (Ayish, 2001). The Arab world adopted a more autocratic version of this broadcasting ethos.

Already by the 1970s, Arab publics experienced some exposure to Western media that frequently drew unfavourable comparisons for indigenous news programming that was clearly poorly resourced and of lower quality in terms of production standards and journalism (Ayish, 2001). During the 1980s and 1990s, public sector broadcasting in the western world also faced growing competition from new private broadcasting operations that were unconstrained by government-imposed public sector broadcasting requirements (Achilles and Miege, 1994). These services operated via technology platforms such as cable and satellite that were not controlled by government regulators as terrestrial transmission system had been.

By 1991, even the Arab world had its first taste of satellite TV when London-based Middle East Broadcasting Centre (MBC) established a footprint in the Middle East. Arab audiences sought out satellite dishes, even in those countries where initially they were banned. This meant that they could obtain reception of international satellite news broadcasts and circumvent traditional government censorship of such exposure. Arab governments recognized that they could not prevent their citizens from gaining access to news uploaded from outside their national borders and realized instead that they must compete with their own versions of these news channels (Alterman, 1998).

Over the last decade of the twentieth century, therefore, further Arab-owned and operated satellite TV services followed including Al-Jazeera that was launched in 1996 (Kraidy, 1998a). Initially, these government-controlled satellite TV news services were still utilized – as previous news vehicles had been – as propaganda tools. Exposure to non-Arab channels led Arab audiences to question the diversity and quality of news provision both in terms of news content and presentation formats (Ghareeb, 2000). Eventually, as more privately owned and operated satellite TV services emerged, some Arab states, especially in the Gulf region, recognized these wider audience needs and relaxed some editorial controls allowing these services to enjoy greater freedom. We examine the reasons for this later in this chapter.

The growth of commercial TV in the Arab world provided audiences with a greater diversity of programming and more especially eventually made available new formats for news presentation (Ayish, 2001). The adoption of satellite technology has been central to the expansion of news provision in the Middle East and North Africa (Amin and Boyd, 1994; Barkey, 1996; Schleifer, 1998; Sakr, 1999).

Although rapid expansion of satellite TV took place after 1995, it was nearly 20 years earlier when the first seeds were sown politically for a satellite broadcasting system at around the time of the formation of the Arab States Broadcasting Union (ASBU) in 1969 (Boyd, 1999). Subsequently, the Arab Satellite Communications Organization (ARABSAT) became established in 1976 with most finance originating from its wealthiest partner, Saudi Arabia. The first satellite with an Arab world footprint was successfully put into orbit in 1985 (ARABSAT 1-B) (Amin and Boyd, 1994). The latter was switched off in 1993, but further satellites (2-A and 2-B) were placed in geostationary orbits over the Middle East in 1996. A further generation satellite (3-A) was established in 1999 (Kraidy, 2002).

The significance of the First Gulf War

The 1991 Gulf War in which allied forces launched a military attack on Saddam Hussein's Iraq to force its withdrawal from occupation of Kuwait introduced a new style of news coverage of war and according to some writers provided the catalyst that triggered significant media developments within the Arab world (Ghareeb, 2000; Mellor, 2007). At least 1,400 journalists from around the world were stationed in the Gulf states during the build-up to the war, with many working for pan-national satellite TV operators (Gantz, 1993). The reporting of the 1991 Gulf War established TV as the primary news medium of that era (O'Heffernan, 1993).

Unlike previous conflicts in Vietnam and the Falklands, mass publics all over the world were furnished with live, on-site reports of the action as journalists became 'embedded' with the military and were able to report and film from the front line. CNN emerged as a key player in this setting. Its feeds provided from within Iraq enabled it to become a primary supplier of film and narrative for other longer established news brands. The public were transformed from passive recipients of historical accounts relayed via asynchronous reporting, so characteristic of previous war reporting, to eyewitnesses who could keep abreast of the latest events no matter which time zone they lived in.

Following this conflict, news media mushroomed across the Arab world both on a local and pan-national scale. Such developments were manifest in terms of new national and local newspapers and more specially satellite TV channels. The new channels with a news focus adopted formats that modelled in many ways the services offered by CNN (Mellor, 2005). Not only were there more newspapers, but also many newspapers that pre-dated the 1991 conflict grew bigger. The news menu expanded such that not only was there more 'hard' news about serious issues, but also more 'soft' news such as human interest stories. The emergence of a more diverse news agenda again signalled an influence of western media on the editorial decisions of Arab newsmakers.

The role modelling impact of Western journalistic practices was further mediated via Arab journalists who learned their trade in the west or in Arab journalism schools with Western orientations (Ayish, 2001). Furthermore, western news providers such as the British Broadcasting Corporation (BBC), CNN and National Broadcasting Company (NBC) launched their own Arab language news services (Mellor, 2007).

The evolving news landscape in the Arab world

Journalism in the Arab world evolved through a number of stages even before the digital technology developments of the New Millennium era emerged. Mellor (2007) invoked Bourdieu's field theory to explain the genesis of Arab news media systems and their integration with existing political, economic and social settings within Arab nations. Status differences emerged between print and broadcast media for the journalists working in them. TV journalists in the Arab world might develop a high public profile but enjoy lesser professional status than their print counterparts because of the historical standing of each medium.

Field theory articulates the different domains within which organizational practices of a specific business sector, such as news media can develop and establish their own niche positions. With news, in addition to the traditional differentiation between print and broadcast, further distinctions can be drawn on the basis of geographical or market scale – local, national, international. Variances can occur across the 'fields' in terms of the social and cultural capital practitioners can accrue among their audiences or markets and their peer groups. The capital or status acquired by journalists can also vary with the developmental stage of the nation state within which they work. The latter can mediate the degree of influence they have and the nature of that influence, as defined in political or social terms. In some countries, journalists of high status, can influence or shape public opinion on issues. In others, professional practice constraints or simply the extant political milieu restricts or prevents this type of influence from emerging.

Mellor (2007) argued that one type of analysis that is needed of Arab journalism is one that attempts to articulate and understand the extent to which news media influence social and political changes in this part of the world. Given the events of the so-called Arab Spring in 2011, this analysis would seem to be of paramount importance.

The evolution of Arab media, however, has not just represented a response to changing political and social values and structures across the Middle East and North Africa (MENA), it also reflects an influence of changes in journalism practice in the Western world and the infiltration of Arab news markets by non-Arab news suppliers, particularly those operating on satellite TV platforms. Global news operators such as the BBC and CNN have left their mark on news audiences in the MENA region and perhaps more importantly on Arab news professionals themselves. The importance of these international news operators on the world scene, and especially of CNN, became acutely apparent during the first Gulf Conflict involving Iraq in 1990–1.

'Arab' identity and news media

Arab news media have developed both within and across nation states since before the era of satellite technology and the Internet. Media systems have not all developed at the same pace within Arab countries and the prevalence in the first instance of the press was associated with levels of literacy (Tash, 1983). Broadcasting of news also emerged for different reasons across Arab nations. In Saudi Arabia, for instance, it represented a response from government to growing popularity of foreign programmes (Sreberny-Mohammadi, 1998).

Despite the many local news media developments that surfaced across the twentieth century, there was a sense for a long time that journalism could play a part in defining a regional pan-Arab identity (Mellor, 2005). This challenge has been taken up more recently by Al-Jazeera. The Qatar-based satellite TV service has aspirations, however, not simply to cultivate this identity across the Arab world, but to project it beyond as a news provider that sits side by side with established global brands such as the BBC and CNN.[1] The prominence of Al-Jazeera, however, has led to it often overshadowing other important developments in analyses of news media in the Arab world (Armbrust, 2005; Guaaybess, 2008). Widespread political, economic and social developments in the Arab world have combined with technological developments to drive changes to its media structures and providers and these must be seen as being more diverse than the emergence of a single, high profile satellite TV news service (Ayish and Sakr, 2010).

Al-Jazeera superseded earlier local news media by demonstrating the kind of news coverage that could be achieved when broadcasters were freed from the shackles of government censorship. Following the example set by CNN during the first Gulf war, the Qatar-based channels provided real-time coverage that drew in news consumers and rendered them eyewitnesses to events almost as they happened. This sort of coverage was difficult for government operated channels where cautious owners wished to pre-check content before allowing it to be broadcast (Horan, 2010). With fast-moving events involving conflicts that could affect Arab citizens own security and quality of life, it was clearly advantageous to have access to a news source that could provide up-to-the-minute breaking news reports.

Attempts to create a pan-Arab identity have not been straightforward and have enjoyed limited and, sometimes only temporary impact. In relation to these attempts involving news media, this difficulty of achieving success stems from the diverse and heterogeneous nature of Arab audiences from different Arab countries. Tribal differences and local dialects mean that localized news interests remain paramount despite shared concerns about issues such as the Israel–Palestine conflict that frequently embrace the world stage. Language variations across Arab states not only interfere with the ability of pan-Arab audiences to follow the news that is transmitted in one dominant form of Arabic, but are also with local cultural identities that underpin distinctive localized news preferences (Suleiman, 2003).

Challenges to establishing an effective pan-Arab news identity

If a common pan-Arab standard for journalism is to emerge it will be essential, first of all, to identify where the relevant commonalities of interest and concerns in terms of news issues can be found and what are the common-alities of acceptance of different styles of news delivery across the MENA region. Then, there is a separate consideration of the impact of established global news players from the Western world that operates Arab news ser-vices of their own. Should Arab-originated news services seek to compete head-on with the BBC and CNN or should they seek to offer something differ-ent? One observation has been that while western Arab news services cover Arab world news stories, they do so in a manner that adopts Western values in the way certain events are interpreted. Thus, competing Arab news ser-vices might report these same events and use similar production techniques, but place stories in a different cultural frame and one more consonant with Arab sensibilities and values (Ezzi, 2004; Mellor, 2007).[2]

Another important aspect of pan-Arab news reporting is that it is invariably originated and uplinked from a single Arab country that will often have its own political agenda. One consequence of this factor is that the service will steer clear of being critical about its own country. This observation has been made about Al-Jazeera in relation to its host country, Qatar (Zayani, 2005).[3]

Social divisions and the rewards that are available to journalists in differ-ent media may also influence the nature of news provision and where these vary in magnitude between Arab countries can undermine the establishment of a pan-Arab news identity. Broadcast journalism is often more lucrative than print journalism and hence the flow of talent tends to be unidirectional. Although the status of print might once have been sufficient to ensure talent retention, this factor is not always sufficient today.

Another factor is the differential social and political status of men and women in the Arab world. More women are training and working as journal-ists in the Arab news media than ever before. Many have complained however that they do not enjoy the same status as their male counterparts. The social status differentials that characterize their domestic lives also permeate the workplace for women journalists (Mellor, 2007). Nevertheless, some female journalists working for TV news broadcasters have acquired role model status among the general public for their own gender and represent female ideals for men in their audiences (Mellor, 2007).

Some investigators have found that women journalists in the Arab world are often better educated than male counterparts and that female journal-ism students outnumber males in many journalism schools (Wright, 2004). Despite their higher credentials, women journalists remain insecure about their chances of career progression as compared to their male colleagues (Al-Qadry and Harb, 2002). This perception has been borne out by audits of the distributions of male to female journalists in senior positions in news media organizations (Sakr, 2001). Furthermore, when women do achieve senior positions, these are often restricted to specialist areas of reporting deemed to be appropriate for their gender, such as women's or children's issues (Abdel Rahman, 2002).

Although satellite TV has opened up the airwaves across the Arab world compared with the pre-satellite era, Arab governments still retain a significant level of control over media uplinked from within their national borders. It has also been noted that some Arab countries display different standards in terms of tolerance of political criticism, allowing satellite news operators greater latitude to be critical of other Arab nations while still constraining this coverage in respect of the treatment of the national government (Kraidy, 1999).

The real challenges for privately operated news media are economic ones. Government operated broadcasters have the security of reliance on considerable government funding. Commercial services must compete for funding in an increasingly crowded open marketplace. Furthermore, across much of the Arab world, the advertising industry has not yet reached a level of maturity to provide levels of income needed to sustain state-of-the-art news gathering and reporting facilities. The absence of reliable market research data also means there is no currency available to measure the effectiveness of advertisements aired on broadcast platforms (Fakhreddine, 2000).

Audiences and pan-Arab news provision

As noted earlier, the 1991 Gulf War opened the eyes of the world and Arab audiences to a different style of conflict reporting. The CNN provided attention-grabbing, live coverage of rocket attacks and bombing of Baghdad and of events at the frontline once the land-based allied military invasion of Iraq was underway. For Arab audiences, this type of coverage, broadcast into their homes from outside their national frontiers provided a type of news that was unconstrained by their governments. It generated a hunger for more coverage of this type (Ayish and Qassim, 1995; Ghareeb, 2001; Semati, 2001). It triggered a demand for satellite TV. This appetite for new services was fuelled also by the fact that government-controlled or privately own loyal news operations were for a long time characterized by narrowly defined, carefully scripted newscasts that focused on coverage of the head of state, government announcements and events (Alterman, 1998; Ayish, 2002).

This demand was met by a range of services, including: (1) propagandist government-controlled TV channels; (2) private commercial channels that followed the style of western channels; and (3) reformist government-controlled channels that modeled key aspects of Western-style channels though were

funded still by ruling authorities (Ayish, 2002). The hunger among Arab publics for news services in their own language that offer the range and quality of news provision observed on international TV channels located in the west such as the BBC and CNN provided the right climate of interest for the launch of new more liberal TV news services in that region (Ayish, 2002).

When it was launched in 1996 Al-Jazeera saw an opportunity to fill this newly emergent news market in the Arab world. After the events of 11 September 2001, it became the highest profile satellite TV news channel of the Arab world. Privately owned and operated from within Qatar, it provides a service of rolling and regularly update news interspersed with other factual programmes, modelled to a significant extent on the BBC's world news service and CNN. Indeed, many initial recruits to the staff of Al-Jazeera were former employees of the defunct BBC's Arabic channel (Sakr, 2005). By 2009, over half (55%) of a sample of adults from six Arab countries (Egypt, Jordan, Lebanon, Morocco, Saudi Arabia and United Arab Emirates) identified Al-Jazeera as the TV services they watched the most for international news (see Horan, 2010).

Al-Jazeera has triggered much debate outside and across the Arab world about the quality of its news provision. It has attracted distrust among people from outside the Arab world (Gunter, 2005). Whether this reaction stemmed from personal experience or negative press reporting of the channel in the West, however, is difficult to unravel.

Even within the Arab world, Al-Jazeera has met with a mixed reception. Supporters have praised its objectivity compared to traditional, government-controlled news services and also acknowledge that it broadcasts newsworthy stories (Miles, 2006). According to some observers, Al-Jazeera's willingness to report and discuss topics that traditional Arab TV news would steer away from, including women's rights and the efficacy of Arab foreign policy, created more open public debate that could eventually benefit Arab societies (El-Nawawy and Iskander, 2002; Zayani and Sahraoui, 2007). Its independence from government influence also meant, for many of its viewers, that the channel tells stories more accurately and allows viewers to make up their own minds about the credibility of its reporting (Rampal, 2006).

Criticisms of Al-Jazeera have challenged its presentation style and story choices and what has been seen as its negative way of presenting the Arab world (Al-Mawari, 2001; Ulian, 2001). It has also been criticized within the Arab world for its treatment of heads of state and its willingness to tackle subjects that other Arab news organizations would never dare to cover (El-Nawawy and Iskander, 2002; Falk, 2003). In contrast to its supporters' opinion that Al-Jazeera has fostered open debate of difficult issues to enhance civil society in the Arab world (El-Nawawy and Iskander, 2002), critics have challenged whether the channel has represented a platform of effective debate on political issues that have real and current relevance to Arab peoples (Al-Zubaidi, 2004).

Studies of its news output have concluded that Al-Jazeera embraces sensationalism in its news coverage and uses glossy production formats to stand out from other Arab news broadcasters (Ayish, 2002; Falk, 2003). While adopting Western style production techniques, its notion of objectivity is distinctly not 'Western' and for that reason it has been challenged for being anti-Western in some of its coverage (El-Nawawy and Iskander, 2002). Research has emerged to show that Arab viewers of Al-Jazeera in Kuwait valued its diversity of news provision, sensitivity to difficult issues and independent reporting unencumbered by government regulation or censorship (Jamal and Melkote, 2008).

Although the source of dispute about whether it is a champion of Arab identity or of Arab civil society, there is little doubt that Al-Jazeera has demonstrated that given the financial resources and regulatory freedom, it is possible for an Arab channel to attain global recognition and even to compete with other major international news brands. It success has also reinforced the advantages of independent, privately owned news broadcasters and newspapers. These news outlets have also embraced the internet and maintain their own web sites and blogs that engage readers, listeners and viewers directly enabling them to become actively involved with stories by providing comments of their own (Horan, 2010).

Emergence of new media in the news sphere

The dramatic rise of satellite TV services has transformed the news landscape across the Arab world. Since 2005 however, another news source has emerged with even more dramatic effect – the internet. Initially, Arab nations lagged behind the rest of the world in their adoption of the internet. One of the key delimiting factors was the technical difficulty of using the Arab language in this environment. Another factor was the availability and cost of connections to the internet. Once these factors had been resolved, Arab citizens quickly and actively embraced the online world. By mid-2011, it was estimated that there were 72.5 million internet users in the Middle East, a penetration level of 33.5 per cent (Internet World Stats, 2011). Middle Eastern Arab countries display considerable variation in internet penetration: 69 per cent -United Arab Emirates; 66.5 per cent – Qatar; 53.7 per cent – Palestine;

53.5 per cent; 48.4 per cent – Oman; Bahrain; 43.6 per cent Saudi Arabia; 42.4 per cent – Kuwait; 29 per cent – Lebanon; 26.8 per cent – Jordan; 19.8 per cent – Syria; 9.7 per cent – Yemen; 2.8 per cent – Iraq.

As internet penetration has grown so too has the position of the web as a news source. This phenomenon has been characterized by the rapid rise in online newspapers and citizen journalism. One survey conducted across four Arab countries in 2009 revealed that readership of online newspapers had overtaken the offline newspapers in Egypt (50% versus 34%) and was as popular as offline reading in Jordan (51% saying they read online and offline). Although lagging behind readership of offline newspapers (61%) in the UAE, nevertheless more than half of those surveyed (53%) claimed to read online newspapers. Finally, in Saudi Arabia, online readership (44%) was found to be closing ground on offline readership (48%) (Ghannan, 2011).

It was estimated that by 2010, there were 40,000 active blogs in the Arab region. There were also an estimated 17 million users of Facebook. Many of these users include journalists (Ghannan, 2011). A number of local social media platforms have become established in countries such as Jordan and Lebanon, such as Aramran.com, 7iber.com, Ammannet.net, Ammonnews.net and Now Lebanon.com, that offer news in text and video formats. These citizen-driven news sources represent an alternative information stream about current events to the largely government-sponsored and controlled newspapers and broadcasters.

Bloggers and social networkers were prominently engaged in not just reporting but also actively orchestrating the uprisings that began across the MENA from late 2010 through to the summer of 2011. Despite the focus of this book on the changes to mainstream news media, the rapidly evolving role of online news and citizen journalists cannot be ignored. Some commentators have referred to digital media as 'liberation technology' for the roles they have played as catalysts of popular uprisings in the Arab world (and other regions) (Diamond and Plattner, 2012). Other scholars have advised caution in assigning significant causal agency to the internet and associated communication systems in the context of the sorts of political and social changes that occurred in the Arab over the 2010–12 period (Lagerkvist, 2010). Certainly second generation web applications such as microblogging and social media sites played a part in assisting with the orchestration of political activism and in circumventing government-controlled media in disseminating publicity about events on the ground to the outside world; the principal drivers of change were the people who used these technologies. The events of the Arab Spring had their genesis in public discontent with their ruling classes and the social and economic opportunities provided for ordinary people in their societies that had festered over many years. Even so, new technologies linked to the internet played a critical role as communication channels that enabled formerly disparate individuals to become organized swiftly into groups with a common purpose (Howard and Hussain, 2012). We will return to these developments in Chapter 9.

The book

Chapter 2 by Khalid Al-Jaber and Barrie Gunter examines evolving media systems in the Middle East. This chapter presents an overview of the media systems and news markets in the six GCC (Cooperation for the Arab States of the Gulf) countries – Bahrain, Kuwait, Oman, Qatar, Saudi Arabia and the United Arab Emirates. It traces news market histories and examines the nature of recent news media developments and the challenges these are presented to news operators, governments and media regulators. There are questions about the relative importance and credibility of sources that arise from a much expanded news marketplace with a larger and more diverse range of news suppliers. The chapter examines the changes that have taken place in news provision in the Middle East with particular reference to the growing influence of new satellite TV news services in the GCC region.

Chapter 3 by Ahmed Al-Rawi and Barrie Gunter examines changes to televised news provision in Iraq. This country has experienced considerable national turmoil over the past two decades as a result of its involvement in a number of regional conflicts. Political regimes have been challenged and overthrown and the country's governance has been temporarily taken out of its own hands. During this time the news media have played a critical role in keeping its own citizens and those from elsewhere informed about the latest events. The chapter traces the developments in news media structures and operators within Iraq and examines the news market that is taking shape as the country rebuilds after the 2003 war. A number of different vested interests and political factions have interacted or dominated at different times since the war to shape the regulation and nature of news provision in the country.

Questions have been raised about the impartiality of news coverage in Iraq, especially that occurring on TV. The chapter examines these events and the status of news provision in Iraq at a crucial time when the country is in the process of rebuilding, economically and politically. It also draws on new research into the representation of news on TV in Iraq to consider the nature of news provision that has been emerging in this country following the recent war.

Chapter 4 by Zaki Nussibeh and Roger Dickinson presents an overview of developments in Palestinian media in the last four decades. The first part describes the Palestinian media during the Israeli occupation of the West Bank and Gaza strip in 1967, summarizing issues of news sources, regulation and patterns of news consumption. The second part describes the media after the establishment of the Palestinian National Authority in 1993 and the emergence of Palestinian autonomy. It reviews the state of the media under two authorities: the Israeli and the Palestinian and describes the introduction of satellite TV and the first Palestinian TV channel.

The third part of the chapter covers the period after June 2007 when two seats of Palestinian government were established, one in Gaza and the second in Ramallah. During this period, the internet has played an increasingly important role and has given journalists the opportunity to communicate without censorship. In addition to several newspapers, the Palestinian Satellite channel (Felestin) in Ramallah, and (Alaqsa) in Gaza became the mouthpieces of the two political parties (Fatah and Hamas). This part of the chapter will also contain a brief review of the media's role during the Israeli attack on Gaza at the end of 2008.

Chapter 5 by Hamza Mohammed and Barrie Gunter describes media systems and developments in Egypt. Once totally controlled by government, independent sources of news supply have been permitted in Egypt. What is the nature of these changes to the news media landscape in this country? What challenges do they present to the new and established media and to government? The chapter examines these questions, examines the position that Egyptian news media have reached, and considers whether expanded news supply in Egypt is reflected in a more diverse news agenda. New research is presented that examines links between different patterns of news consumption and public news agendas.

Chapter 6 by Mokhtar Elareshi and Julian Matthews examines the changing news landscape in Libya prior to the internal conflicts that occurred in 2011. Libya's news coverage was until recently dominated by local news services. The news was mostly parochial and local and the choice of news providers was extremely limited. All this is now changing largely due to the introduction of satellite TV to the country. This has brought a number of international Arab-language and English-language news services to Libya and stimulated news appetites of which the local news audiences had previously been unaware.

These changes have given rise to important questions about what types of news are really of most importance to the people of Libya. The new services also pose a potential threat to the older, local news services that may need to revise their self-images and seek to carve out new niches for themselves in a more competitive news marketplace. Elareshi and Matthews present an analysis of these developments and present some original research on the impact of these changes on the news consumption habits of young people in the country.

Chapter 7 by Khalid Al-Jaber and Barrie Gunter describes how new developments in news media have impacted upon news consumption patterns in the Arab World, taking the GCC states as a starting point for their analysis. The emergence of new developments in Arab news services has reconfigured the shape of the news media landscapes in many Arab countries. What do these changes mean for the way people consume news in these countries. Have some new news operators superseded older news suppliers? Has the market fragmented into distinct niches with specific news brands being valued and used for particular types of news? This chapter presents findings from new research in the Arab world that has explored the nature of news consumer markets in the GCC countries and the motives associated with use of specific news suppliers.

Chapter 8 by Ebrahim Al-Shaikh and Vincent Campbell presents new evidence concerning the role played by the news media in the political socialization of young people in Bahrain. The rapid growth of new sources via traditional and new news media has created many fresh opportunities for news consumers to obtain news information in a range of different formats and an increased array of perspectives. This raises questions about the impact of this expanded news provision on the public's political awareness. The news media have long been identified in the western world as playing a significant role in the political socialization of young people. News media not only keep people informed about the latest political developments but can also impart knowledge about the political systems and processes that shape the governance of a country. The study reported in this chapter investigated these issues in the context of Bahrain at a time when its population has access to a growing number of news providers via new TV services and the internet.

Finally, in Chapter 9 Roger Dickinson and Barrie Gunter draw together what has been learned from the analyses provided in the earlier chapters of this book. It revisits specific news developments and news consumption patterns that have been surfacing across the Arab world to discuss the key changes that have occurred to examine their degree of consistency in different countries. Dickinson and Gunter also make comparisons between news developments in the Arab world and the West to consider the lessons that might be learned in Arab countries from western experiences of rapid changes in media landscapes. From this analysis, the authors consider the directions in which news provision may develop in the future.

Notes

1 Al-Jazeera's original service is now known internally as 'Al-Jazeera Arabic' to distinguish it from its other services: Al-Jazeera English, Al-Jazeera Balkans, and the forthcoming Al-Jazeera Turkish and Al-Jazeera Kiswahili services.

2 It has been suggested that because Arabic services often depart from the conventional Western news media agenda they are able to gain access where Western organizations cannot. Frequently cited is the example of the reporting of the battle for Fallujah during the Iraq war in 2004. Western media organizations were embedded with American troops while some Arabic news organizations were reporting from inside the city. Controversially, their coverage was at odds with the Western narrative of 'surgical' strikes and limited casualties.

3 The point is a controversial one: Al-Jazeera English broadcast several reports during the Arab Spring that were openly critical of Qatari foreign policy and the station has frequently questioned Qatari government policy (regarding immigrant labour law, for example). Al-Jazeera has claimed editorial independence from the Qatari government from its inception, although the Wikileaks cables released in 2010 claimed that the station had been used as a 'bargaining chip' in negotiations over foreign policy (www.guardian.co.uk/world/2010/dec/05/wikileaks-cables-al-jazeera-qatari-foreign-policy).

References

Abdel Rahman, A. (2002) *Issues of the Arab Region in the Press in the 20th Century.* Cairo: Al Arabi Press.

Achilles, A., and Miege, B. (1994) The limits to the adaptation strategies of European public service television. *Media, Culture and Society*, 16(3), 31–46.

Alterman, J. (1998) *New Media, New Politics? From Satellite to the Internet in the Arab World.* Policy Paper No.48, Washington, DC: Washington Institute for Near East Policy.

Al-Mawari, M. (28 December 2001) Mohammed Jasim Al-Ali: The Qatari government helped us financially and we put her on the map. *Al-Bayan.*

Al-Qadry, N., and Harb, S. (2002) *Female and Male Journalists in the Television.* Beirut: Arab Cultural Centre and Lebanese Women Researchers.

Al-Zubaidi, L. (2004) *Walking a Tightrope: News Media and Freedom of Expression in the Arab Middle East.* Ramallah: Heinrich Boll Foundation.

Amin, H. (2001) Mass media in the Arab states between diversification and stagnation: an overview. In K. Hafez (ed.), *Mass Media, Politics and Society in the Middle East.* Creskill, NJ: Hampton Press, 23–42.

Amin, H. Y., and Boyd, D. A. (1994) The development of direct broadcast television to and within the Middle East. *Journal of South Asia and Middle Eastern Studies*, 18(2), 37–50.

Armbrust, W. (2005) Letter from the editor: Al-Jazeera is not a medium. *Transnational Broadcasting Studies*, 1(2), 1–4.
Ayish, M. (2001) American-style journalism and Arab world television: An exploratory study of news selection at six Arab world satellite television channels. *Transnational Broadcasting Studies*, 6(6). Available at: www.tbsjournal.com/Archives/Spring01/spr01.html (accessed 15 February 2013).
— (2002) Political communication on Arab world television: Evolving patterns. *Political Communication*, 19, 137–54.
Ayish, M., and Qassim, A. (1995) Direct satellite broadcasting in the Arab gulf region: Trends and policies. *Gazette*, 56, 19–36.
Ayish, M., and Sakr, N. (2010) Editorial: Dynamics of developments in Arab broadcasting. *Middle East Journal of Culture and Communication*, 3, 3–7.
Bakr, Y. A., Labib, S., and Kandil, H. (1985) *Development of Communication in the Arab States: Needs and Priorities*. No. 95. Paris, France: UNESCO.
Barkey, M. (12–14 January 1996) Satellite TV: On the eve of revolution. *Arab ad.*
Boulos, J. C. (1996) *La Tele: Quelle histoire* [*Television: What a Story*]. Beyrouth: Fiches du Monde Arabe.
Boyd, D. A. (1991) Lebanese broadcasting: Unofficial electronic media during a prolonged civil war. *Journal of Broadcasting and Electronic Media*, 35(3), 269–87.
Boyd, D. (1999) *Broadcasting in the Arab World: A Survey of Electronic Media in the Middle East*. Ames, Iowa; Iowa State University.
Diamond, L. (2012) Introduction. In L. Diamond and M. F. Plattner (eds), *Liberation Technology: Social Media and the Struggle for Democracy*. Baltimore: Johns Hopkins University Press, pp. ix–xxvi.
Diamond, L., and Plattner, M. F. (eds) (2012) *Liberation Technology: Social Media and the Struggle for Democracy*. Baltimore: Johns Hopkins University Press.
El-Nawawy, M., and Iskander, A. (2002) *Al-Jazeera: How the Free Arab News Network Scooped the World and Changed the Middle East*. Boulder, CO: Westview Press.
Ezzi, A. R. (2004) *Arabs and the Satellite Media*. Al Mostaqbal Al Arabi Series, 34, Beirut: Centre for Arab Union Studies.
Fakhreddine, J. (2000) Pan-Arab satellite television: Now the survival part. *Transnational Broadcasting Studies*, 5, www.tbsjournal.org.
Falk, W. (18 April 2003) The impact of Al-Jazeera. *The Week Magazine*, p. 11.
Gantz, W. (1993) Introduction. In B. S. Greenberg and W. Gantz (eds), *Desert Storm and the Mass Media*, pp. 1–15. Cresskill, NJ: Hampton Press.
Ghannan, J. (3 February 2011) *Social Media in the Arab World: Leading Up to the Uprisings of 2011*. Washington, DC: Center for International Media Assistance.
Ghareeb, E. (2000) New media and the information revolution in the Arab World: An assessment. *The Middle East Journal*, 53(3), 395–418.
— (2001) Al-Jazeera moved the waves and created a revolution in the Middle East. *Al-Rayah*, p. 25, 21 February.
Guaaybess, T. (2008) Orientalism and the economics of Arab broadcasting. In K. Hafez (ed.), *Arab Media: Power and Weakness*. New York: Continuum, pp. 199–213.

Gunter, B. (2005) Trust in the news on television. *Aslib Proceedings*, 57(5), 384–97.

Hafez, K. (2001) Mass media in the Middle East: Patterns of political and societal change. In K. Hafez (eds), *Mass Media, Politics and Society in the Middle East*, Cresskill, NJ: Hampton Press, pp. 1–20.

Hafez, K. (2006) Arab satellite broadcasting; Democracy with political parties. *Transnational Broadcasting Studies*, 15, www.tbsjournal.com/Archives/Fall05/Hafez

Horan, D. (2010) *Shifting Sands: The Impact of Satellite TV on Media in the Arab World*. Washington, DC: Center for International Media Assistance, 29 March.

Howard, P. N., and Hussain, M. M. (2012) Egypt and Tunisia: The role of digital media. In L. Diamond and M. F. Plattner (eds), *Liberation Technology: Social Media and the Struggle for Democracy*. Baltimore: Johns Hopkins University Press, pp. 110–23.

Jamal, A., and Melkote, S. R. (2008) Viewing and avoidance of the Al-Jazeera satellite television channel in Kuwait: A uses and gratifications perspective. *Asian Journal of Communication*, 18(1), 1–15.

Kraidy, M. M. (1998a) Satellite broadcasting from Lebanon: Prospects and perils. *Transnational Broadcasting Studies*, 1, www.tbsjournals.org

— (1998b) Broadcasting regulation and civil society in post-war Lebanon. *Journal of Broadcasting and Electronic Media*, 42(3), 387–400.

— (1999) State control of television news in 1990s Lebanon. *Journalism and Mass Communication Quarterly*, 76(3), 485–98.

— (2002) Arab satellite television between regionalization and globalization. *Global Media Journal*, 1(1), www.repository.upenn.edu/asc_papers/186

Lagerkvist, J. (2010) *After the Internet. Before Democracy*. Bern, Switzerland: Peter Lang.

Mellor, N. (2005) *The Making of Arab News*. Lanham, MD: Rowman and Littlefield.

— (2007) *Modern Arab Journalism: Problems and Prospects*. Edinburgh: University of Edinburgh Press.

Mernissi, F. (9 September 2007) Der Islam schafft Solidaritat. *Die Tageszeitung*, 9 September.

Miles, H. (2006) Think again: Al-Jazeera. *Foreign Policy*, July/August. Available at: www.foreignpolicy.com/story/cms.php?story_id+3497.

O'Heffernan, P. (1993) Sobering thoughts on sound bites seen 'round the world. In B. S. Greenberg and W. Gantz (eds), *Desert Storm and the Mass Media*. Cresskill, NJ: Hampton Press, pp. 19–28.

Rampal, K. R. (2006) Global news and information flow in the internet age. In K. Y. Kamalipour (ed.), *Global Communication*, 2nd edn. Belmont, CA: Wadsworth/Thomson Learning, pp. 105–32.

Rugh, W. A. (1979) *The Arab Press: News Media and Political Processes in the Arab World*. Syracuse, NY: Syracuse University Press.

— (2004) *Arab Mass Media: Newspapers, Radio and Television in Arab Politics*. Westport CT: Praeger Publishers.

Sakr, N. (1999) Satellite television and development in the Middle East. Middle East Report 210 (Spring): 6–8

Sakr, N. (2000) Optical illusions: Television and censorship in the Arab world. *Transnational Broadcasting Studies*, (5). Available at: www.tbsjournal.com.

— (2001) Seen and starting to be heard: Women and the Arab media in a decade of change. *Social Research*, 69(3), 821–51.

— (2005) Maverick or model? Al-Jazeera's impact on Arab satellite television. In J. K. Chalaby (ed.), *Transnational Television Worldwide: Toward a New Media Order*. London: I.B. Tauris.

Schleifer, S. A. (1998) Media explosion in the Arab world: The Pan-Arab satellite broadcasters. *Transnational Broadcasting Studies*, 1(1). Available at: www.tbsjournal.com/Archives/Fall98/fall98.html (accessed February 2013).

Semati, M. (2001) Reflections on the politics of the global 'rolling news' television genre. *Transnational Broadcasting Studies*, 6. Available at: www.tbsjournal.com.

Sreberny-Mohammadi, A. (1998) The media and democratization in the Middle East: The strange case of television. *Democratization and the Media*, 5(2), 179–99.

Suleiman, Y. (2003) *The Arabic language and National Identity: A Study of Ideology*. Edinburgh: University of Edinburgh.

Tash, A. (1983) *A Profile of Professional Journalists Working in the Saudi Arabian Daily Press*. Unpublished PhD dissertation. Southern Illinois University.

Ulian, H. (14 October 2001) Al-Jazeera in the sea of Kabul and a race toward the war's rewards. *Al-Qabas*, p. 21.

Wright, L. (2004) The kingdom of silence: A reporter at large. *The New Yorker*, 79(41).

Zayani, M. (ed.) (2005) *The Al-Jazeera Phenomenon: Critical Perspectives on New Arab Media*. London: Pluto Press.

Zayani, M., and Sahrauoi, S. (2007) *The Culture of Al-Jazeera. Inside an Arab Media Giant*. New York: MacFarland and Co Inc.

2

Evolving News Systems in the Gulf Countries

Khalid Al-Jaber and Barrie Gunter

This chapter presents an overview of the media systems and news markets in the six GCC (Cooperation for the Arab States of the Gulf) countries – Bahrain, Kuwait, Oman, Qatar, Saudi Arabia and the United Arab Emirates. These six Arab monarchical states have been economically joined since 1981 in the GCC. All these Gulf countries share a regional culture that is sometimes referred to as 'khaleeji (Gulf) culture'. They all speak the Gulf dialect of Arabic and share similar styles of cuisine, dress and music (Hourani, 1991).

All of the Arab states of the Gulf have greatly relied economically on oil and gas reserves. This has turned them into the wealthiest nations in region with per capita incomes higher than those of their Arab neighbours in the Middle East and North Africa (MENA). However, to meet indigenous labour shortages they host large numbers of temporary, non-citizen-status, economic migrants from South Asia, Southeast Asia and Africa. In the past there were also significant numbers of immigrants from other Arab countries such as Egypt, Jordan, Palestinian and Yemen (The Columbia Encyclopedia, 2008).

All six GCC states are monarchies with limited political representation. However, Kuwait and Bahrain have legislatures with popularly elected members. Oman has an advisory council that is popularly elected and in the United Arab Emirates – which is in fact a federation of seven monarchical emirates – the Federal National Council also functions only as an advisory body and has a portion of its members elected from a small electoral college nominated by the seven rulers. In Qatar, an elected national parliament is written into the new constitution which was released in 2003, but no elections have yet been held. However, women in Qatar were granted the right to vote and be elected in Qatar's first democratic 'municipal elections' from 1999, even before women in Kuwait were granted the right to vote and stand for election in 2006 (Auter and Al-Jaber, 2003; The Columbia Encyclopedia, 2008).

This chapter will examine the news media histories of the GCC countries culminating in the emergence of new digital media transmitted via satellite broadcasting and the broadband internet. It will also discuss the challenges that these developments have posed for the governments of these states.

Media developments in the GCC states

Traditionally mass media in GCC countries have been government-owned and operated. They have privileged concerns about the image of the state, most often equated with that of its ruler, an unelected monarch. Recent developments in communication technologies, most visibly manifest with the emergence of satellite TV channels, have changed the media landscape of these countries and impacted upon the media consumption patterns of their indigenous populations (Boyd, 1999; Iskander, 2007).

Accompanying satellite TV transmissions have been the steady penetration of the broadband internet and advanced mobile telephones that are also capable to intersecting with the internet. Among the outcomes for media consumers have been significant expansion of choice of entertainment and information content to which they can gain access, greater control over access, and exposure to content over which state governments have diminishing direct control (Ghareeb, 2000; Guaaybess, 2002).

The new communication media have proven to be popular and the new content they convey has created a more competitive media marketplace within the region, not least in respect of the provision and consumption of news. Such changes have forced governments, regulators and policymakers, and media operators themselves to rethink their policies and practices. Competition from the new media, loss of control over the information flow, criticism of inefficient national television (TV) systems, erosion of audience loyalty and the clamouring by entrepreneurs for a role in emerging pan-national commercial media operations have led to the establishment of a new media environment in all GCC countries (Rugh, 2004).

All this represents a significant shift from how the media used to look in the Middle East. Rugh (2004) described Arab media even in the last quarter of the twentieth century as being under tight government control. Effectively, the media served as an extension of government and were carefully monitored to ensure they never strayed from the ruling party line in any news stories they published and never criticized government. In this regard, there were minimal differences between the Arab States.

By the early twenty-first century however the same author observed changes starting to emerge in the way the media were conceived by Arab governments, often accompanied by new expectations of the media on the part of Arab citizens (Rugh, 2004). Governments still retained overwhelming control over the media, largely exercised through ownership of media infrastructures, but in some cases were allowing limited freedom of expression within news reporting. The emergence and popularity of satellite TV was identified as a key instrument of change in this context.

As more new media operations emerged that were privately owned, there was a growing expectation on the part of media owners and their audiences that there should be greater plurality in news provision, both in terms of content and production style (Ghareeb, 2000). Developments such as these that began in the GCC countries also started to spread to other Arab nations. This trend was facilitated by the migration of media operations from other parts of the Arab world to set up bases in Dubai which adopted a more open attitude to the media.

The dominant satellite TV channels came to be associated with the GCC countries as a result of Saudi investments in operations such as Middle East Broadcasting Corporation Orbit, Arab Radio and Television Network, Showtime and Dubai Media City. These channels form part of a framework called the Arab Satellite Communications Organization (ARABSAT) owned by the governments of Saudi Arabia, Kuwait and Qatar. Although expanded media infrastructures have permitted the flow of much more media content to Arab audiences, a clear vision of how this will serve Arab peoples or help to create a distinctive Arab identity that can be promoted across the Arab world and beyond has yet to materialize (Guaaybess, 2002; Rugh, 2004).

Despite the emergence of a buoyant private sector, commercially funded media operations in the Arab world are dominated by those based in the Gulf. Although governments may no longer enjoy controlling ownership of these companies, they can still impose local censorship laws that place restrictions on what news providers can publish or broadcast (Boyd, 1999).

Journalists and other media personnel working in the Gulf area do not enjoy freedom of association or the protection of professional trade unions. Although some loose professional communities have been established, these do not enjoy the status of the counterparts in the west. There is lack of balance between nations and regimes that prevents opening channels for dialogue and serious discussion of issues for serving the common interests (Rugh, 2004).

Journalism in the Gulf has undergone three important phases, the first of which started with the publication of the *Journal of Kuwait* in 1928. This publication moved from Kuwait to Bahrain just one year after its inception. Bahrain was the site of another newspaper launch in 1939 with the launch of Al-Bahrain. This publication had an influential role in supporting the United Kingdom against Nazi Germany.

The second phase occurred between 1949 and 1956 and was characterized by the emergence of a number of newspapers, magazines and periodicals across the Gulf, and especially in Bahrain. Perhaps the most important publication at this time was the *Voice of Bahrain*, a news magazine which specialized in tackling current issues of the day and recruited well-educated writers to produce high quality reporting that could enrich the cultural and social awareness of local populations. The publication's activities were curtailed by censorship and other government-imposed restrictions that undermined its prominence. It was not until the 1970s that the Gulf press began to assert greater influence as more writers move to Kuwait where they enjoyed relatively greater freedom of expression than elsewhere in the Arab world.

A third phase in the development of printed news media in the Gulf states saw print journalism challenged by broadcast journalism that had been invigorated in the 1990s with the emergence of satellite transmission platforms. The role played by journalism also became redefined with the coverage provided by Western media, and especially Cable News Network (CNN), of the first Gulf war in Iraq. This conflict received more direct eyewitness coverage than any one previously with journalists becoming embedded with the military and enabled to report live from the frontline.

Kuwait, Qatar and the United Arab Emirates recognized the significant role that could be played by a private press which was independent of the direct intervention of the state. Meanwhile, though unwilling to embrace privatized media to that extent, Saudi Arabia sought to create public–private media partnerships that could source and transmit news beyond its national borders. These initiatives resulted in the spread of international Arab press and the emergence of celebrity newsmen whose views influenced the public opinion locally and abroad.

The press and other news publications

The Gulf press was born at the beginning of the twentieth century in Saudi Arabia, Kuwait and Bahrain. The press spread to Oman, Qatar and the United

Arab Emirates in the early 1960s and 1970s. The first Saudi newspaper was *Al-Hijaz* which was launched in 1908, followed by newspapers in Kuwait in 1928, Bahrain in 1939, the United Arab Emirates in 1966, Oman in 1970 and finally Qatar in 1972 (GCC Publications, 2004).

The number of published newspapers dramatically increased at the end of the twentieth century facilitated by technological developments in publishing and printing. Daily newspapers, magazines and other publications emerged across all the Gulf countries. By 2002, for instance, there were 176 news publications in Saudi Arabia, 80 in Kuwait, 72 in the United Arab Emirates, 27 in Oman and 22 each in Bahrain and Qatar (GCC Publications, 2004). Some newspapers are published in languages other than Arabic, the most important of which is English.

Freedom House (2009), an institute that assesses the degree of freedom in the world's nation states, indicated that Kuwait ranked first among the Gulf region states in terms of the degree of freedom accorded to its indigenous press and the second among all Arab countries. It was categorized, however, only as a 'partially free country'. As for other Gulf countries, they were classified as 'non-free countries' and all ranked outside the top 100 countries on this scale. The Reporters Without Borders annual report for 2009, which summarizes the nature of the media in different countries indicated that there were signs of evolution in freedom of the press in the Arabian Gulf region, but noted that the GCC states still have a long way to go. The next sections of this chapter examine individual Gulf nations and the nature of their news media and journalism.

The Kuwaiti press

The first pamphlet published in Kuwait was a monthly magazine known as the *Journal of Kuwait*, owned by Sheikh Abdul Aziz Al-Rashid in 1928. Following this came the *Kuwait Journal* in 1954 and *Al-Arabi* in 1958. The first press law to regulate the relationship between the press and the state was not issued, however, until 1956. The Kuwaiti press can be divided into pre-independence press and post-independence press. The pre-independence period marks the beginning of specialized press during which a newspaper was no longer a collection of jokes, stories and features. Instead, it became a chronicle of daily events together with critical analysis and interpretation.

The post-independence press refers to the period after 1961 which witnessed the issuance of press law to boost press activity in Kuwait. *Al-Arabi* magazine in December 1958 represented the first indication of what could be possible. The daily journal called Public Opinion issued on 16 April 1961, however, is considered to mark the beginning of journalism in its modern sense. Since that time, the number of daily newspapers and weekly magazines in Kuwait increased significantly.

The Press and Publications Law No. 8 of 1979 entrusted to the Directory of Publications and Distribution (DPD) a number of competences related to supervising the activities of the press and their distribution in Kuwait. This law charged the DPD with regulating the press, but at the same time providing the necessary facilities to underpin the production of newspapers, to create some stories via press releases, and facilitating the flow of employees into the news media (GCC Publications, 2004).

Since the beginning of the booming publication services market, the Kuwaiti government started publishing newspapers and magazines but they were suspended because they could not compete with privately owned newspapers and publications. Newspapers and magazines in Kuwait are published in quite a few languages including English, French and Urdu, with more than 15 daily newspapers published in Arabic. The most popular Arabic daily newspapers in Kuwait are *Al-Rai Ala-Am* (Public Opinion) which was founded 1961, *Al-Seyassah* (Policy) established in 1965, *Al-Qabas* (Starbrand) which was launched in 1972, *Al-Watan* (The Homeland) which started in 1974, and *Al-Anbas* (The News) which began publishing in 1976. After a series of amendments made to the Press and Publications Law in 2007, other newspapers were published which included: *Alam Alyoum, Al Jareeda, Al Wasat* and *Annahar.*

The Qatari press

Print and publication media started in Qatar with the governmental publication of an official gazette that contained the laws and Emir's decrees in 1961. Qatar established its Department of Information in 1969, which issued *Doha* magazine the same year; the Ministry of Education issued *Education* magazine in 1970. In the same year, *Al Urooba Press* and *Gulf News*, a bimonthly English language magazine, were launched as the first private publications in Qatar (Auter and Al-Jaber, 2003).

There are three main Qatari daily newspapers, namely: *Al-Raya, Al-Sharq* and *Al-Watan.* Prior to these newspapers, there was a publication titled *Al-Arab* which started in 1971 and ceased publication in 1996 only to be resumed again in 2008 (GCC Publications, 2004). The oldest of the other three publications is *Al-Sharq* whose first issue came out in September 1978 followed by *Al-Raya* (launched 10 May 1979) and then *Al-Watan* (3 September 1995). In addition to Arabic newspapers, the *Gulf Times* newspaper is published in English by Al-Raya Press. It was published for the first time on 10 December 1978 and was followed by the *Peninsula* newspaper in 2001 issued by Al-Sharq Press, while the Al-Watan Press issued the *Qatar Tribune* in September 2006. Magazines publishing news in Qatar cover many subjects: politics, business, social, finance, health, arts and entertainment.

The Qatari government provided financial support for local newspapers since it first established its Ministry of Information and Culture. However, this support stopped in 1995. Censorship was lifted from the local press from October 1995 by virtue of Law No. 5 of 1998 which abolished the Ministry of Information and Culture and distributed its competencies and transformed some of its directories to independent bodies. At this time also the National Council for Culture, Arts and Heritage was established. This left the press and publication media essentially free from government interference and many national and international newspapers and magazines started to appear in the Qatari market such as the *New York Times, the Washington Post, Time magazine, Financial Times* and *Alquds Alarabi* (Auter and Al-Jaber, 2003).

The Emirates press

The press started in the United Arab Emirates later than in the other Gulf countries. Some UAE emirates initiated early newspapers that did not last long. In 1927, for example, Ibrahim Mohamed Al-Madfa'a issued a bi-weekly newspaper called *Oman*, in collaboration with some poets and writers from the region. *Oman* was handwritten with five printed copies that were traded among the literate people of the country. The newspaper contained excerpts from the news published in other Arab newspapers especially Egyptian and Iraq ones, which tended to arrive in Sharjah, several weeks after their release, in addition to a host of local news, information about the prices of commodities and Bedouin tales.

Oman ceased publication only one year after its launch. Subsequently, a group of young writers based in Dubai and Sharjah issued a daily bulletin written by hand which they called *The Sound of Sparrows*. In addition there were a number of leaflets and posters that were posted in the markets containing advertisements in English on the arrival timetables of ships coming from India and Iran.

In January 1965, the Dubai Municipality Media Directory issued a bulletin under the title of *Dubai News*, to be followed by the Emirate of Ras Al-Khaimah which issued a similar magazine in 1968. The two publications continued to be published for a long time until after the establishment of the state of the United Arab Emirates. The Sharjah emirate followed in the footsteps of Dubai and Ras Al-Khaimah and from 1970 published *Al-Shurooq*, a monthly magazine produced by two brothers, Treim and Abdullah Omran. This publication, however, was short lived. The Omran brothers then launched a second magazine *Al-Khaleej* in October 1970 which was edited in Sharjah, printed in Kuwait, and shipped by air to Sharjah. This newspaper subsequently ceased publication.

On 20 October 1969, the weekly *Al-Ittihad* newspaper was published by the Department of Information and Tourism in Abu Dhabi, and turned into a daily newspaper on 20 April 1972, to be followed by *Al-Wahda* in August 1973 which was owned and edited by Mr Rashid Oweidha. More newspapers followed. *Al-Fajr* came out in March 1975, owned and edited by Mr Obeid Al Mazrui. *Al-Khaleej* was revived in April 1980 in Sharjah, to be followed by the *Al-Bayan* daily that was issued by the Dubai Information Department in May 1980 (GCC Publications, 2004).

The Bahraini press

Bahrain is a leading country in the Gulf in terms of promulgating legislation regulating press, printing and publication. The first Act to regulate the press goes back to 1930, which was known as the Press Regulation Law. In 1979, a comprehensive law was issued that contained detailed principles governing the press, printing, publishing and circulation (GCC Publications, 2004).

The beginning of the breakthrough in the Bahraini press occurred when *Bahrain* newspaper was issued by Abdullah Al-za'id between 1939 and 1944 to tackle political, cultural, literary and domestic social news and to support the Allied forces at war against Germany in the 1940s.

Newspapers of the 1950s in Bahrain played a prominent role, especially *Al-Qafila, Al-Watan, Al-Mizan* and *Al-Shu'la* which published only one edition, in fighting colonialism, spreading national awareness and supporting the revolution of 1952 in Egypt and in criticizing the political situation of the British protectorates in the Gulf region. Such was their impact on public opinion that the British ordered them all to cease publication in 1956. Subsequently, the following two decades witnessed the publication of relatively low profile newspapers and political journals that touched only tangentially on local issues and focused mainly on reporting pan-Arab and foreign news.

The 1970s and 1980s are considered to be the period of maturity of the literary and cultural movement in Bahrain and saw the emergence of varied newspapers such as the *Akhbar Al-Khaleej* daily in 1976, the English language

Gulf Daily in 1978, and the *Al-Ayyam* daily in 1989. The 1980s witnessed dynamic cultural change embodied by the publication of cultural periodicals such as *Akhbar Al-Tarbiya* in 1981, *Al-Watheeqa* in 1982 and *Al-Muhami* edited and published by Bahraini lawyers in 1982. A literary magazine, *Kalemat*, was issued in 1983 by writers and dealing with cultural issues. More magazines were issued side by side with *Kalemat*, namely, *Afaqun Amniyya, Panorama Al-Khaleej* and *Bahrain Charity*.

The Omani press

Press history in Oman is relatively short because until 1970, no newspapers were published except for the news release of the Omani Oil Company entitled *News of our Company* in 1967 that covered corporate news only. On 25 July 1970, and only two days after the ascension of Sultan Qaboos to the throne, a newspaper entitled *Oman News* was printed on stencil paper in Arabic and English and contained news of the Sultanate in addition to Sultani decrees and government resolutions (GCC Publications, 2004).

Al-Watan was the first and most important Omani daily newspaper. The inaugural issue came out on 28 January 1971. It is published by Omani Press for the Publication and Dissemination Corporation. *Al-Watan* was published in more than one Arab capital. In the early 1970s, it was published in Beirut then transferred to Kuwait in 1974 due to the Lebanese civil war. Then it migrated to Oman after the establishment of the International Press Corporation and was eventually published by its own press from 1988.

Oman Daily is considered to be the first state-run newspaper published in the Sultanate of Oman and started on 18 November 1972 on the occasion of the Second National Day celebrations. It was committed to come out every Saturday on a temporary basis until 11 November 1975 when it started to be published twice a week, (Saturdays and Tuesdays) so as to stay more up to date with the important events in the country. On 29 May 1972, however, Sultan Qaboos Bin Saeed introduced Law No. 49 of 1980 establishing the Oman Press which separated the newspaper from the General Directorate of Information and Tourism.

The Times of Oman was the first English-language newspaper in the Sultanate debuting on 23 February 1975 as a weekly paper published every Thursday. It included a variety of articles covering local affairs and offering a special service for the expatriate community. Starting from 1 January 1991, it became a daily newspaper issued by Dar Muscat for press, publishing and distribution.

The Saudi Arabia press

The first press activity in the Arabian Peninsula started with the introduction of printing machines in 1908 when several newspapers were published during the late Ottoman era. Most of these newspapers disappeared soon after their launch for many reasons including the volatility of the political situation in Hijaz and financial problems (GCC Publications, 2004).

During the Ottoman era, newspapers were published in Mecca, Jedda and Medina between 1908 and 1912. These included *Hijaz, Hijaz Reform* (The Sun of Truth), *Safa'a Al-Hijaz* and *Al-Madina Al-Munawwara*. The entry of King Abdulaziz bin Abdulrahman to Mecca marks the real beginning of Saudi media in general and the Saudi press in particular, as evident in the initiative of publishing the *Umm Al Qura* daily in Makkah in 1924. This publication emerged around the same time as a number of miscellaneous periodicals.

The Printing Presses and Publications Law was introduced four years after the publication of *Ummu Al-Qura* and was in force for ten years. It was then succeeded by another law that reached assent 1940 which included 36 articles that marked the beginning of the development of Saudi media structures and institutions. At this time, Saudi radio was in its infancy under the management and supervision of the Ministry of Finance, while the press was under the supervision and management of the Ministry of Foreign Affairs. A number of further Saudi newspapers were published, some of which are still published while others have gone out of business such as *Hera'a, Al-Dhahran, Al-Fajer Al-Jadeed, Qaseem* and *Commercial Week*. Some newspapers of that time are still leading newspapers today such as *Al-Madina* which was first issued in 1937 first in Medina and then in Jeddah; *Al-Bilad* daily which was first issued in 1964 in Mecca; *Okaz* which debuted its publication in 1960 in Jeddah; *Al-Jazirah* which was first issued in 1965 in Riyadh; *Al-Riyadh* newspaper, which came out first in 1965 in Riyadh; *Asharq al-Awsat* which was first published in 1978 in London; followed by *Al-Riyadh, Jeddah* and *Al-Watan* which were published in 2000 in Abha.

Radio broadcasting services

Radio services have become more entrenched in the Arab world since the late 1950s and 1960s. This development was followed the spread of TV broadcasting in the Gulf region during the 1970s and 1980s. Radio stations broadcast news around the clock, but mainstream newscasts were usually transmitted between 12 noon and 12 midnight (Boyd, 1999).

Gulf radio stations broadcast detailed bulletins specializing in politics, economy, sports, culture, science, in addition to independent programmes comprising 'Light on Local and Arab Press' and reports of radio correspondents in the Arab world and reports of news agencies. Radio broadcasts in the Gulf region can be heard via the internet (GCC Publications, 2004).

Saudi Arabia was the first country to establish a wireless network in 1932, while broadcasting to the public began in 1949 in Jeddah. At that time, it was called Radio Mecca and heard only in the Hijaz. On 23 August 1979, broadcasting was unified under the name of 'Saudi Arabia from Riyadh' and started live broadcasting for more than 20 hours a day. By 1980 the broadcasting system in Saudi Arabia had become a match for the radio systems in most developed countries of the world in terms of signal strength and clarity of reception.

Public broadcasting in Bahrain and Kuwait began in 1941 during World War II and continued until 1945. In July 1955, the Public Bahrain Broadcasting Station was opened to broadcast for four hours only per day, though gradually increasing its broadcast hours across the 1960s. At the beginning of 1990, Bahrain Radio became a 24-hour radio broadcaster on short-wave.

Kuwait official radio began broadcasting on 12 May 1951 with its recurrent slogan 'This is Kuwait'. The year 1961 represented an important turning point in the history of Radio Kuwait, as it marks Kuwait's independence, and radio played a significant role before the spread of TV by providing news, programmes, and speeches by the rulers of Kuwait demanding independence and not to be either a part of Iraq or a colony of Britain. During Iraqi invasion in 1990, Radio Kuwait continued broadcasting from Saudi Arabia. However, after liberation and by the end of 1991, all channels had started operating again from Kuwait.

In Qatar the first to broadcast in the country in the early 1960s was Mosque Radio which covered part of the area of the capital, Doha. On 25 June 1968, Qatar Radio was established and the Big Mosque Radio continued to broadcast for a few more months after the establishment of the official Qatar Radio until the acquisition of live transmission facility in Qatar Radio. The Qatar Broadcasting Service (QBS) began airing radio programmes in Arabic languages. English, Urdu, and French programmes were added to the line up in 1971, 1980 and 1985 respectively. There is no private radio in Qatar, it being entirely state-run. However, international radio stations such as the British Broadcasting Corporation (BBC) and Voice of America, and Radio Sawa, which is publicly funded by the Broadcasting Board of Governors and the United States Congress, are available (Auter and Al-Jaber, 2003).

In the United Arab Emirates, Abu Dhabi Radio was set up on 25 February 1969 and subsequently changed its name on 2 December 1971 to the Voice of the United Arab Emirates from Abu Dhabi. Prior to that, Dubai Radio was set up bearing the name of Voice of the Coast first broadcasting from Sharja in 1966. It later changed its name to Dubai Radio. In addition, Ras Al-Khaimah Radio started its broadcasts in September 1972, while Umm Al-Quwain Radio began its official broadcasts in March 1978.

Radio in Oman is entirely government funded, is free of advertising, and is overseen by the Ministry of Information. Oman Radio began broadcasting on 30 July 1970 for a period of five hours a day to cover the capital Muscat. On 25 November 1975 the station moved to a new site in Salalah. The BBC utilizes Masirah Island off the coast of Oman for a medium-wave relay station to boost the signal for its Arabic, Farsi, Hindi, Pashtu, English and Urdu programmes. The eventual plan is to move the relay station from the island to the Omani mainland (Boyd, 1999).

TV broadcasting services

TV transmission in Saudi Arabia started in 1965 to cover the major cities of the Kingdom through the TV transmitters. In December 1967 a TV station was set up in Medina followed by Qassim station in July 1968 and by Dammam station in November 1969 to cover all the cities of the eastern region and most of the Arabian Gulf. Subsequently, these were joined by the Abha station in 1977 to cover the surrounding areas. Saudi TV broadcasts through four satellite channels. The first and second channels broadcast in English with news bulletins in French. In addition there are Arabic news and sports channels. The first channel and the sports channel broadcast their programmes via land transmission in addition to their satellite transmission (Boyd, 1999; GCC Publications, 2004).

TV broadcasting in Kuwait began in 1957 and transmitted only animation and feature films to the northern and eastern regions of the country. In 1964 it expanded to cover all the areas of Kuwait. Kuwait's TV consists of four terrestrial channels and a satellite TV channel together offering political, religious, scientific, cultural and recreational programmes.

Qatar TV Broadcasting started in 1970 and transmissions were initially confined to afternoons between 3 p.m. to 7 p.m. in monochrome. Transmissions extended to nine hours per day by 1974 at the time of the introduction of colour. It continued to develop until 1982 when Channel 2 in English was launched to broadcast cultural programmes, sporting and other events. In 1998, satellite transmissions were introduced to Qatar to broadcast for more than 18 hours a day. All TV channels were government-owned except Al-Jazeera satellite news channel, which was introduced in 1996. Al-Jazeera was considered a private entity even though the Qatari government originally financed it.

In the United Arab Emirates there are four popular TV stations, Abu Dhabi, Dubai, Sharjah and Ajman. TV began transmission from Abu Dhabi in monochrome on 6 October 1969. Colour TV transmissions began on 4 January 1974 using the PAL system via a main transmission station in Abu Dhabi and relay stations in other cities. Dubai TV began broadcasting in 1976. Sharjah TV was inaugurated in February 1989 and Ajman TV station in February 1996.

Bahrain TV started broadcasting for five hours a day in 1973. The first satellite TV transmissions began in October 1996. Bahrain Radio and TV became an independent public body in January 1996.

Finally, Oman began TV transmissions in 1974 covering the capital only. In 1975 it was extended to cover the capital and other parts of the country.

It is worth noting that media laws and regulations in the Gulf States do not allow private ownership of radio and TV stations except in Dubai which overcame such restrictions and established Dubai Media City. This area is a free zone where media services including satellite TV stations and production and other services are licensed, overriding the local laws and regulations that would restrict their operations in other parts of the Arab world.

National news agencies

All Gulf Arab states own national news agencies aimed at collecting and disseminating news about them as well as other countries in the world, and they often rely on the news and information from international and national news agencies.

The role of Arab news agencies is to provide an interface between Arab states and the rest of the world. They are an extension of government and generate stories that have the purpose of highlighting government accomplishments in different domains, as well as fostering relations with authorities and media figures abroad. A news agency undertakes to exchange and transfer services and cooperation with national, pan-Arab and international parties, in addition to reporting local and international events and distributing and marketing these reports. It also conducts research projects and produces specialized newsletters and other visual and printed news. In addition, a news agency provides governmental bodies with news through its reporters locally and abroad and monitors all news related to the country in pan-Arab and international media and news networks and the internet. Furthermore, an agency follows up professional and technological advances in media. The first news agency in the Gulf area was established in Saudi Arabia in 1971, followed by others in Qatar in 1975, Kuwait and the United Arab Emirates in 1976 and finally in Bahrain in 2006 (GCC Publications, 2004).

Satellite TV channels in the Arabian Gulf

Audio-visual media in the Gulf Arab countries have evolved greatly since the end of the twentieth century. This development has been evident in the growing number of satellite TV channels and the improved quality of programmes aired by these channels. Another important factor has been the emergence of the private sector as a partner to national governments in respect of the operation and ownership of TV stations which have, for a long time, been the preserve of the official public sector in Gulf Arab states. The provision of adequate funding to operate high quality satellite TV services is a challenge for private enterprises in the Arab states just as it is in other parts of the world. The involvement of governments can therefore help to underwrite costs. Although such support would normally be exchanged for editorial control, Arab governments have increasingly come to recognize the benefits of a more hands-off approach to dealing with TV news operations (Ayish, 2001; Rugh, 2004; Mellor, 2005).

The allied operation 'Desert Storm' to liberate Kuwait from Iraqi occupation in 1991 constituted a turning point for public media in the Gulf region and taught Arab governments some valuable lessons. First, it made the people in charge of media realize the vital role that cross-border TV stations, such as CNN, can play in wars in the sense that they control the flow of information, thereby controlling public opinion at the national and international levels regarding the conflict in the area. The 'CNN effect' was noted in several countries around the world. Even in its home country, the United States, the channel broke new ground in the nature of its war coverage. Its 24-hour news cycle meant that it had an enormous amount of airtime to fill compared with the other major TV networks. It deployed many more reporters to the Middle East at the time of the 1991 Gulf conflict and took a lead in breaking news. Despite the increased news coverage of the major networks at this time, CNN was found to have presented more event-oriented coverage of the war than other TV channels (Wicks and Walker, 1993).

Second, officials in the Gulf region realized that they can utilize media to shape public opinion regarding national issues. This realization coincided with the emergence of new digital technologies that enhanced the development of new media operations within the private sector. Such operations opened up a different type of media service for Arab audiences from those to which they had become accustomed under purely authoritarian media regimes. Nation states in the Middle East also recognized that more open media systems could be used to advance their economic objectives through the creation of profitable new businesses and platforms that could be utilized to reach out to the non-Arab world with messages designed to enhance Arab identity and to cultivate a more positive brand image (Zayani, 2005; Lynch, 2006).

After the first allied war against Iraq, the Gulf countries competed in the launch of the satellite TV channels to reach the masses of Arabs everywhere starting from the Kuwaiti satellite channel 1991 followed by Abu Dhabi TV (1992) and Dubai Satellite Channel (1992) and Al Bahrain, Saudi Arabia channels I and II (1995) and Al-Jazeera news TV channels. In November 1996 Al-Jazeera, which means 'the island' in Arabic, was introduced in Qatar as the first Arab news satellite channel. The channel was financed by 500 million riyals from the Qatari government ($137 million), and it also has relied on advertising and viewer revenue (El-Nawawy and Iskandar, 2002).

The Gulf countries were the first in the Arab world to involve the private sector in the TV industry through launching several media enterprises with local funding. The first of these new TV channels to see the light of day was MBC from London in 1991 as an arm of the Saudi Media Company 'ARA' broadcasting from outside the Arab World. MBC introduced varied entertainment programmes new to the Arab viewer after half a century of official media whose main concern was glorifying the ruler and promoting his policies which created a sense of boredom and futility among Arab viewers (Boyd, 1999).

In 1994, Orbit Radio and TV launched its satellite channels from Italy to put the Arab viewer face-to-face with the Western entertainment programmes and news unseen before in the Arab media environment. This network also introduced Arab viewers to subscription TV services for the first time. By the end of the 1990s, viewers in the Gulf region had access to dozens of TV entertainment channels that offered music, drama and comedy broadcasting from the region or from abroad (Rugh, 2004).

One of the most important outcomes of this developmental phase was a changing concept of TV in the Gulf region from being a tool for political propaganda into a source of entertainment, cultural enrichment and education for the masses (Miles, 2005). TV has become an important fixture in modern Arab households enabling people to keep pace with economic, social and cultural developments experienced by the region (Sakr, 2001).

Developments involving satellite TV have not just brought many new forms of entertainment to audiences in the Arab world they have also promoted the launch of many new news channels. Researchers and analysts agree that the Arabian Gulf region is unique among Arab countries by its satellite news channels that present news and analyses with a high level of professionalism and objectivity (Guaaybess, 2008). Most prominent among these channels are Al-Jazeera, Abu Dhabi and Al-Arabiya which are the best representatives of this emerging generation of TV channels marked out by boldness in tackling controversial issues with a high level of professionalism (Ayish, 2001).

If debate in the wake of the Gulf War in 1991 pivoted around what came to be known as the 'CNN effect', it revolved in the wake of events of 11 September 2001 around the 'Al-Jazeera effect' (Seib, 2008). Such was its perceived significance that the USA administration resorted to counteracting this effect by establishing the Al-Hurra satellite TV channel to compete in the same media marketplace (Miles, 2005; Seib, 2008).

Al-Jazeera managed to find a foothold on the international media map. Its reporting outraged many Arab and foreign countries which accused it of transcending the boundaries and professional standards in dealing with issues and events (Miles, 2005). Nevertheless, one cannot but acknowledge that the channel has stirred the stagnant water of media in the Gulf region and the wider Arab World and has played a leading role in challenging the operators of the dominant news media in the region to adopt a different approach to news reporting.

Al-Jazeera's news service provides a diversity of factual content. If one watches 'With Haikal' documentary, one can get the impression that the channel is Nasserite in its orientation whereas 'Witness to the Age' or 'Without borders', a contrary impression arises that Al-Jazeera is anti-Nasserite and sympathetic to the 'Muslim brotherhood' Movement. A viewer of 'More Than One Opinion' by Sami Haddad could get the impression that the channel is liberal whereas 'Opposite Direction' by Faisal Al-Qasem leaves the impression that it is pan-Arab nationalist, while 'Islam and Life' by Yousef Al-Qardawi suggests that the channel is a moderate Sunni channel. 'Open Dialogue' by Ghassan Bin Jeddu makes the channel look like a Shiite pro-Iran channel. Thus, Al-Jazeera is an open space that accommodates all the colours of the spectrum (Mellor, 2005; Miles, 2005; Zayani, 2005). The question that arises here is: is it possible to maintain such diverse ideological perspectives under the same roof within one editorial framework?

The proliferation of satellite TV news channels reflects the depth and nature of the political transformations in the region after the events of 11 September 2001 and subsequent Allied occupation of Iraq. The Arab region in general and the Gulf region in particular found themselves in the heart of the international conflict led by the United States labelled 'the war on terror'. At the same time, these states have found themselves under pressure to embrace political and economic and social reforms. Initially these pressures were external to the Arab world, but the uprisings of the Arab spring in 2011, bore witness to internal pressures for change (Mellor, 2005; Miles, 2005).

There is no doubt that these changes, whether they are sourced from abroad or from within, require the ruling political elites in the region to search for local solutions rather than submit to external prescriptions for change imposed by force from outside the border. The growing role of satellite TV news channels can be conceived as one of the internal tools for change to contain the tensions resulting from external pressures. These channels may be able to create an environment of interaction and dialogue that can provide local alternatives to political, economic and social problems without any need for external pressure. Satellite TV news services can play an important role in promoting a state of equilibrium in the community that enables the region's nations to handle the input of international politics and the local environment without the need to make huge sacrifices to ensure their survival and prosperity (El-Nawawy and Iskandar, 2003; Seib, 2008).

Media challenges in the Gulf

The press, publications and media broadcasting industries and services in the Arab world particularly in the Arab States of the Gulf countries are on the verge of changes, challenges and transformations of unprecedented magnitude. Interwoven transitions ranging from political 'opening' to economic boom, from the emergence of internal security concerns to the advocacy of the right to know, are combining to direct Gulf-based media through shifting sands (Khalil, 2006).

Since the emergence of new communication technologies and the access to satellite TV news channels, new terminology has spread to the Arab masses by covering issues such as alternative media, new media, public participation in decision-making, administrative corruption, voting patterns in elections, human rights and civil society, pressure groups, government transparency and accountability, the free market economy, money-laundering, rights of women and children, domestic violence, rights of defendants, banning torture in prisons and so on. These subjects were not generally covered in the traditional, government-controlled press and local TV news services (El-Nawawy and Iskandar, 2003; Mellor, 2005). Satellite TV news channels have, for instance, hosted Israeli officials and analysts, a practice initiated by Al-Jazeera in a dramatic development that made Israel appear closer and its democracy a model dreamed of by some Arabs. Opposition politicians have found platforms on satellite TV news channels, private and public alike (Miles, 2005; Zayani, 2005).

Prior to the spread of satellite TV stations and new media, Arab ruling regimes used to have the final say regarding social change and they would introduce any change gradually without consulting the masses. The spread of satellite TV stations has enabled government opposition figures to have their messages heard as well in a way that used to be classed as an infringement on national sovereignty and the government's control of information (Lynch, 2006). Yet, some of these TV stations, especially the ones with widespread audience reach, are owned by businessmen close to the ruling regimes. This fact inevitably raises doubts about their editorial independence from government.

A positive outcome of Arab news satellite news stations is that their impact has started to influence different Arab issues and political institutions. Arab leaders began to see programmes depicting views that formerly lay off the political map. Transmissions from Arab satellite stations also began to reach the foreign political establishment. For instance, Al-Jazeera and Al-Arabia aroused the ire of the US administration after the invasion of Iraq in March 2003 and put it in a state of permanent criticism of their detailed coverage of the war for exposing the facts in terms of both number of innocent civilian deaths or the death toll among US forces and its allies because of the escalation of resistance, to the extent that prompted then Secretary of Defence Donald Rumsfeld to warn Al-Jazeera and Al-Arabia not to continue their coverage of the war and to accuse them of incitement against US troops (Sakr, 2007; Zayani, 2007).

The impact of new media and satellite news channels, including those aligned with the Arab governments, has had unexpected negative consequences that have acted as a catalyst to demands for political and societal changes. Such has been the pace of the demand for change that some incumbent political administrations have been perceived as slow to respond to the public's wishes (Mellor, 2005).

In this way the new Arab media have virtually revolutionized the Arab world, and began working to break down the authoritarian communication system based on one point of view representing the 'sacred point of view of the regime'. They have prompted governments to meet the upcoming danger by issuing laws to regulate satellite transmissions, most important of which is 'a document of principles regulating space transmission of radio and TV in the Arab countries' proposed by the Arab information ministers meeting in Cairo upon an initiative by Egypt in 2008. The issuance of this document aroused much controversy since it came from the ministries of information targeting the most popular media outlet: TV, and touching the most sensitive issue for citizens which is public freedoms, particularly, freedom of thought and query (Ghareeb, 2000; Alterman 1999; Rugh, 2004).

A key issue for Gulf administrations arising from the growing appeal of new media and satellite TV channels is concern about the potential impact, culturally and socially, of foreign TV channels. Exposure of Arab publics to non-Arab ways of life via satellite TV transmissions could cause people to question their satisfaction with local political, economic and social circumstances and to seek a break with specific cultural traditions.

References

Alterman, J. (1999) Transnational media and social change in the Arab world. *Transnational Broadcasting Studies*, 3. Available at: www.tbsjournal.com.

Auter, P. J., and Al-Jaber, K. (2003) Qatar media/Al-Jazeera TV. In D. DesJardins (ed.), *World Press Encyclopedia*, 2nd edn, pp. 759–62.

Ayish, M. (2001) American-style journalism and Arab World television: An exploratory study of news selection at six Arab World satellite television channels. *Transnational Broadcasting Studies*, 6. Available at: www. tbsjournal.com/Archives/Spring01/Ayish (accessed 18 December).

Boyd, D. (1999) *Broadcasting in the Arab World: A Survey of Electronic Media in the Middle East*. Ames, Iowa; Iowa State University.

El-Nawawy, M., & Iskander, A. (2002) *Al-Jazeera: How the Free Arab News Network Scooped the World and Changed the Middle East*. Boulder, CO: Westview Press.

— (2003) *Al-Jazeera: The Story of the Network that is Rattling Governments and Redefining Journalism*. Boulder, CO: Westview.

GCC Publications (2004) *Media Institutions in the Arab countries of the Gulf Cooperation Council (GCC): Radio, TV, and News Agencies*. Secretariat General. Riyadh, Saudi Arabia.

Ghareeb, E. (2000) New Media and the information revolution in the Arab world: An assessment. *Middle East Journal*, 54, 395–418.

Guaaybess, T. (2002) A new order of information in the Arab broadcasting system. *Transnational Broadcasting Studies*, 9 (Fall/Winter). Available at: www.tbsjournal.com/Guaaybess.html

— (2008) Orientalism and the economics of Arab broadcasting. In K. Hafez (ed.), Arab Media: Power and Weakness. New York: Continuum, pp. 199–213.

Hourani, A (1991) *A History of the Arab Peoples*. Cambridge: Harvard University Press, Belknap Press.

Iskandar, A. (2007) Lines in the sand: Problematizing Arab media in the post-Taxonomic era, *Arab Media and Society*. Available at: www. arabmediasociety.com/.

Khalil, J (2006) News television in the Arabian Gulf .Period of transitions. *Global Media Journal*, 5(8). Available at: www.lass.calumet.purdue.edu/cca/gmj/index.htm.

Lynch, M. (2006) *Voice of the New Arab Public: Iraq, Al-Jazeera and Middle East Politics Today*. New York: Columbia University Press.

Mellor, N. (2005) *The Making of Arab News*. Lanham, MD: Rowman and Littlefield.

Miles, H. (2005) *Al-Jazeera: The Inside Story of the Arab News Channel that is Challenging the West*. New York: Grove Press.

Rugh, W. A. (2004) *Arab Mass Media: Newspapers, Radio, and Television in Arab Politics*. Westport, CT: Praeger.

Sakr, N. (2001) *Satellite Realms: Transnational Television, Globalization and the Middle East*. London: IB Tauris.

— (2007) *Arab Television Today London*. UK: I.B. Tauris and Co. Ltd., pp. 137–64.

Seib, P. (2008) *The Al-Jazeera Effect: How the New Global Media Are Reshaping World Politics*. Washington, D.C. Potomac Books, Inc.

The Columbia Encyclopedia (2008) *The Columbia Encyclopedia*, 6th edn. Columbia University Press.

Wicks, R. H., and Walker, D. C. (1993) Differences between CNN and the broadcast networks in live war coverage. In B. S. Greenberg and W. Ganz (eds), *Desert Storm: and the Mass Media*. Hillsdale, NJ: Lawrence Erlbaum Associates, pp. 99–112.

Zayani, M. (2005) *The Al-Jazeera Phenomenon: Critical Perspectives on the New Arab Media*. Boulder, CO: Paradigm.

3

News in Iraq

Ahmed Al-Rawi and Barrie Gunter

Iraq has experienced considerable national turmoil over the past two decades as a result of its involvement in a number of regional conflicts. Political regimes have been challenged and overthrown and the country's governance temporarily taken out of its own hands. During this time the Iraqi news media has played a critical role in keeping its own citizens and those from elsewhere informed about the latest events.

This chapter will trace the developments in news media structures and operators within Iraq and examine the news media landscape that is taking shape as the country rebuilds after the 2003 war. A number of different vested interests and political factions have dominated the scene at different times since the war to shape the regulation and nature of news provision in the country. Questions have been raised about the impartiality of news coverage in Iraq, especially that occurring on television.

This chapter will examine these events and the status of news provision in Iraq at a crucial time when the country is in the process of rebuilding, economically and politically. It will also draw on new research into the presentation of news on Iraqi television post-invasion.

Early history of Iraqi media

The history of the Iraqi media goes back to the nineteenth century. One of the first Iraqi newspapers is called *Azzawra* which was first published in 1869.

The first Iraqi radio transmission took place during the rule of King Faisal I on 22 March 1932 (al-Rawi, 2010: 191). Faisal's son, Ghazi, was personally inter-ested in the news media especially the radio. After becoming King in 1933, Ghazi established the Zuhoor Palace Radio in 1936 transmitting from one of the royal palaces in Baghdad (192). In relation to television transmission, Iraq had one of the first television stations in the Arab world, broadcasting first in 1954 although regular programmes were only aired from 1956 (Boyd, 1982: 111; al-Rawi, 1992: 103, 106; 2010: 11, 201–2; de Beer and Merrill, 2004; Rugh, 2004: 2). At almost every revolution Iraq witnessed after the fall of the monarchy in 1958, the official TV station became the main focus for revolu-tionaries keen to reach the general public (Rugh, 2004: 7).

During the Ba'ath Party rule (1968–2003) the Iraqi media were completely controlled by the government and Iraqi journalists were expected to write in line with the policies of the party. Investigative journalism was not widely practiced and there was a low tolerance for criticism of the government.[1] As a result, Iraqi daily newspapers such as *al-Iraq*, *al-Jamhurryyah*, *al-Qadissyyah* and *al-Thawrah* looked very similar, regularly publishing large photographs of Saddam Hussein on their front pages and carrying similar if not identical reports and news stories. Any kind of intentional or unintentional deviation from the party's line was considered a crime punishable by imprisonment, torture or, in some cases, death. As Kim and Hama-Saeed (2008) put it, media channels were 'subordinate to state interest and were harnessed to serve only one political party, Ba'ath' (579–80). Reporters Sans Frontières' (RSF) (2002) described Saddam Hussein as a 'predator of press freedom' who managed the country's media with 'an iron fist and has given them the single mission of relaying his propaganda' (RSF, 2002: 1–3). Iraq was not unique in the Arab region in this respect, of course; other countries followed similar media policies. The 2003 United Nations Arab Human Development report observed that the Arab media were characterized by their authoritarian traits: 'media discourse mostly excludes the other point of view, keeping it away from the public mind' (UNDP, 2003: 62).

The Iraqi media were also banned from including any kind of sectarian or racist remarks against Iraqis in their reports in order to prevent public dis-order or internal conflict. With the ethnically and religiously rich diversity of Iraq's population, the use of language that distinguished Iraqis in terms of, for example, their membership of the Shia or Sunni Muslim sects was strictly prohibited (Bengio, 1985: 13). The social and political risks of highlight-ing the religious differences among Iraqis were well understood by the Iraqi government.

Under the Ba'ath Party rule there were four official television channels: two Iraqi national channels, Iraqi Satellite TV and Ashabab (youth) TV. Ownership of satellite television equipment was banned and any individual caught receiving satellite transmissions was either fined or imprisoned. After 1991 the situation in Iraqi Kurdistan was different. The number of partisan Kurdish television channels exceeded 20, broadcasting from the northern region of Iraq in which Kurds had their own relative independence from Baghdad (RSF, 2002: 2). The 'mountain journalists' of Kurdistan were well-known throughout the 1990s for propagandizing against the central government and encouraging Kurds to join the Kurdish armed militia, the Pashmerga. Since 1991 all Kurdish media outlets have been affiliated with political parties, the Patriotic Union of Kurdistan (PUK) and Kurdistan Democratic Party (KDP) being the most dominant.

Iraqi media after 2003

After the occupation of Iraq by the US-led forces in March 2003, the country's political, social and media systems changed dramatically. The newly appointed US administration, the Coalition Provisional Authority (CPA), sanctioned the creation of political/religious parties but banned the activities of the Ba'ath Party, hurriedly dissolved the Ministry of Information, the Iraqi army and security forces and prohibited their members from joining the newly established official bodies. The result was chaotic: the new parties whose heads and members mostly resided outside Iraq came with their own sectarian or ethnic agendas, while hundreds of thousands of young Iraqis remained unemployed and many faced continuous humiliations at the various US-controlled detention centres scattered across the country. Under the new political system Iraqis, including journalists, became polarized towards their own sect, ethnic group or tribe, seeking protection amid the overwhelming lack of security. The Iraqi media suffered from this new reality and became divided along these polarized lines.

In terms of the official US policy, the US government and its president ideally wanted to 'support a free, independent, and responsible Iraqi media (including television, radio, and print) that delivers high-quality content and responsible reporting throughout Iraq' (Bush, 2005). Following such a policy, the CPA expressed its desire to create 'an environment in which freedom of speech is cherished and information can be exchanged freely and openly' (CPA, 2003). The new media slogans were so powerful that even the US Civil Administrator to Iraq, Paul Bremer, prided himself on the difference between Iraq in the past and the current time, saying: 'under the last regime, it was illegal to criticize the government. Now you are free to criticize whomever or whatever you want' (Jayasekera, 2003). Yet in reality, the CPA acted violently against any media outlet that criticized the Coalition forces by either closing down newspapers and TV stations or arresting and interrogating journalists.

Within the context of this new media scene, Iraqis at first began to publish newspapers and magazines without any kind of censorship. Some positive outcomes were seen, such as the freedom to watch satellite television and the ability to browse the internet with fewer restrictions (Prusher, 2003, 6 April; al-Rawi, 2011). Internet users in Iraq, for example, numbered around 50,000 by the end of 2004 and about 170 internet cafés were operational by July 2006 (OpenNet Initiative, 2007: 2).

Iraqi journalists, who were either ignorant of the principles of good journalism during the previous era or were new to the profession, followed 'confused, mediocre journalistic standards' (Kim and Hama-Saeed, 2008: 581). Further, the majority of Iraqi journalists felt cornered because they were either pressured by their own religious or tribal community or by US soldiers, militias, insurgent groups or Iraqi security forces. As a result Iraq became known as the most unsafe country in the world for journalists for several years running.

In 2003 the CPA created the Iraqi Media Network (IMN) with the help of exiled Iraqis with the aim of becoming an independent media outlet. It also established the Communication and Media Commission (CMC) to regulate the work of media channels and telecommunication companies operating in Iraq. Before it was dissolved, the CPA transferred its control over IMN and CMC to the authority of the Iraqi government and its prime minister (CPA, 2004).

IMN was expected to become a public service media channel similar to the BBC or the US PBS. With a $6 million monthly budget, the first programme of IMN radio was aired on 10 April 2003 and its TV station, Iraqia channel, began broadcasting on 13 May (Dauenhauer and Lobe, 2003; Williams, 2003). Several problems arose soon after but one of the most significant was caused by the fact that the overwhelming majority of staff members working at IMN were Shiites and this affected the kind of messages the network aired to the public. However, the main problem was that the CPA's direct interference in IMN's work meant that it quickly became dependent on state policies and reliant on the official line (al-Rawi, 2011). This was despite CMC's regulation that IMN must remain independent and should not 'advocate the positions or interests of any particular political, religious, commercial or other party. In doing so, the IMN must ensure the public is aware of different points of view in order to create informed public opinion' (Communications and Media Commission, 2007: 14). The regulations also stated that clear policies must be observed in order to ascertain that 'programmes about religion or religious groups are accurate and fair. The belief and practice of religious groups must not be misrepresented. Programmes must not denigrate the religious beliefs of others' (Communications and Media Commission 2007: 14).

When the CPA was dissolved, IMN became more pro-Shiite than before especially so as the most powerful Iraqi politicians were Shiites (Cochrane, 2006; Metcalf, 2006). After the creation of the Interim Iraqi government, IMN came under the control of Prime Minister Iyad Allawi, who used it as a platform to propagate his party's polices. Allawi was a Shiite secular leader and he tried to prevent IMN from becoming divided along sectarian lines. To secure greater media control Allawi created the Higher Media Commission (HMC). By appointing his friend and media advisor, Ibrahim al-Janabi, as its head, Allawi attempted to impose his authority over IMN and other media channels. The prime minister displayed to journalists a steely resolve to control the news agenda and repeatedly attacked those who disagreed with him. During the state emergency rule, al-Janabi insisted that any kind of criticism against the prime minister or government performance could not be tolerated.

When the Shiite Dawaa Party member, Ibrahim Ja'afari, became the second prime minister in April 2005, the political situation in Iraq changed. Iraq witnessed the worst sectarian clashes after the bombing of the Shiite Samara shrine in 2006. As for IMN, it was restructured by 'hiring and firing editors, and directing editorial policy' (Levinson, 2006). As already stated, the overwhelming number of staff working at IMN was Shiite and the new management was loyal to different political parties. This turned IMN into a tool used by powerful Shiite parties such as Dawaa that is currently led by Nouri Maliki, the Muqtada Sadr movement and the Supreme Council of the Islamic Revolution in Iraq (SCIRI) (now called the Islamic Supreme Council of Iraq (ISCI) and led by Ammar Hakim).

In 2007 the CMC published a report on IMN's activities and expressed the serious need to have 'internal pluralism' that could be achieved by 'the inclusion of women and representatives of Iraq's various ethnic, religious and political groups – among members of its board and management and among its reporters and on-air personalities' (Communications and Media Commission, 2007: 42). Among the more popular programmes aired were Shiite religious sermons, flagellation processions, interviews with Shiite religious scholars and the infamous 'Terrorism in the Grip of Justice'. The latter programme aired confessions of alleged Sunni insurgents who were captured by US and Iraqi security forces. Without a trial, the confessions were focused on the assumed crimes committed by those insurgents, while clear signs of torture were seen in almost all of the interviewees. The programme was aired at 9 pm, TV prime time, and it usually implicated Syria and the news channel Al-Jazeera to be behind the violence in the country (Stalinsky, 2005).

In brief IMN's pro-Shiite editorial policy played a large role in polarizing post-invasion Iraqi society, marginalizing the Sunni masses and turning them against the Iraqi government. For example, the Iraqi Sunni politician, Saleh al-Mutlaq, expressed his concern over the sectarian tension in the country and pointed his finger directly to IMN because it helped 'turn Iraqi society into a sectarian society' (Levinson, 2006). Other Iraqi media channels followed the IMN example, ultimately increasing the overall tension (Roug, 2006).

Finally, when Nouri Maliki came to power, he followed Allawi by creating his own media body that was expected to oversee and monitor the activities of IMN and other media outlets. The National Media Center (NMC) was established in 2007 and Maliki appointed his media advisor, Ali Hadi al-Musawi, as its head. During Maliki's rule, a new phenomenon appeared which reflected the method used by the Iraqi government to silence the opposition. Many libel suits were filed in Iraqi courts against Iraqi journalists who challenged the official authority and pointed out its shortcomings. The prime minister, for example, filed a defamation suit against Ayad Zamili who mentioned that Maliki's chief of staff favoured his own relatives when he hired them for governmental posts. Zamili posted his article on a German-based website called 'Kitabat' (RSF, 20 May 2009). In addition, al-Diyar TV aired a news report taken from a newspaper about the alleged corruption of the director of real estate in the Ministry of Transportation. The channel was ordered to pay 10 million Iraqi dinars in April 2009 for defaming the reputation of an Iraqi official by airing 'false' information (Journalistic Freedoms Observatory, 2009).

Other setbacks in the media scene followed. Similar to the situation under the Ba'ath Party rule, the Iraqi government decreed that all publications imported from abroad must be checked before they were allowed into the market (Middle East Online, 14 August 2009). Other proposed manuscripts and book drafts must be inspected before giving printing rights to publishing houses (Al-Hayat, 2009). Finally, internet access also became restricted to websites that did not endanger the state's security. Access to websites that had sectarian, pornographic and terrorist overtones was prohibited (Salaheddin, 2009).

To sum up, there were some positive gains for the Iraqi media after the 2003 invasion: a plural and diverse media system was introduced and journalists' pay increased. Yet, there were many losses and negative outcomes: the polarization of journalists, the sectarian media that played a role in dividing the Iraqi society and the increasing risks of violence and intimidation against journalists. The following section reports on an analysis of newscasts aired by four Iraqi TV stations. This is based on the findings of a study designed to enhance our understanding of the kind of media messages being broadcast in post-invasion Iraq. The data were collected at the time of the 2010 Iraq general election. This event and the campaign that preceded it provided an opportunity to capture a sample of politically charged news coverage and to examine whether the nature of this coverage varied between TV channels with distinctive political and religious allegiances. More broadly it also facilitated an analysis of the status of broadcast journalism in Iraq.

Broadcast news coverage of a political election in Iraq

The research reported below investigated the tone of topics coverage in the evening newscasts of the government-run Iraqia channel, Furat (Shiite led by SCI), Hurria (Kurdish led by Jalal Talabani) and Baghdad (Sunni led by Ayad Samarai) over 14 days that preceded polling day on the 7 March 2010. In total, 56 evening newscasts were selected that yielded a sample of 857 news stories relating to the election. These stories aggregated to 33.73 hours of programme running time. The research considered two major research questions: how did these channels frame issues in the election campaign? And which issues were made prominent?

A hierarchical analysis of programme content was undertaken on three levels: (1) programme level, (2) story level and (3) sub-story-level. The programme level analysis measured the total number of news stories contained in each broadcast, the frequency of occurrence of specific news topics, the total amount of airtime time allotted to each news story topic and the number and types of news formats used. The news topics were: political differences, security/terrorism, democracy, public services, corruption/violence, national unity/political dialogue, election fraud, federalism, supporting electoral slate, Iraqi High Electoral Commission (IHEC) and other. There were eight formats differentiated, informed by the work of Grabe and Bucy (2009): newsreader (talking head); voice-over; voice-over-sound-on-tape (VO/SOT); recorded interview; live interview; package; film report (reporter unseen) and in-studio interview.

The story level analysis examined the presence/absence of: (1) narrative references to political candidates; (2) featured film/images of the candidates; (3) featured interviews with the candidates. This analysis shed light on the emphasis placed by each TV channel on specific political candidates over others.

The sub-story level of analysis focused on the treatment given to candidates featured within stories. Verbal references to them were classified as 'positive', 'neutral' or 'negative' via a predetermined lexicon of terms. Further codes measured whether a political candidate was featured alongside a rival candidate and the spatial relationship between them. Finally, camera shots (camera angle and use of close-ups) were classified in relation to specific candidates.

The main evening newscasts were chosen from different phases of the election campaign and from three different channels as follows: Baghdad on 22 February, Iraqia on 25 February and Hurria on 2 March. The coding frame was pretested with two coders and a high average reliability coefficient (alpha = 0.86) was achieved.

Topic profiles of TV news in Iraq

Beginning with the programme level analysis of the newscasts, the total sample of 857 stories was distributed fairly evenly across the four TV channels: the Sunni Baghdad channel (n = 234); the Shiite channel, Furat (n = 221); the Kurdish TV Hurria (n = 201) and the state-run Iraqia channel (n = 201).

Based on the raw data collected, the Hurria channel owned by Jalal Talabani, the head of PUK and the current President of Iraq, aired less air time and fewer stories. The PUK's main target audience is Kurdish speakers, so it seemed that Hurria paid less attention to producing Arabic news and reports on the election than did the other channels. This was also evident in the major type of news formats used as will be explained below. Unlike Hurria channel, Baghdad TV was the only Sunni channel whose sponsors were represented in the government, and it was the sole television medium used by Ayad al-Samarai and his slate.

Distribution of news topics

This section discusses the distribution of news topics along the four channels (see Table 3.1). In general, Iraqia TV showed the most emphasis among the other channels in airing stories related to 'IHEC' and 'other'. Iraqia TV closely followed the Iraqi government's policy to cover IHEC's activities and urge Iraqis to vote in the election. On the other hand, the Kurdish Hurria TV showed the least keenness in promoting its Kurdish sponsors in terms of the number of stories, airtime and news formats. Also, the channel was closer to Iraqia TV in many aspects, particularly the amount of coverage of 'IHEC' and 'other' topics. This is mainly due to the fact that both channels are closely affiliated with the Iraqi government. The only topic that Hurria TV showed more interest in airing was 'federalism', though Baghdad TV shared with it

TABLE 3.1 Number of topics' references

Topics	Iraqia	Furat	Baghdad	Hurria	Total
1. Political differences	12	37	30	19	98
2. Security/terrorism	59	41	87	48	235
3. Democracy	24	34	9	22	333
4. Public services	4	39	65	21	129
5. Corruption/violation	3	6	27	8	44
6. National unity/political dialogue	13	24	30	13	80
7. Election fraud	31	61	38	25	155
8. Federalism	0	2	7	7	16
9. Supporting electoral slate	0	106	141	43	290
10. Iraqi High Electoral Commission (IHEC)	78	39	46	50	213
11. Other	115	81	88	103	387

the same number of stories. This is understandable since Hurria channel is owned by a Kurdish party that strongly advocates federalism.

Turning to Furat TV, its coverage showed it to be a partisan channel that was attempting to promote its sponsor. There was a clear one-sided view of the events and topics covered as the other opponent parties or slates either did not appear on the channel or were criticized. The channel showed the highest degree of emphasis on airing the topics of 'political difference', 'democracy' and 'election fraud'.

As for Baghdad TV, it was not very different from Furat TV: the priority was to promote their parties and cover the activities of their candidates. Both channels were concerned with covering the performance of the government headed by the prime minister who was one of their stronger political opponents. Baghdad TV was ahead among the other channels in the attention it gave to the topics of 'security/terrorism', 'public services', 'corruption/violation', 'national unity/political dialogue', 'federalism' and 'supporting electoral slate'.

The pair-wise, non-parametric Mann–Whitney tests were computed. The results showed that the highest degree of difference among the paired channels was between Baghdad and Iraqia channels as eight topics showed significant differences in terms of the number of stories. This was expected because the two channels stand at opposite poles in relation to the whole political process and other vital issues.

Amount of airtime devoted to news topics

This section discusses the distribution of airtime devoted to the different topics covered by the channels (see Table 3.2). Iraqia TV showed the highest amount of emphasis in relation to the time allotted to the topic of 'IHEC'. This is expected because as the state-run channel Iraqia TV is more concerned with airing the announcements made by IHEC to inform the public about any major development in the electoral process. What is striking is the fact that Iraqia TV downplayed the importance of many topics by exhibiting the least airtime of the four channels. These topics include 'political differences', 'public services', 'corruption/violation', 'national unity/political dialogue' and 'federalism'. By ignoring many important issues that trouble Iraqis on a daily basis, the channel aimed at projecting a brighter view of the events than the reality on the ground.

TABLE 3.2 Time allotted to topics in minutes

Topics	Iraqia	Furat	Baghdad	Hurria	Total
1. Political differences	26.1	172.4	133.6	56.6	388.6
2. Security/terrorism	116.9	135.2	303.3	79.2	634.7
3. Democracy	57.1	127.9	28.06	47.2	260.4
4. Public services	12.2	151.4	235.8	40.1	439.6
5. Corruption/violation	5.2	48.9	101.6	11.4	167.1
6. National unity/political dialogue	26.1	94.8	118.3	27.1	266.3
7. Election fraud	88.2	214.4	147.2	39.9	489.7
8. Federalism	0.0	2.6	31.21	9.1	43.0
9. Supporting electoral slate	0.0	325.2	443.3	72.1	840.6
10. Iraqi High Electoral Commission (IHEC)	207.0	142.2	169.3	67.7	586.2
11. Other	247.4	201.0	303.1	146.2	897.7

As for Furat TV, it showed the greatest emphasis in terms of the time allotment to the topics of 'political differences', 'democracy' and 'election fraud'. Except for democracy, it was expected that the channel would highlight the issues of 'political differences' and 'election fraud' due to the animosity between Hakim's slate and that of Maliki. In other words, Furat wanted to show that there were serious political divides and election fraud taking place because of the policies of Maliki's party.

Further, Baghdad TV emphasized the topics of 'security/terrorism', 'public services', 'corruption/violation', 'national unity/political dialogue', 'federalism', 'supporting electoral slate' and 'other' more than the other channels. Except for 'supporting electoral slate', 'other' and to a certain extent 'national unity/political dialogue', most of the topics cited above were covered in a negative manner which reflected the ideological background of the channel. Finally, Hurria TV did not show any topic emphasis over the other channels investigated in this study. Again, this reflects the channel's lack of interest in airing Arabic programmes that promote the election and its candidates.

The results of pair-wise, non-parametric t-tests showed that the highest degree of difference among the paired channels being investigated was between Baghdad and Hurria channels: nine topics showed significant differences in terms of the time allotment. Again, this is expected because Baghdad channel seems to be against the policies of the Iraqi government unlike Hurria channel whose owner represents the whole government.

In conclusion, based on the number of stories, time allotment and type of news formats, we can see that Baghdad TV came ahead of Furat in its effort to cover the election and promote its political sponsor. Iraqia channel came third in its emphasis on covering the election but not on promoting candidates, while Hurria TV placed last in promoting its political bloc and the least interested in covering the election. In order to further understand the way these topics were covered, it is important to know the tone of coverage to give us an idea about the way these topics were framed by these four channels.

Story analysis: Candidates' coverage

The second stage in the content analysis of newscasts was centred on the stories themselves. Using a separate coding frame, the research analysed the stories by highlighting their prominence: time allotment, number of stories and format type. Though there was usually a close correlation between the number of stories and time allotment, there were some variations due to the nature of the stories presented.

This section will discuss the stories that featured narrative references to political candidates. Baghdad TV scored the largest number of stories with 164 and highest time allotted with 524.5 minutes that presented narrative references to candidates representing the Iraqi Accord Front (IAF), the slate that sponsors the channel. The stories constituted 69.7 per cent of the total number of stories aired by the channel. Baghdad TV rarely referred or assigned much time to other competing political blocs. Just five stories (running time of 14.25 minutes) were devoted to other parties/groups.

Furat channel came second in rank in terms of the number of stories and time allotted to its party's candidates. The channel aired 120 stories (377.7 minutes) on the party's candidates. The stories made up 54.2 per cent of the total number that were analysed for this channel throughout the period of study. Further, the channel also aired five stories (7.7 minutes) that carried narrative references to Sadr's movement/candidate. This was understandable because Hakim and Sadr formed the Iraqi National Alliance (INA) from its inception, so the two Shiite groups stood together against other competing political blocs.

Hurria TV aired 43 stories (54.8 minutes) on the Kurdish Alliance (KA) constituting 21.3 per cent of the total number of stories aired by the channel. The channel devoted six stories (6.7 minutes) to Allawi's bloc, two stories to Maliki's slate (1.8 minute) and two others to Hakim's alliance (1.9 minute). There were four references to Allawi's al-Iraqia slate (6.7 minutes) because some of its candidates were subjected to the de-Ba'athification process in order to exclude them from running in the election. In fact, this move created a great deal of controversy about the credibility of the government and its Accountability and Justice Commission which was led by Ali al-Lami, being himself a candidate running in the election.

Finally, Iraqia TV did not allot more emphasis to one political group over any other. Four stories (1.7 minute) were devoted to Allawi's bloc. However, the dominant issue related to this political group was the law suits filed against some of its candidates. In presenting the different political blocs, the channel established itself as the most balanced and objective among the four channels.

News formats

Further story level analyses centred on the extent to which stories featured film reports or still images of candidates sponsoring the channels. This analysis examined the presence/absence of: (1) narrative references to political candidates; (2) featured film/image of the candidates; (3) featured interviews with the candidates. This analysis sheds light on the tendencies of each channel either to promote its political candidates or to pay attention to other candidates from different parties eager to speak about their political programmes. The presence of film footage or still images can enhance the visibility of news stories to the audience and be used to emphasize particular elements of a story (see Gunter, 1997). Finally, interviews have been found to have greater effects on viewers than the other format types examined in this study (Detenber et al., 1998; King and Morehouse, 2004: 304; Grabe and Bucy, 2009). Viewers tend to see candidates as being more significant when they are presented on TV. If they are repeatedly shown on screen candidates tend to become more important too (McCombs and Shaw, 1972). Certainly, conducting interviews with political candidates is indicative of attention and emphasis given by the channel to the politician because they entail a per-sonalized encounter with the candidate giving him/her the chance to voice the political programme and thereby to become closer to the viewer. Less importance and influence is found in the moving film shown, but the latter can enhance story recall by viewers more so than still images or the narrative references to the candidate (Gunter, 1979).

Film and stills

On the measure of the use of picture formats, Baghdad TV was ranked first with the largest number of stories and greatest amount of air time allotted to such production treatments. The 160 stories (518.8 minutes) constituted 68.08 per cent of the total number of stories aired by the channel for 14 days. Again, Furat TV was ranked second on this measure with 114 stories (358.11 minutes) that comprised 51.5 per cent of the total number of stories. Hurria channel was ranked last with 33 stories (53 minutes) that formed 16.4 per cent of the total number of stories.

In general, the number of stories and time allotment that featured film footage or still images of candidates from other blocs were less than the number of stories and time allotted to featuring purely narrative references to candidates. As cited earlier, presenting a film or still image on television can have more impact on the viewers than just making a narrative reference (see Gunter, 1997). Hence, three out of the four channels discussed (the exception being Iraqia TV) sought to stress the importance of their own candidates by paying less or no emphasis on candidates from other parties.

Looking at inter-channel differences further, it emerged that Maliki's slate was covered equally by the four channels. In general TV channels largely favoured their own candidates, but some also covered other candidates as well. The significant differences were mainly centred on the slates that sponsor the respective channels such as Hakim's slate covered by Furat

TV, Talabani's group presented by Hurria, and Samarai's party covered by Baghdad TV. As for Sadr's group, Furat TV was the only channel that showed a significant difference from the rest of the channels.

Candidate interviews

Further analysis dealt with the number of stories and time allotted to interviews with political candidates. Once more, Baghdad TV ranked highest with the largest number of stories and time allotment compared with the other channels. There were 126 stories containing candidate interviews (429.58 minutes) making up 53.6 per cent of the total number of stories aired on its IAF candidates. Furat TV ranked second airing 42 stories (147.5 minutes) featuring candidate interviews, making up 19 per cent of the total number of stories broadcast. Hurria channel aired only 16 stories (35.6 minutes) featuring such interviews, accounting for 7.9 per cent of stories aired.

It is noteworthy that the number of stories and time allotted to featuring interviews with candidates from other political blocs were less than the number of stories and time devoted to featuring narrative references and films or images of their own political candidates.

As mentioned earlier, conducting interviews with candidates is seen as a very effective tool for involving news viewers (King and Morehouse, 2004). Furat TV, for example, never showed a story that contained an interview with a candidate from other blocs, not even from Sadr's movement. Hurria TV only aired an interview with a representative of Hakim's INA and two interviews with representatives from other smaller parties that lasted 298 seconds in total. Finally, Baghdad TV aired two interviews which took five minutes with candidates from other parties that seemed to be weak in influence.

In terms of 'other parties', Hurria and Baghdad TV seemed to be more relaxed in airing interviews with candidates in this category. On the other hand, Hurria showed one short interview lasting 2.4 minutes with Hakim's bloc. This might have been due to the channel's awareness that future alliances must be established with other parties in order for the Kurds to get some political gains when the parliament is established. The events following the general election support this explanation since the KA made an alliance with INA and Maliki's State of Law slate which all formed a majority in the Iraqi Parliament.

In relation to further inter-channel comparisons, there were just a few notable differences: Hakim's group was preferred by Furat TV; the Talabani's party by Hurria and the Samarai's slate by Baghdad TV. The slates mentioned here were the actual sponsors of the respective channels, so it became very clear that these channels favoured their own political parties.

In summary, looking at the data on stories featuring narrative references to political candidates, film/images of the candidates and interview with the candidates, Baghdad TV showed the greatest variance in coverage followed by Furat TV and then Hurria channel, while Iraqia TV was not directly involved in the promotion of political candidates. As expected, most of the channels examined in this study showed obvious bias towards their own respective sponsors. They then largely negated the existence of other political factions and preferred to air favourable views of the parties that sponsored them.

These findings give some clear indications about the (non-)application of good principles of journalism especially in respect of neutrality and impartiality. The findings show that most of the major Iraqi TV channels were only concerned about presenting their own agendas and conveying favourable ideas about their own preferred candidates/sponsors rather than offering more balanced coverage or criticizing their own parties.

Candidates' attributes

Within news stories about the election, further analyses were computed to explore the way political candidates were treated. One key analysis was the valence of the treatment given to each candidate, meaning whether they were treated in a neutral, positive or negative fashion. To facilitate this analysis, story references to candidates were assessed in terms of their use of neutral/positive/negative descriptors, adjectives and expressions.

Iraqia TV largely refrained from covering the activities of political candidates; however, there was some coverage of Allawi and his slate. Five negative references were made in comparison to three neutral ones. The Iraqi President Talabani and the Parliament speaker Samarai both received one neutral reference. Maliki was mentioned on a daily basis and mostly in a positive way.

On Furat TV, the concentration of references was on Hakim's slate (the channel's sponsor) with 124 positive attributes. However, there were also ten negative references to Maliki's slate. This was largely due to the fact that Maliki decided to withdraw from the Shiite alliance that was formed in 2005 in order to present himself as a unifier of Iraqis whether they were Sunnis or Shiites. Maliki tried to include Sunni figures in his slate (such as the senior members of the Awakening Council of Anbar). This move angered Hakim and his bloc who responded with an antagonistic attitude towards Maliki and his slate. Other references made by Furat TV included nine positive ones on Sadr and his bloc (reflecting the fact that the two groups had formed an alliance).

On Baghdad TV there were few negative references to political blocs. The largest number of positive references occurred for Samarai's bloc (n = 639) (the channel's sponsor) and eight for other slates. Finally, there were seven neutral references to Samarai's bloc.

The last channel investigated was Hurria TV. In terms of positive references, there were 38 for Talabani's slate (the channel's sponsor), seven for Allawi's bloc and four for Hakim's. As mentioned earlier, the Kurds did not focus on Talabani and his slate because there were investing in other Kurdish-language channels. As for the positive references to other blocs, it seems that the channel had in mind the idea of future alliances with other slates without which the Kurds could not form a majority in the Parliament. There were few negative references, too. The highest number of such references was centred on Talanabi's slate (n = 10), Maliki's slate (n = 6) and Allawi's bloc (n = 3). Finally, neutral attributes were given to Talabani (n = 12), while Sadr and Samarai got one reference each.

TABLE 3.3 Kruskal-Wallis and Mann-Whitney tests: Ranking of candidates' positive attributes

	Iraqia TV No. of References	Furat TV No. of References	Baghdad TV No. of References	Hurria TV No. of References	Chi-square	Asymp. Sig.
Maliki	0[a]	0[a]	0[a]	0[a]	0.00	$p < 1.000$
Allawi	0[a]	0[a]	0[a]	7[a]	6.54	*$p < 0.055$
Hakim	0[a]	124[b]	0[a]	4[a]	63.36	**$p < 0.000$
Sadr	0[a]	9[b]	0[a]	0[a]	5.76	$p < 0.124$
Talabani	0[a]	0[a]	0[a]	38[b]	19.70	***$p < 0.000$
Samarai	0[a]	0[a]	639[b]	0[a]	326.67	****$p < 0.000$
Others	0[a]	0[a]	8[a]	0[a]	2.66	$p < 0.447$

Note: Scores that share the same superscript are not significantly different at the $p < 0.05$ level.
*$p < 0.055$ (Allawi: There are significant differences in covering this candidate/slate among the channels).
**$p < 0.000$ (Hakim: There are significant differences in covering this candidate/slate among the channels).
***$p < 0.000$ (Talabani: There are significant differences in covering this candidate/slate among the channels).
****$p < 0.000$ (Samarai: There are significant differences in covering this candidate/slate among the channels).

In order to examine the details of the differences in covering the candidates among the four channels, a series of Kruskal–Wallis and Mann–Whitney Tests were computed. There were no significant differences in use of negative references for candidates across the four TV channels. There was just one significant difference in respect of use of neutral references in respect of coverage of Talabani and his slate which was due to Hurria TV's high number of neutral references to its sponsor.

Turning to positive references, a number of significant differences occurred (see Table 3.3). These differences occurred for Hakim, Talabani and Samarai. They reflected the heavy focus on positives for each of these political parties by their sponsored TV channels: Furat, Hurria and Baghdad channels respectively.

Candidates' spatial relationship

A further sub-story level analysis explored each candidate's spatial relationship with others within the sampled news programmes. Murphy (1998) classified the spatial relationship of a candidate with others into five categories following the study of Patterson and McClure (1976): 'candidate shown alone', 'touching distance to audience', 'speaking distance', 'public distance', 'further' or 'unable to determine' (1998: 35–6). Indeed, there is a strong link between the way a candidate is shown on screen and the effect on the viewer. For example, there is more influence on the viewer if the candidate is shown in touching or speaking distance to the audience (Patterson and McClure, 1976). This study added 'candidate shown with others' which carries similar weight to the previous two techniques since the candidate is not always shown speaking to the audience. Public distance was the classification assigned when the candidate appeared on a stage that was above the level of the audience. This technique is less intimate and has a lesser influence on the viewer because the candidate is made to look isolated from the people around. The same argument is applied to a candidate 'shown alone'.

Across the four TV channels candidates were more likely to be 'shown alone' (249 candidate appearances) than alongside another candidate, regardless of the spatial distance between them. When two or more candidates were featured, they were most likely to be shown at a 'public distance' (127 appearances), followed by 'shown with others' (111 appearances), 'touching distance' (35 appearances) and 'speaking distance' (29 appearances). This pattern was consistently applied across the three TV channels sponsored by political candidates. Relevant depictions of candidates on Iraqia TV were rare.

Baghdad TV was most likely of all channels to prefer to show candidates on their own ($n = 153$). This was true for all the major political candidates featured in this analysis such as Hakim, Mahdi, Al-Amri, Talabani, etc. Furat TV preferred to use a 'public distance' format ($n = 66$). Hurria TV also preferred to show candidates on their own ($n = 29$) but displayed candidates much less often than Baghdad TV and Furat TV. As a reminder, Baghdad, Furat and Hurria channels focused their coverage on their own candidates and largely ignored the others as mentioned above; hence, Table 3.4 deals with the candidates

TABLE 3.4 Candidates' spatial relationships

		Iraqia	Furat	Baghdad	Hurria
Candidate 1	1. Shown alone	4	43	107	21
	2. Shown with others	1	31	45	19
	3. Touching distance to audience	0	10	21	0
	4. Speaking distance	0	2	22	0
	5. Public distance	0	65	36	5
	6. Further or unable to determine	0	0	0	0
Candidate 2	1. Shown alone	1	12	30	5
	2. Shown with others	1	0	7	2
	3. Touching distance to audience	0	0	3	0
	4. Speaking distance	0	0	4	0
	5. Public distance	0	1	14	0
	6. Further or unable to determine	0	0	0	0
Candidate 3	1. Shown alone	0	5	17	4
	2. Shown with others	0	0	4	1
	3. Touching distance to audience	0	0	2	0
	4. Speaking distance	0	0	1	0
	5. Public distance	0	0	6	0
	6. Further or unable to determine	0	0	0	0

whose slates sponsor the channels, except for Iraqia TV that showed films/ stills of Maliki, Talabani and Samarai once each and Allawi twice.

Camera angles

The final phase of analysis in this coding frame was related to the camera angles used when a candidate(s) is shown. Kepplinger (1982, 1983) investigated how some camera angles used in filming candidates can influence TV viewers' impressions of those candidates. The results of that study showed that the positive effect of the camera angle is achieved when the camera is held at eye level. This is probably due to the viewer's feeling of being equal with and close to the candidate. Low angles have a negative impact on the viewer. Graber examined how camera angles can influence the manner by which the audience comprehend the message; for example, 'audiences are likely to pay more attention to close-ups' (2001: 197). Grabe and Bucy confirmed that:

> when candidates are portrayed in close-up shots that promote emotional involvement and establish social proximity between televised subjects and viewers. . . . By minimizing the psychological distance between viewing audiences and actors on the political stage, television prompts viewers to regard candidates in personal terms, fostering familiarity and trust. (2009: 153)

In other words, there is more 'visual weight' with the camera's close-up and eye-level positions which add more importance to the candidate and show a clear production bias.

As expected, we find in Table 3.5 that Baghdad TV showed more emphasis on its IAF's candidates by showing them more than did the other channels in close-up and at eye-level. This was not only confined to the first candidates but also to the second and third candidates when available. In the second rank was Furat TV, followed by Hurria channel.

To sum up, Baghdad TV was more fervent in its emphasis on the importance of its candidates than the other channels at all the production levels. The channel aired more stories and used more 'favourable' techniques than the others in terms of the number of political affiliates interviewed, its candidates' spatial relationship with others and camera angles (eye-level view and close-up). Based on the same criteria, Furat TV claimed second rank in relation to the attention given to its candidates, while Hurria channel came third. As for Iraqia TV, the main emphasis was on the topics aired rather than

TABLE 3.5 Camera angles

	Iraqia	Furat	Baghdad	Hurria
Candidate 1. Eye level	5	117	153	41
Candidate 2. Eye level	2	13	44	7
Candidate 3. Eye level	0	5	25	5
Candidate 1. Full top view	0	1	1	0
Candidate 2. Full top view	0	0	0	0
Candidate 3. Full top view	0	0	0	0
Candidate 1. Bottom view	0	0	3	0
Candidate 2. Bottom view	0	0	2	0
Candidate 3. Bottom view	0	0	1	0
Candidate 1. Close-up	0	98	130	27
Candidate 2. Close-up	1	13	34	5
Candidate 3. Close-up	0	5	21	4

political candidates. Based on the data reported above, we can conclude that all the TV channels examined in this study showed some kind of imbalance and subjectivity in either covering topics or candidates. Balance is measured by counting the negative and positive references to topics/candidates, and what we observed was that all the channels, except in few cases, tended to either align with the positive or negative sides.

The Iraqi media after 2010

After the re-election of Maliki as prime minister in 2011, several protests were organized in different parts of Iraq demanding an end to corruption and job-lessness. Many Iraqi news outlets were highly critical of the government and some political parties for their alleged role in the deterioration of living standards and the spread of lawlessness. As a result, several journalists were beaten in Basrah in March 2011 and the office of the Journalistic Freedom Observatory was destroyed by security forces in Baghdad. In the Kurdish city of Sulymaniah, Voice Radio together with Nalia Radio and Television were stormed by men wearing security uniforms and were closed down for airing the protests that were held against the main political party (Barzanji, 2011; Tawfeeq, 2011). Human right groups criticized the Kurdish authorities for arresting activists and limiting freedom of expression.

Iraq continues to be regarded as one of the most dangerous countries in the world for journalists to work in. More than 230 media personnel died since the beginning of the US invasion in 2003, including journalists and their assistants, and hundreds of journalists have been forced to flee to neighbouring countries (RSF, 2009, 2010). According to the Committee to Protect Journalists (CPJ), 136 journalists were killed as a direct result of their media work; 90 per cent among them were Iraqis (CPJ, 2008). For four consecutive years, Iraq has the highest number of murdered journalists whose cases have not yet been resolved. From 2001 to 2011, 92 journalists have been killed, but the government is either 'unable or unwilling to prosecute the killers' (CPJ, 2011). Iraq is regarded as 'the world's biggest market for hostages. Over 93 media professionals were abducted' from 2003 to 2010 'at least 42 of whom were later executed. Moreover, 14 are still missing' (RSF, 2010). In fact after 2003 Iraq became the worst country in the world to live in not only for journalists but also for people as a whole. The Global Peace Index of 2010 mentioned that Iraq came in number 143 and ranked as the worst country in the world in terms of the lack of security and peace (Institute for Economics and Peace, 2010).

This study and the developments that occurred after 2010 clearly indicate the disappointing reality of the Iraqi media and the illusion that real democratic change has taken place in Iraq. Media outlets are dependent on their political sponsors and Iraqi journalists are mostly governed by the editorial policies of their newspapers and TV stations rather than by the principles of good journalism. Further, each TV channel seemed to be addressing its own sect or ethnic group as if other minorities did not exist. Although they claimed to be impartial and objective, the results showed that TV news services were far from this and showed strong allegiance to their partisan or religious affiliations. These channels were rather reserved in showing the negative attributes of other candidates/slates, perhaps because they either feared retribution, libel suits or death threats that are so common in contemporary Iraq.

Note

1 Despite this, many Iraqi journalists attempted to abide by the principles of good journalism and observe balance, impartiality and objectivity, while others even attempted to criticize Saddam Hussein's regime (al-Rawi, 2012).

References

Al-Hayat (2009) Iraqi official censorship on imported books. 22 July. Available at: http://ksa.daralhayat.com/ksaarticle/40272 (accessed 31 December 2009).

Al-Rawi, K. H. (1992) *History of Radio and Television in Iraq* (in Arabic). Baghdad: Dar al-Hikma for Publishing and Distribution.

— (2010) *The History of the Press and Media in Iraq from the Ottoman Period until the Second Gulf War, 1816–1991* (in Arabic). Damascus: Dar Safahat lil Dirasat wa Al-Nashir.

— (2011) Iraqi women journalists' challenges and predicaments, *Journal of Arab and Muslim Media Research*, 3(3), 223–36.

— (2012) *Media Practice in Iraq*. Hampshire: Palgrave Macmillan.

Barzanji, Y. (2011) Gunmen in Iraq attack Kurdish TV station that showed protest. *The Associated Press*. 20 February.

Bengio, O. (1985) Shi'is and politics in Ba'thi Iraq. *Middle Eastern Studies*, 21(1) (January), 1–14.

Boyd, D. A. (1982) *Broadcasting in the Arab World: A Survey of Radio and Television in the Middle East*. Philadelphia: Temple University Press.

Bush, G. W. (2005). Iraq strategy. November. Retrieved on 12 June 2009. http://georgewbushwhitehouse.archives.gov/infocus/iraq/text/iraq_strategy_nov2005.html.

Coalition Provisional Authority (2003) Prohibited Media Activity. CPA/ORD/10 June 2003/14.

— (2004) Transition of Laws, Regulations, Orders, and Directives Issued by the Coalition Provisional Authority. CPA/ORD/28 June 2004/100.

Cochrane, P. (2006) The 'Lebanonization' of the Iraqi media: An overview of Iraq's television landscape, *Transnational Broadcasting Studies*, 16. Available at: www.tbsjournal.com.

Communications and Media Commission (2007) *Policy Recommendations Concerning Broadcasting in Iraq*. Stanhope Centre for Communications Policy Research, January.

CPJ (Committee to Protect Journalists). (18 December 2008) Special reports: For sixth straight year, Iraq deadliest nation for press. Available at: http://cpj.org/reports/2008/12/for-sixth-straight-year-iraq-deadliest-nation-for.php (accessed 25 June 2009).

— (2011) Special reports: Getting away with murder: CPJ's 2011 impunity index spotlights countries where journalists are slain and killers go free. Available at: http://cpj.org/reports/2011/06/2011-impunity-index-getting-away-murder.php#index (accessed 5 August 2011).

Dauenhauer, K. and Lobe, J. (2003) Iraq: Massive military contractor makes media mess. *IPS*. Available at: www.ipsnews.net/interna.asp?idnews=19661 (accessed 25 June 2009).

De Beer, A. and Merrill, J. (2004) *Global Journalism: Topical Issues and Media Systems*. Boston: Pearson Education.

Detenber, B. H., Simons, R. F. and Bennett, G. G., Jr. (1998) Roll 'em!: The effects of picture motion on emotional responses, *Journal of Broadcasting and Electronic Media*, 4, 113–128.

Grabe, M. and Bucy, E. (2009) *Image Bite Politics: News and Visual Framing of Elections.* New York: Oxford University Press.

Graber, D. A. (2001) *Processing Politics: Learning from Television in the Internet Age.* Studies in Communication, Media and Public Opinion. Chicago: University of Chicago Press.

Gunter, B. (1979) Recall of television news items: Effects of presentation mode, picture content and serial position, *Journal of Education Television*, 5, 57–61.

— (1997) *Measuring Bias on Television.* Bedfordshire: University of Luton Press.

Institute for Economics and Peace (2010) Global peace index. Available at: http://economicsandpeace.org/wp-content/uploads/2011/09/2010-GPI-Results-Report.pdf (accessed 10 February 2013).

Jayasekera, R. (2003) Gives with one hand,takes away with the other. *Indexonline.* Available at: www.indexonline.org/news/20030611_iraq.shtml (accessed 13 June 2003).

Journalistic Freedoms Observatory (JFO) (19 April 2009) A satellite channel must pay a fine for a defamation case. Available at: http://www.jfoiraq.org/newsdetails.aspx?back=1andid=557andpage=5 =EF=BB=BF (accessed 8 July 2009).

Kepplinger, H. (1982) Visual biases in television coverage, *Communication Research*, 9, 432–46.

— (1983) Visual biases in television campaign coverage. In E. Wartella, C. Whitney and S. Windahl (eds), *Mass Communication Review Yearbook*, vol. 4. Beverly Hills, CA: Sage, pp. 391–405.

Kim, H. S. and Hama-Saeed, M. (2008) Emerging media in peril: Iraqi journalism in the post-Saddam Hussein era, *Journalism Studies*, 9(4), 578–94.

King, David C. and Morehouse, David (2004) Moving voters in the 2000 presidential campaign: Local visits, local media. In David A. Shultz (ed.), *Lights, Camera, Campaign: Media, Politics, and Political Advertising.* New York: Peter Lang, pp. 301–18.

Levinson, C. (2006) Iraq's 'PBS' accused of sectarian slant, *The Christian Science Monitor.* Available at: www.csmonitor.com/2006/0110/p06s01-woiq.html.

McCombs, M. E. and Shaw, D. L. (1972). The agenda-setting function of mass media, *Public Opinion Quarterly*, 36, 176–87.

Metcalf, Steve (2006) Analysis: Iraq's media three years on. BBC. Available at: http://news.bbc.co.uk/2/hi/middle_east/4884246.stm (accessed 7 July 2009).

Middle East Online (2009) Iraqi journalists protest 'intimidation', censorship. Available at: www.middle-east-online.com/english/?id=33720 (accessed 31 December 2009).

Murphy, J. (1998) An analysis of political bias in evening network news during the 1996 presidential campaigns. Unpublished PhD Thesis. University of Oklahoma Graduate College.

OpenNet Initiative. (2007) *Iraq.* Available at: http://opennet.net/sites/opennet.net/files/iraq.pdf (accessed 3 August 2009).

Patterson, T. E. and McClure, R. D. (1976) *The Unseeing Eye: The Myth of Television Powers in the National Politics.* New York: G.P. Putnam's Sons.

Prusher, I. (2003) Free media blossom in Iraq city. *The Christian Science Monitor.* 29 April.

Roug, L. (28 March 2006) Unfair, unbalanced channels. *Los Angeles Times*. Available at: http://articles.latimes.com/2006/mar/28/world/fg-media28 (accessed 5 July 2009).

RSF (Reporters Sans Frontières) (24 April 2002) Iraq 2002 annual report. Available at: www.rsf.org/Iraq-annual-Report-2002.html (accessed 3 July 2009).

— (20 May 2009) News website latest target in government's legal offensive against independent media. Available at: www.rsf.org/News-website-latest-target-in.html (accessed 10 July 2009).

— (2010) The Iraq war: A heavy death toll for the media, 2003–2010. Available at: http://en.rsf.org/IMG/pdf/rapport_irak_2003–2010_gb.pdf (accessed 7 September 2010).

Rugh, W. A. (2004) *Arab Mass Media: Newspapers, Radio, and Television in Arab Politics*. Wesport: Praeger Publishers.

Salaheddin, S. (2009) Iraq to impose controls on internet content, sparking freedom of speech debate. *AP*, 4 August.

Stalinsky, S. (2005) Reality TV, Iraq-style. *FrontPageMagazine.com*. Available at: www.frontpagemag.com/readArticle.aspx?ARTID=9083 (accessed 6 July 2009).

Tawfeeq, M. (7 March 2011) Two students killed in Sunni neighborhood of Baghdad. CNN. Available at: http://articles.cnn.com/2011–03–07/world/iraq.violence_1_baghdad-s-zafaraniya-civilians-falluja?_s=PM:WORLD (accessed 26 March 2011).

UNDP (United Nations Development Programme) and Arab Fund for Economic and Social Development (2003) Arab human development report: Building a knowledge society. Available at: www.arab-hdr.org/publications/other/ahdr/ahdr2003e.pdf (accessed 12 December 2009).

Williams, D. (18 August 2003). U.S. taps media chief for Iraq; regulation attempted without appearing heavy-handed. *The Washington Post*, A14.

4

The Development of the Palestinian News Media

Zaki Hasan Nuseibeh and Roger Dickinson

This chapter describes the history and development of the Palestinian media and their impact on the Palestinian people and the wider international community. As will become clear, these media have faced many challenges and restrictions since their birth, but they continue to thrive nonetheless.

For more than a century the Palestinian media have not been free. Palestinians (whose population in 2012 numbered roughly 4 million) have been ruled by successive occupying forces and their media remain obstructed externally and internally – by both Israel and the Palestinian National Authority, the latter having controlled some areas of the West Bank and Gaza Strip since the beginning of the twenty-first century after the implementation of the Oslo Accords. The Palestinian media are currently divided to serve two factions (Fatah in the West Bank and Hamas in the Gaza Strip) in a country which has yet to achieve either independence or national unity. However, Palestinian media have developed and now exist in multiple forms. There are numerous newspapers, radio and terrestrial and satellite television channels as well as internet-based media currently serving Palestinian people across the occupied territories.

Perhaps because of their unique and troubled history Palestinians seem always to have been eager to follow the news. As a recent report put it: 'Palestinians are hungry for news: 36 per cent of Palestinian adults surveyed by NEC said they always follow the news, while 57 per cent said they sometimes do and only 6 per cent said they never follow the news' (Near East Consulting, 2010: 5). The Palestinian press has evolved through seven, sometimes distinct, sometimes overlapping, stages in its history: the Ottoman Empire (1876–1914), the British Mandate (1919–48), Israeli rule (1948–), Jordanian and Egyptian rule over the West Bank and Gaza Strip (1948–67), Israeli occupation of the West Bank and Gaza (1967–), the Palestinian Authority (1995–), the Palestinian dispute and division between the Palestinian National Liberation Movement (Fatah) and the Islamic Resistance Movement (Hamas) (2007–).

The Palestinian press during the Ottoman empire

Newspapers were first published in Arabic in Jerusalem in 1876 when the Ottoman authorities issued the official daily *Al Quds Al-Sharif* (Jerusalem) in both Arabic and Turkish. 'Most historians agree that the first newspaper was printed in Jerusalem in 1876, where two newspapers were being published sporadically by the Ottoman governor' (Khouri, 1976, 3). *Falasteen* (Palestine, first published in 1911) was the most important newspaper for Palestinians of the period. It was founded by cousins Issa and David Al-Issa, but was closed down by the Ottoman authorities shortly afterwards (20).[1] This situation remained until 1914 and the collapse of the Ottoman Empire. Newspapers reopened a few years afterwards under the British Mandate (1919–48).

The Palestinian press during the British Mandate

During the British Mandate in Palestine, more regulations were imposed resulting from the Publication Law of 1933 which represented the first legal basis on which to control the media. Article 19 gave the High Commissioner the right to issue a decree suspending a newspaper if it published material that might endanger public order (Sisalem, 1996).

The peak of the British Mandate regulations came in 1945 via the Defence (Emergency) Regulations which included tight restrictions and granted wide power to the Mandate authorities to increase their control and censorship over publications and the exchange and circulation of ideas and information. Article 87 allowed the censor, who was appointed by the High Commissioner, to prohibit 'the publishing of matter the publishing of which, in his opinion, would be, or be likely to be or become, prejudicial to the defense of Palestine or to the public safety or to public order' (Anon, 1945). During this period

Palestine witnessed a movement of cultural and intellectual activities which were focused in three cities: Jaffa, Jerusalem and Haifa. Kabha notes that the number of Palestinian newspapers in the period between the two world wars had reached 48, of which 12 were dailies. Most of these were published in Jaffa (17 newspapers in total), Jerusalem (16) and Haifa (11) (2004).

In addition to the printed press, in 1936 the British Mandate established Palestine's first official radio service. This was broadcast from Jerusalem in Arabic and, while mainly serving the political goals of the British Mandate, broadcasters aimed to 'enrich their programmes with cultural variety presenting Arab culture' (Najjar, 2005: 288–9). Despite the constraints the media played an important role in Palestinian national politics and were a significant mobilizing tool playing a significant role in propagating Palestinian nationalism (Khalidi, 1997). Political leaders and, later, political parties utilized newspapers to promote their views and engage in debate during this period. A major issue that drew the attention of journalists and was covered extensively in newspapers was the matter of Jewish immigration (mainly from Europe) to Palestine. As Khalidi shows, the media of the 1930s warned of the political, social and economic implications of Jewish immigration, and journalists sought to raise public awareness of the need for opposition to British policies regarding Israel (ibid.). The state of Israel was established in 1948. This was followed by the annexation of the West Bank to the Hashemite Kingdom of Jordan in 1950.

The Palestinian press during 1948–67

Jordan's first Press and Publications Law was created in 1955. It imposed tight restrictions on the freedom of speech. At that time there were four newspapers, two emigrating from Jaffa to the Arab part of Jerusalem (*Al Difaa* – Defense – and *Falasteen*), and two others (*Al Jihad* – Holy War and *Al Manar* – The Beacon). In February 1967 the Jordanian government published the second Press and Publications Law, cancelling the law of 1955. Article 25 of the new law granted authority to the Jordanian Cabinet to abolish the issuing of licenses for printed publications, or to suspend them if it was found that they 'adopt a line that threatens the national entity, endangers the safety of the state, and violates the constitutional basis of the kingdom'. It also reduced the number of newspapers in Jerusalem and in Amman through forced mergers when it gave permission to publish only to two newspapers, one in Jerusalem (*Al Quds* which arose from the merger of *Al Difaa* and *Al Jihad*), and the other in Amman (*Falasteen* and *Al Manar* merging to form *Al Dustor* – The Constitution).

The Palestinian press during 1948-67 (Gaza under Egyptian administration)

After the establishment of the Jewish state in 1948 the Gaza Strip remained under Egyptian administration. In June of that year the Egyptian government strengthened the Press and Publications Law that had been imposed under the British Mandate. The Palestinian press in the Gaza Strip was affected greatly by Egypt's political currents of the time. Several newspapers were published in Gaza in the period between 1954 and 1967. The most prominent and stable was first a daily newspaper, *Al Tahrir* (Liberation), established in 1958 and chaired and edited by the Arab nationalist lawyer Zuhair Al Rayyes. *Al Tahrir* became a weekly newspaper published in conjunction with the Egyptian *Akhbar Al Yawm* (Today's News) with the name *Akhbar Falasteen* (Palestine News). The last issue of *Akhbar Falesteen* appeared on 5 June 1967 at the start of the six-day war.

Palestinian press during 1948-67 (The Arab press in Israel)

In Israel, two Arabic-language newspapers were published during this period: *Al Ittihad* (The Union) – the newspaper of the Communist Party of Israel, and *Al Yawm* (Today). *Al Ittihad* was the only Arabic newspaper that had continued without interruption since 1944; all others had ceased publication. According to Masalha, *Al Yawm*, was launched in 1948 in Jaffa by the Mapai party, the Israeli party in power, under the cover of continuing the Arab press in Palestine. 'It was an integral part of the Hebrew *Davar* newspaper [. . .] which facilitated and contributed to the editing and translating of news and views from Hebrew into Arabic. *Al Yawm* had used the offices and printing presses of *Falasteen* after the latter's staff migrated to Jerusalem' (Masalha, 2007).

Palestinian media in the occupied West Bank and Gaza under Israeli occupation

After the six-day war the West Bank and Gaza Strip were left without a local Arab newspaper, although *Al Ittihad* and *Al Yawm* continued to be published in Israel. *Al Ittihad* soon began to call for Israel's withdrawal from all territories occupied in 1967, and to campaign for a Palestinian state with East Jerusalem as its capital, alongside the state of Israel, whose capital would be the western part of Jerusalem – a call that later became a Palestine Liberation Organization (PLO) demand. Otherwise the people of the West Bank and Gaza found themselves without a newspaper that would express their views and truly represent them until November 1968 when Mahmoud Abu Zalaf,[2] the owner of *Al Quds*, obtained an Israeli license to allow the paper to be re-published in East Jerusalem. Since that time *Al Quds* has continued to be published and has enjoyed one of the highest circulations in the West Bank.

The publishing of *Al Quds* in East Jerusalem laid the foundation for a new era in the city, for in the years to follow East Jerusalem became the cultural capital for all Palestinians. Other Palestinian newspapers and magazines soon started to publish there. Some were published daily, such as, *Al Nahar* (Daytime), *Al Sha'ab* (The People) and *Al Fajr* (The Dawn), while several others were published weekly. Although all of these newspapers were issued under Israeli occupation, there was variation in their political tendencies and orientations. Initially *Al Quds* continued to call for an end to the occupation and for reunification with Jordan (a large photograph of King Hussein of Jordan had appeared in a front-page story on the first day *Al Quds* was published under the occupation).

Later, in 1986, the paper changed direction and, alongside *Al Ittihad*, became a supporter of the establishment of a Palestinian state in the West Bank and Gaza Strip with its capital in East Jerusalem. A number of factors led to these changes, not only at *Al Quds* but also in the overall political climate that emerged in the occupied territories. First, there was a gradual deterioration of the influence of senior supporters of the Jordanian regime who were forced to stay in their towns and villages. Second, there was the emergence of the PLO as the sole legitimate representative of the Palestinian people after it received recognition from the Arab summit in Morocco in 1974. The emergence of resistance inspired a new generation of Palestinians to reject the old ways of thinking and to demand the return of the name of Palestine.

In 1986 the journalist and businessman Othman Hallaq first published *Al Nahar* in Jerusalem. This paper was loyal to Jordan, replacing *Al Quds* in that role which by then was supporting the PLO, itself joining two other titles, *Al Fajr* and *Al Sha'ab*, which the PLO had begun to finance in the early 1970s. During this period, there was no Palestinian radio service in the occupied territories and the population listened to various services including *Radio Israel* and the *Voice of Palestine* which were broadcast from abroad. As far as television was concerned, Palestinians watched programmes transmitted from Jordan and Israel, while those in the Gaza Strip were also able to receive programmes from Egypt.

The press in the Gaza strip under Israeli occupation

No local newspaper was published in the Gaza Strip during the first ten years of the Israeli occupation. In the mid-1970s some local weekly magazines and newspapers were published in Jerusalem and distributed in the region. A number of journalists and editors from Gaza contributed news stories and articles to newspapers published in Jerusalem during this period.

The Israeli regulations

Under Israeli military rule, the Palestinian media entered a new era of regulation with different foundations but with the same if not greater levels of restriction. The Defence (Emergency) Regulations of 1945 shaped the Israeli approach towards its own press, but they were unable to deal with the Palestinian publications in the occupied territories. The Israelis therefore added certain military orders to limit freedom of expression still further. Military Order 50, for example, requires that a permit be obtained for the importation and distribution of publications; Military Order 379 gives the Israeli army the power to confiscate any publication which does not have the required permit. Military Order 101 forbids the publication of anything that contains any article with 'political significance' without a license. 'Political significance' is not defined and it is left to the judgement of the military court to determine whether a publication is in violation of the order.

In addition to these formal controls there have been many reported instances of official harassment of journalists with arrests on varying charges and the use of detention and house arrest. Akram Haniya,[3] the editor of *Al Sha'ab*, for example, was deported from the West Bank in 1986 because of his 'affiliation' with the PLO (Committee for the Protection of Journalists/ Article, 1988).

The Palestinian press in the diaspora

Those Palestinians who fled their country after the establishment of Israel and after Israel's occupation of what remained of Palestine in 1967 used 'refugee media' to express their views and defend their cause wherever they found an opportunity. *Al Difaa* moved from Jaffa to Egypt for several months, but eventually returned to East Jerusalem to express the Palestinian view. The PLO helped to maintain a strong Palestinian media which moved with it wherever it went. It reached a peak during the PLO presence in Lebanon – the only Arab country that enjoyed democracy and freedom of expression at the time. During that period, every Palestinian faction had a newspaper or magazine to express its views.

In January 1972 the Palestinian National Council launched an official weekly magazine representing the PLO. *The Palestine Revolution* was edited by Kamal Nasir[4] who was then spokesman for the Executive Committee of the PLO. Nasir said in this context: 'we have to realize that the revolution without ideology is a bunch of gangs, and the magazine is the rhetoric of our revolution' (Nasir, 1972, quoted in WAFA/Palestinian Information Centre, 2012).

In the same year, the PLO established the Palestinian News Agency, WAFA. It also launched Radio Palestine which was based in Cairo. Although these Palestinian institutions succeeded in creating an independent Palestinian media system, the PLO did not differ in principle from other Arab regimes in using their media in pursuit of their political objectives.

The Palestinian Authority

After the signing of the Oslo agreement between the PLO and the government of Israel in 1993, parts of the occupied territories came partially under the Palestinian Authority (PA). This agreement and the establishment of the PA marked a major change in the landscape of the Palestinian media which affected all the newspapers, weeklies and periodicals of the PLO. It also marked the advent of new media forms that had not previously existed under Israeli occupation. This stage following Oslo was characterized by a pronounced increase in the number of newspapers, weeklies and periodicals (Jamal 2003, 24).

The PLO's financial crisis following the 1990–1 Gulf War meant that at the beginning of the 1990s only two newspapers were being published in Jerusalem: *Al Quds* and *Al Nahar*. The crisis had forced the PLO to end its financial subsidies of privately owned publications such as the daily *Al Fajr* and *Al Sha'ab* and the weekly *Al Bayader al Siyasiyya*, which represented the political views of the main PLO faction, Fatah. The absence of public reaction to the closures reflected not only the artificial nature of these newspapers but also the psychological readiness of the Palestinian public for a new phase in history bearing the possibility of a peaceful settlement (Jamal, 2000).

For more than two decades, the city of Jerusalem had been the cultural capital of the occupied West Bank and Gaza, and the newspapers and magazines that were published there and distributed across the country were highly influential. During that period, The Orient House, led by late Palestinian politician Faisal Husseini, had become a place of pilgrimage for foreign diplomats (despite the opposition of the occupation), and the Palestinian National Theatre (Al Hakawati) had been founded as the first national theatre in the occupied territories. Following the establishment of the PA, Jerusalem lost this prestige in favour of the new Palestinian 'capital', Ramallah.

The PA began publishing two daily newspapers there, *Al Hayat al-Jadeedah* (*New Life*) and *Al Ayyam* (*The Days*) in 1994–5. The chief editor of *Al Hayat al Jadeedah* was Nabil Amro, a former PLO ambassador to Moscow. *Al Ayyam* introduced new printing and layout technology. This paper, a more sophisticated version of the recently closed *Al Sha'ab* and *Al Fajr* in terms of content and closeness to the leadership, followed the PA line even while maintaining a critical distance. Its editor Akram Haniya, had been a senior adviser to PA chairman Yasser Arafat (Jamal, 2000).

As well as the new dailies, the Palestinian Broadcasting Corporation (PBC), which was in charge of radio and television, was set up by Arafat even before his arrival in Gaza. The radio service began to broadcast from Jericho in July 1994 while the television station began in 1996. Although television broadcasting was split between the West Bank and Gaza, the main decisions concerning news and its interpretation were made in the basement of Arafat's headquarters, where the television offices were located (Jamal, 2000).

Arafat was fully aware of the importance of the media in shaping public opinion. He used the media from the trenches of resistance, to the arenas of civil war in Jordan, and during Israel's siege in Beirut and the air raids on Hammam el Shat in Tunisia. The Palestinian newspapers, which Arafat sponsored in the occupied territories, were the voice of the PLO, a voice which stood in the face of what Israel called the 'Jordanian option' – the idea that the Palestinian territories should be returned to Jordan. In June 1994 the Ministry of Information 'was formally established by virtue of a presidential decree' (Palestinian Authority Ministry of Information, 2009).

Since then the media available to Palestinians have steadily expanded. There are currently 31 separate television channels in the West Bank and Gaza Strip. All, with the exception of *Al Quds Educational TV*, depend almost entirely on revenues from advertising for their programmes (NGOs provide some of their output). The levels of production and the prices charged for advertising slots vary widely from one station to another (Batrawi, 2001).

A recent survey of the Palestinian television audience found that the five most watched television channels were the Qatar-based news channel

Al-Jazeera (31% had watched the day before the survey), the Palestinian Authority station Palestine TV (18%), the Dubai-based MBC entertainment channels (18%), Al Arrabiyah news channel (also owned by MBC) (7.5%), and Abu Dhabi TV (5%). These channels are all available via satellite which is widely used by households in both the West Bank and Gaza (Near East Consulting, 2010).

In the last decade of the twentieth century the renewed opportunities for a peaceful solution to the conflict appeared to make Palestine an attractive region for economic investment. In 1995 a number of private business people and several corporate and institutional shareholders established PalTel in Jericho city. The company was licensed on the basis of an agreement with the PA as a public shareholding company with a capital of 45 million Jordanian Dinars, increased to JD 67.5 million by the PA General Assembly. In January 1997 PalTel started managing and operating the telecommunication sector in Palestine, providing all types of communication services: fixed, mobile, data systems and internet (Palestinian Telecommunication Company, 2012).

The PA regulations

While these developments led to freedom of expression in some areas, there were restrictions in others and Palestinians had to learn to live with a new kind of censorship. In addition to routine control of news and advertising by the Israeli military on operational or religious grounds, coverage critical of the Palestinian President and his family, criticism of political decisions, and criticism of the Oslo agreement were all forbidden. However, while the newspapers of the PA in Ramallah understood the rules of the game, as did the state radio and television services, the two newspapers which remained in Jerusalem, *Al Quds* and *Al Nahar*, and the newspapers and magazines of the Islamic movements, were in a difficult situation where there was neither overt censorship nor complete freedom of speech. As Jamal notes, these papers at first followed a liberal editorial policy that attempted to capture the public mood, dwelling less on the policies of the occupying force and more on issues relating to the establishment of the Palestinian state.

The limits of tolerance soon became clear. The pro-Jordanian *Al Nahar* criticized the PLO for compromising fundamental issues and for 'selling out' to Israel as well as for the way Oslo was negotiated, particularly the PLO's failure to coordinate with the other Arab countries, especially Jordan.

On 28 July 1994, shortly after the establishment of the PA Ministry of Information, *Al Nahar's* administration was informed that the paper would not be allowed into the areas controlled by the PA. Technical reasons were cited – the paper had not applied for a permit to distribute in the autonomous areas – but the real reason was clear. (Jamal, 2000: 48)

The Palestinian Press and Publications Law was issued in 1995 and appeared, on the surface, to safeguard media freedom. There are, for example, specific clauses concerned with freedom in news reporting and the issuance of licenses for journalists. However, a number of taboos can be identified in the Law. There are clauses preventing, for example, the dissemination of confidential information from police and public security forces; the publication of material that includes contempt of religions and sects; the publication of anything that could be detrimental to national unity or likely to sow hatred, discord or disharmony; the publication of material that may stir sectarian strife among members of the community and the publication of the proceedings of secret sessions of the National Council or the Council of Ministers.

The Law has been criticized on a number of grounds. One refers to the onerous obligations on printers outlined in Article 33 which states that 'the owner or manager of a printing house must submit to the Department of Publications four copies of any non-periodical publications printed in his place prior to distributing them' (de Jonge, 2010: 12). The Law makes no provision, on the other hand, for the right of citizens to have access to information.

The Press and Publications Law has had a profound effect on Palestinian media freedom. After the Law's publication *Al Nahar* continued to have difficulties with the PA until it was forced to close in 1997. Journalists working for *Al Quds* have been detained and several newspapers and magazines of the Islamic movement have fallen foul of the Law. *Al Watan* (*The Homeland*), for example, a newspaper affiliated to Hamas, was established in April 1995 and closed down the following December, its operations having been temporarily suspended twice by the Palestinian security forces in the meantime. *Al Risala* (*The Message*), a weekly newspaper published by the National Islamic Salvation Party, first appeared in January 1997 and was closed for the first time by the Palestinian police in September of that year for a period of three months. The same happened with *Al Istiqlal* (*Independence*), a political weekly affiliated with the 'Islamic Jihad' faction. This paper first appeared in October 1994. In February 1995 members of the PA security forces raided the paper's offices, confiscated material, arrested six employees (who were later detained for periods ranging from 23 days to 3 months) and closed it down for one and a half months. The paper was closed for a second and final time in July 1998.

Self-censorship

Subsequent to several incidents in which the PA reacted severely to the media, newspapers began to establish their own system of self-censorship. This has become a common practice among Palestinian journalists. In addition to the traditional Israeli restrictions on the Palestinian press such as closure of newspapers, detention of journalists, denying journalists their press cards (which are essential for travel), the PA's methods of control have found their way not only into newspapers offices but also, it seems, into the minds of Palestinian journalists.

The January 2006 elections and the victory of Hamas

The death of Yasser Arafat, Chairman of the Palestinian National Authority, had a significant impact on the PA. Despite his disagreement with the various Islamic movements, particularly Hamas, who refused to recognize the Oslo Accords and continued armed operations against Israel, Arafat had been strong enough to maintain some sort of national unity. As part of its boycott of the Oslo agreement, Hamas refused to participate in the elections of the Legislative Council in 1996, and refused to participate in presidential elections after Arafat's death in 2005. However, after winning elections for municipal and local councils and student unions and committees, and noting the Palestinian people's anger at corruption among members of the PA and their relative lack of political achievement, Hamas participated in the elections of the Legislative Council in early 2006.

Although it did not expect victory in these elections, Hamas obtained 74 of the 132 seats in the Legislative Council (56%), while Fatah obtained 45 (34%) (Central Elections Commission, 2012). The result was an internal Palestinian conflict in June 2007 during which Hamas succeeded in defeating the PA security services and establishing a secure stronghold in the Gaza Strip. This situation led to the creation of two governments, the Ramallah government led by Fatah and the Hamas government in Gaza.

The year 2007 was subsequently one of the worst for the Palestinian press since the establishment of the PA in 1994. There were reportedly more than 250 violations of media freedom committed by the Palestinian parties due to the intensification of hostilities between Fatah and Hamas during the year (Palestinian Centre for Development and Media Freedoms, 2008). As a result the Palestinian media split into two: those under the control of the Palestinian

National Authority (Fatah) in Ramallah, and those under the control of Hamas in Gaza. In addition, both Fatah and Hamas banned newspapers that they saw as being affiliated to or supportive of the opposing side. Newspapers published on the West Bank (*Al Quds, Al-Ayyam* and *Al-Hayyat*) are not available in the Gaza Strip, while *Al-Risala* and *Filasteen*, published in Gaza, are not available on the West Bank. As well as restrictions on the printed and audio-visual media, bloggers (especially those active in the Gaza Strip) have also been harassed.

Palestinian media coverage since the internal split has also been characterized by increased cautiousness and self-censorship. According to Walid Batrawi, a freelance Palestinian journalist,

> after the split in June 2007 between the West Bank and the Gaza Strip, the media in general turned to report issues that are unlikely to be criticized or opposed by their government or public. Reporting on the division between the West Bank and the Gaza Strip and about the Israeli occupation characterized the Palestinian media in the past two years. Social and other issues were rarely covered. (Batrawi, 2011)

The internal division has paralysed the Palestinian legislature and thus blocks attempts to develop a new regulatory framework for the media (Near East Consulting, 2010: 13). A report by the Palestinian Centre for Human Rights shows that the events that followed the Palestinian division led to a negative change in Palestinian media discourse which it describes as moving from incitement to defamation (Palestinian Centre for Human Rights, 1995). This, coupled with structurally malfunctioning media institutions, has resulted in a failure of independent media (Othman and Oudih, 2007: 197).

Palestinian media professionals have also been widely affected. A recent report quotes Adel Zanoun, a reporter with Agence France Press in Gaza:

> There is no doubt that the internal Palestinian division negatively impacted Palestinian media. The most important impact was the gradual retreat among journalists from ethical, professional and objective values and standards to political agendas, and the consequent exploitation of the news outlets in the respective areas. As such, many of the news outlets contributed, by agreeing to be a tool of the division, in strengthening the division itself. (Near East Consulting, 2010: 12)

The Palestinian media have thus been transformed into media of factions. The Islamic satellite channel Al-Aqsa in Gaza and Al Quds in Jerusalem support Hamas, while the various Palestinian television channels that were intended

TABLE 4.1 Attacks on the Palestinian media 2010

Type of attack	Israeli	Palestinian	Total
Physical attacks on personnel	89	10	99
Detention	19	17	36
Arrests	18	14	32
Summons for investigation	3	17	20
Raids	0	8	8
Prevention of coverage	3	4	7
Travel restrictions/deportation	3	3	6
Destruction of property	3	0	3
Threats	1	2	3
Closures/blockades	0	2	2
Equipment confiscation	0	1	1
Frequency disruption	0	1	1
Total	139	79	218

Source: Near East Consulting, 2010: 11.

to be the voice and image of all Palestinians are broadcast from Ramallah and have supported Fatah. According to Near East Consulting, this situation has increased the suffering of Palestinian media which now have to deal with three censoring authorities – Israel, Hamas and Fatah. Attacks on the press and the media in general remain frequent in the Palestinian territories. Table 4.1 lists attacks against the media committed by both the Israeli Army and the Palestinian forces in the West Bank and the Gaza Strip in 2010.

The internet

Since the beginning of 2008 most Palestinian newspapers have been available online. This has enabled readers who have access to the internet to read these papers free of charge and to be free of the restrictions imposed on newspaper distribution in the territories. The internet quickly opened a window for Palestinian media which realized the need to speed up the transfer of news and information and make use of the interactive online spaces provided by the new environment where audiences are able to express opinion and interact in response to unfolding events. The growth of the internet has also led to the emergence of a number of specialist sites that focus on law, human rights and on economic, financial and health and welfare issues.

These sites enjoy a certain amount of freedom of expression and there are several that follow the lives of Palestinian people and society and their problems. These include the Arabic Media Information Network (AMIN), Electronic Intifada, International Middle East Media Center (IMEMC), Maan News Agency, Jerusalem Media and Communication Centre, the Palestinian Initiative for the Promotion of Global Dialogue and Democracy (MIFTAH), Palestine News Network (PNN), Palestinian Information Center, Al Watan Voice, Adalah (the Legal Center for Arab Minority Rights in Israel), the Palestinian Centre for Human Rights and a growing number of others.

In addition the internet has become the space in which Palestinians are able to communicate and associate with their family and friends unencumbered by Israeli security and without the need of travel visas (Palestinian passports are not recognized in many countries of the world). For the people of Gaza, who must often negotiate the Israeli blockade, the internet affords them the freedom to communicate with their loved ones that has often been denied to them in the past.

> The Internet is almost the only way residents of the Gaza Strip can break the isolation in which they live, which could explain the high amount of browsing the network in Gaza. According to a Report of the Palestinian Central Board of Statistics (PCBS) in 2009 57 per cent of the population over ten years of age (for Gaza and the West bank alike) used a computer. 32 per cent of the population over the age of ten used the Internet. It is reasonable to assume that their number has increased since then. The *Wall Street Journal* examined and found that the Gaza Strip is the record holder of Internet users in the Arab world, even more than the Gulf Emirates. (Bin Nun, 2011)

Growth in internet usage in Palestine from 2004 to 2009 is shown in Table 4.2.

According to a survey by Near East Consulting, the majority of Palestinians (70%) have access to the internet, mainly at home (85%), and three quarters use the internet daily. Perhaps surprisingly, there is wider access to the internet in Gaza (76%) than in the West Bank (67%). Young people spend the most time surfing the internet, with 28 per cent of 18–24-year-olds saying they spend more than four hours on the internet every day (Near East Consulting, 2010: 12).

Sixty per cent of Palestinians surveyed use social networks such as Facebook and Twitter: 21 per cent claim to use them 'extensively', 24 per

TABLE 4.2 Access to and use of the internet in Palestine 2004–9

	2004 (%)	2006 (%)	2007 (%)	2009 (%)
Palestinian families who have internet access	9.2	15.9	16.9	28.5
Individuals (aged ten years and older) who use the internet	11.9	18.4	32.2	32.3
Individuals (aged ten years and older) who have email	5.1	10.0	Unavailable	21.3

Source: PCBS, 2009: 31.

cent 'moderately' and 15 per cent 'rarely'. Again, usage is most pronounced among the young with 33 per cent of people aged between 18 and 24 saying they use social networks 'extensively' (5).

Just as the conventional media have often been a battleground over ideas and policies the internet has also on occasion been a place for the display of the horror of internal Palestinian conflict. For example, Fatah and Hamas have each used YouTube as a platform to demonstrate their opponents' inhumanity.

Palestinian media today

At the time of writing (April 2012) there were 192 functioning media organizations in the Occupied Palestinian Territories. Most of these institutions are based in the West Bank and East Jerusalem. There are three main Palestinian newspapers (*Al Quds, Al Ayyam* and the PA (and therefore, Fatah-dominated) daily *Al Hayat Al Jadidah*) and two additional daily newspapers based in the Gaza Strip under Hamas (*Al Resala* and *Felesteen*).

There are more than 70 radio and television stations based in the territories in addition to the Fatah-controlled Palestinian Broadcasting Corporation's Voice of Palestine and the Palestinian Satellite Channel. Palestinians can also receive transmissions from satellite channels based abroad – channels such as Al-Jazeera and Al Arabiya are popular as are the several channels of Jordanian TV. There is also Al Quds Satellite Television based in Lebanon; Al Quds TV, an educational channel owned and operated by Al Quds University in Jerusalem; Palestine Today which is based in London; and there is the Al

Aqsa Media Network run by Hamas and based in Gaza. A new Fatah-backed satellite channel (Al Filastiniyya) began transmitting to the territories in 2009. And there are now numerous media websites springing from the traditional media organizations across the territories and a growing number of online-only news sites that help to inform the Palestinian audience and encourage online dialogue and debate (Abu Sada, 2010).

The occupation of journalism in the region has always been a risky one and the danger journalists face in covering the news in the occupied territories is perhaps greater than it has ever been. The arrest and the expulsion of a large number of journalists and others killed during the performance of their work[5] is however evidence of the Palestinian news media's continuing determination in the face of its many challenges to fulfil their political and social role.

Despite the many restrictions and constraints on their activities and the continuing threat of censorship, the Palestinian media have played an important role in shaping and unifying Palestinian public opinion. The various forms of control imposed upon them over the years have not prevented them from responding to the views of Palestinians even if this has led to temporary, or even permanent, closure of one or more of their institutions. Many commentators have credited the Palestinian media with the preservation of the national identity and the international recognition of the Palestinian people (Abu Sada, 2010). Their impact in the region has been faltering and subject to numerous setbacks but it is nonetheless palpable in many ways. For a long period it was common, for example, for the Israeli media to describe Palestinians in the West Bank and Gaza as the 'Arabs in the Israeli-managed territories'; the phrase 'the Palestinian people' has now become commonplace in the media across the region, whatever their affiliation, location or ownership.

Notes

1 The journalist and historian Omar Saleh Barghouthi writing in the Jerusalem magazine *Mirror of the East* in 1928 described Issa Al-Issa as 'brilliant and bold' in his criticism as he attacked the Ottoman authorities and the Zionist movement. His forthright journalism led to his detention and trial on more than one occasion.

2 Mahmoud Abu Zalaf was born in Jaffa in 1924, moving to Jerusalem after 1948. He established *Al Jihad* in 1951. The paper flourished and was the leading title under Jordanian rule until the forced merger with *Al Difa'a* to form the new title *Al Quds* (the Arabs' name for Jerusalem) in 1967, a few months before the Israeli occupation of what was left of Palestine.

3 Editor of *Al Ayyam*, Haniya was a political advisor to Arafat, a member of the final status talks team, and held a leading role in the Camp David peace

talks. He was previously the editor of *Al Sha'b* for which he was placed under house arrest in August 1980. He was elected to Fatah in 1989 after being deported in 1986.

4   Kamal Butros Nasir was the son of a Palestinian Christian family from Bir Zeit near Ramallah in the West Bank. Born in 1924 in Gaza, he grew up to be a writer, joined the Palestinian revolution and was killed on 10 April 1973, reportedly by Ehud Barak, in the so-called Fardan massacre which also assassinated Kamal Adwan, Mohamed Youssef Najjar and the latter's wife. It is widely believed that Nasir was killed because the Israelis considered his writings to be as dangerous as the armed resistance itself.

5   The Committee to Protect Journalists reports that ten journalists have been killed in the region since 1992 (Committee to Protect Journalists, 2012).

References

Abu Sada, Fadi (2010) Media landscape: Palestine. *European Journalism Centre*. Available at: www.ejc.net/media_landscape/article/palestine/.

Anon (1945) The defence (emergency) regulations, 1945, Supplement No. 2. *The Palestine Gazette* No. 1442, 27 September.

Batrawi, Walid (2001) Private television in Palestine, Unpublished MA dissertation, Centre for Mass Communication Research, University of Leicester, UK.

— (2011) Personal communication with the authors.

Bin Nun, Sagi (2011) 'Code from the trachea', *Maariv*, 8 March 2011.

Central Elections Commission (Palestine) (2012) The second 2006 PLC elections. The final distribution of PLC seats. Available at: www.elections.ps/CECWebsite/events/elections2006/results.aspx (accessed 4 April 2012).

Committee to Protect Journalists/Article 19 (1988) *Journalism under Occupation: Israel's Regulation of the Palestinian Press*. New York: Committee to Protect Journalists.

Committee to Protect Journalists (2012) *10 Journalists Killed in Israel and the Occupied Palestinian Territory since 1992/Motive Confirmed*. Available at: http://cpj.org/killed/mideast/israel-and-the-occupied-palestinian-territory/ (accessed 4 April 2012).

de Jonge, Nona (2010) *Press Freedom in Palestine*. Palestinian Human Rights Monitoring Group. Available at: www.phrmg.org/Sam_Dec2010/Freedom%20of%20Press%20Palestine.pdf (accessed 8 August 2012).

Jamal, Amal (2000) The Palestinian media: an obedient servant or a vanguard of democracy? *Journal of Palestine Studies*, 29(3), 45–59.

— (2003) *State Formation and Media Regime in Palestine*. The Tami Steinmetz Centre for Peace Research, Tel Aviv University.

Kabha, Mustafa (2004) *Under the Eyes of the Censor. The Palestinian Press in the National Movement between the Two World Wars*. The Center for Arabic Literature Studies, Beit-Berl College, Israel (in Arabic).

Khalidi, Rashid (1997) *Palestinian Identity: The Construction of Modern National Consciousness*, New York: Columbia University Press.

Khouri, Yousef (1976) *The Arab Press in Palestine, 1876–1948*. Beirut: Institute for Palestine Studies (in Arabic).

Masalha, Omar Amin (2007) A Glance at the Arab Palestinian press in Israel 2007 (in Arabic). Available at: www.bettna.com/articals2/showArticlen. ASP?aid=484 (accessed 4 April 2012).

Najjar, D. Aida (2005) *Palestinian Press and the National Movement in the First Half of the 20th Century: 1900–1948*. Beirut: The Arab Institution for Research and Publishing (in Arabic).

Near East Consulting (2010) *Survey of Palestinian Media*. Ramallah: Near East Consulting for Fondation Hirondelle.

Othman, Ziyad and Oudih, Ghazi Bani (2007) *Media Plaything and Bloody Discourse in Palestine*. Ramallah: Ramallah Centre for Human Rights Studies (in Arabic).

Palestinian Authority Ministry of Information (2009) *Palestinian Press: Beginning and Development* Available at: www.minfo.ps/arabic/index. php?pagess=mainandid=137 (in Arabic) (accessed 4 April 2012).

Palestinian Central Board of Statistics (2009) *Palestine in Figures 2009*. Available at: www.pcbs.gov.ps/Portals/_PCBS/Downloads/book1661.pdf (accessed 4 April 2012).

Palestinian Centre for Development and Media Freedoms (2008) *More than Two Hundred and Fifty Violations of Media Freedom during 2007. Stained with the Blood of Journalists*. Palestinian Centre for Development and Media Freedoms (MADA) (in Arabic). Available at: www.madacenter.org/index. php?lang=1 (accessed 4 April 2012).

Palestinian Centre for Human Rights (1995) *Critique of the Press Law of 1995*. Available at: www.pchrgaza.org/portal/en/index.php?option=com_contentan dview=articleandid=2913:critique-of-the-palestinian-press-law-of-1995andcat id=50:pchrstudiesandItemid=197 (accessed 4 April 2012).

Palestinian Telecommunication Company (PALTEL) (2012) The Palestinian Telecommunication Co. PALTEL. Available at: www.paltel.ps/index. php?lang=en (accessed 4 April 2012).

Sisalem, M., Muhanna, I. and El Dahdoh, S. (1996) *The Laws of Palestine*, Vol. XXVII. Gaza: Matabi' Mansur.

WAFA/Palestinian Information Centre (2012) *The Palestinian Press in the Diaspora* (in Arabic). Available at: www.wafainfo.ps/atemplate.aspx?id=2473 (accessed 8 August 2012).

5

News Consumption and News Agendas in Egypt

Hamza Mohammed and Barrie Gunter

This chapter will describe media systems and developments in Egypt and their relationship to the extant political systems. Once totally controlled by government, independent sources of news supply have been permitted in Egypt. What is the nature of these changes to the news media landscape? What challenges do they present to the new and established media and to government? This chapter will examine these questions, examine the position that Egyptian news media have reached, and consider whether expanded news supply in Egypt is reflected in a more diverse news agenda. New research will be presented that examines links between different patterns of news consumption and public news agendas.

Undoubtedly, over recent years, Egyptian media have witnessed many significant changes. The post-2000 era media landscape has moved from 'Nasser-style totalitarian government' to more liberal, modernized authoritarian government (Hamdy, 2008). According to Hamdy, in asserting control over the media the Egyptian regime applies a 'carrot-and-stick' approach. Reporting they like is rewarded, reporting they dislike is punished. In the early, 1990s affirming its crucial role as a leader in the media field and a major political player in the Arab world, Egypt established direct broadcast satellite (DBS) technology for the first time in the region. This was followed by the emergence of media privatization, the beginning of private satellite television (TV) channels, the extend of privately owned opposition newspapers, and the introduction of the internet with its massive flows of information (Hamdy, 2008; Khamis, 2008).

The establishment of satellite TV channels in Egypt represented a significant change from the 'monolithic', state-controlled and government-owned media model to a much more 'pluralistic' and varied media land-scape. As a result, the Egyptian media have shifted from total 'state media ownership' and harsh 'governmental domination' to 'private ownership' and 'individual or party control' (Abdulla, 2006; Amin, 2002; Khamis, 2008; Rugh, 2004; Zayani, 2008). This transition has coupled with several changes in the legal sphere of Egyptian media. Rugh (2004) classified Egypt as a country with a media scene that is in a process of transition from an authoritarian to a more liberal system. On the other hand, other scholars classified Egypt as a more in the pre-transition stage (Iskandar, 2006; Mellor, 2005). In both cases the media scene has dramatically changed in Egypt. This transitional era can be described as a period of political reform. As a result, this transition referred to the willingness of the Egyptian regime to accept more criticism and alter-native views. The most obvious feature of this period is the unprecedented freedom of expression that has created a new generation of journalists who are practicing press freedom and criticizing governmental politics.

Taking this into consideration, the first part of this chapter discusses the development of the Egyptian media institutions (press, radio, TV and new media); and the second part examines the relationship between the political regime and the media institutions, including how the regime can control and operate media institutions.

The development of media institutions in Egypt

The Egyptian press

Egyptian newspapers, as in other Arab countries, initially appeared during a period of foreign colonial rule. The newspaper in Egypt is an eighteenth-century phenomenon, with the first newspaper being published in August 1798 under the French occupation. Since the beginning, newspapers have been essential communication tools, due to their effectiveness for Egyptian lead-ers, in the spreading of political and social opinions. For this reason, the first newspapers that appeared in Egypt were not private but official government publications. Napoleon Bonaparte established *Le Courier d'Egypt* as the first newspaper in Egypt. This publication generally dealt with political news and appeared in editions of four pages once every four days to serve the French interests in Egypt (Rugh, 2004). In 1828 Mohamed Ali[1] issued the first Egyptian newspaper called *Al Waqai al-Misreya*, (Egyptian Events), then the first popular newspaper *Wadi an-Neel,* (Nile Valley) was issued in 1867, and this was followed by a number of newspapers that reflected the political, economic, social and cultural conditions. As Dabbous stated:

> The history of the Egyptian press is the history of Egypt. Every political event and reform had its influence on the press. The Egyptian press was the first voice calling for independence, demanding education for the masses, and introducing western thought and ideas (Dabbous, 1994: 61).

Since, the Egyptian press has always been closely tied to politics, so its publications were organized over time by a cycle of laws. The first law on publications was issued on 26 November 1881 as the earliest press legislation in Egypt. According to this law, the publication of newspapers was a right for any individual on condition of having permission from the government. However, this law gave the government the right to close down or confiscate any newspaper violating public order, religion or morals. On 27 February 1936, Decretal Law No. 20 of 1936 on publications and printing houses in Egypt was issued. In 1941, the Syndicate of Journalists was also established (Abd El-Magid, 2001).

Under the British occupation, in 1882, Egyptian newspapers became more popular. They started with the publication of *Al-Liwaa* by Mustafa Kamil in 1900 and was followed by *Muayyad* and *Al Garida* with their subsequent parties emerging. Between 1923 and 1939, the Egyptian press largely enjoyed freedom. With the beginning of World War II (WWII) martial law was re-imposed, which led to the disappearance of several papers (Dabbous, 1994). After the 1952 revolution, various measures were taken by the government to unite the press with the revolution. The 1952 revolution had a political agenda that implied a contradictory approach to basic democratic values. For instance, President Gamal Abdel Nasser used an 'iron fist' policy in dealing with his opponents. He closed a lot of the newspapers that existed before the 1952 revolution. Also, the government imposed heavy financial fines on the newspaper's journalists and many of them were jailed. In sum, Nasser's policy led to a harsh backlash in the margin of freedom enjoyed by various media (Khamis, 2008).

In 1960 the press was nationalized under the Press Organization Law (Law 156, 1960). According to this law the Arab Socialist Union (ASU) owned and controlled the press. No newspapers could be published without the permission of the ASU, which was given power to license press institutions. The main role of Egyptian newspapers during this period was to mobilize public opinion strongly towards the ideology of the revolution. The press system under the 1952 July revolution can be described as a mobilization press. Under this kind of regime the press was discouraged from criticizing the basic policies of the national government, while the major lines of domestic policy are never attacked. The main themes which were stressed by the media at that time were of 'Arab nationalism', 'pan-Arab identity', and 'supporting independence movements' all over the world.

The Egyptian media system under Nasser fitted what Rugh (2004) described as the 'mobilization press' model (Rugh, 1987 2004). When President Sadat came to office, the Egyptian press entered a new phase. The new regime removed direct censorship (while retaining government control of the press) and adopted a multiparty system. In 1980, new legislation was passed to organize the Egyptian press institutions and to give them more independence from the government (Law 148, 1980). This law affirmed that the press is 'an independent popular authority performing its mission freely in the service of the community'.

The new law gave political parties the right to publish their own news-papers, and journalists under Sadat became free to write whatever they wanted as long as they followed the official policy. Although the political regime supported opposition parties and expressed a more open attitude toward the press, it still took a dogmatic approach to the regime/press relationship; the political regime failed to present a democratic environment within which the political parties and their particular affiliated press publications could operate. After the assassination of Sadat on 6 October 1981 Hosni Mubarak came to office. The period of President Mubarak witnessed a number of important developments, which affected the Egyptian media scene and so, deserve further attention and contextualization within the larger picture of the changes in the Arab media scene in the post-1990 era, in general (Khamis, 2008).

Press system and political authority

For some commentators, the mass media system of a nation-state is a prod-uct and a reflection of the character of the political system within which it exists. Severin and Tankard indicated that 'political, economic, and social forces directly affect media content. Media ownership and control affect media content, which in turn determines media effects' (Severin and Tankard, 1992: 285). Hamada (2001) reported that the media in the Middle East are the product of two basic components: colonialism and post-independence cir-cumstance. The mass media as a major source of information in Egypt have been influenced by the political, economic and social events that have taken place there in the last 60 years or so. Post-independence, all Egyptian's media institutions have been under the direct control of all political regimes but this control has differed from one to another.

Press systems before the 1952 July revolution

The political situation before the 1952 July revolution added to the influence of the Egyptian press, because the great national goal of gaining independence from British occupation had united most Egyptians. Hence, all types of journalism (party and individual) seemed to have agreed to work toward achieving that goal (Hafez, 1990). Having been mobilized around liberty, journalism was a politically powerful voice before the 1952 July revolution, largely due to the absence of an efficient broadcasting system.

Before the July revolution and during the two multiparty periods in Egypt (from 1907 to 1914 and from 1922 to 1953), the relationship between journalism and Egypt's political parties was powerful (Negida, 1988).This era witnessed a highly politicized and exciting media environment and a high level of partisanship among both media professionals and media audiences. Just as the political parties in Egypt were established as a result of journalism – the National Party through the *Al-Liwaa* Newspaper, the Omma Party through the *Al-Garida* Newspaper, and the Al-Esslah Party through the *Al-Moaied* Newspaper – Egyptian journalism benefited from and flourished in the presence of political parties in Egypt (Abu-Zeid, 1977, 2000) – each was dependent on the other.

Press systems under Nasser's rule (1952–70)

One of the main goals set by the Nasser's regime when it first came to power was to put an end to the monopolization of capitalist parties. The revolutionary government dissolved all the political parties (Vatikiotis, 1991). In 1956 Nasser created a single party called the Socialist Union, whose task was to operate for the realization of the purposes of the July revolution (The Egyptian revolution) and to encourage efforts for the political, social and economic construction of the state. The ruling party (Socialist Union) fixed the main lines of the new regime. The party was democratic, socialist and cooperative. Nasser's political regime mobilized all the Egyptian mass media to achieve his beliefs. He nationalized mass media institutions and made their main role one of service to the president and his government. According to Amin, 'In 1960 Nasser nationalized the Egyptian press, including all privately owned press organizations, forcing them to surrender their ownership to the National Union (*Al-Ithad Al-Ishtraki*) and re-imposed a censored press system after a brief lifting' (Amin and Napoli, 2000: 179).

In his significant and comprehensive book, *The Functions of the Arab Press in the Arab Society,* Rugh classified the Egyptian press under the mobilization press. The political regime under Nasser considered the press as a very important tool for the mobilization of popular support of their political programmes (Rugh, 1987, 2004). It can be argued, however, that although Rugh classified the Egyptian press under the mobilization system, this classification was perhaps more appropriate in the past (under Nasser's regime), but these days may not be appropriate. While Rugh's study presented a comprehensive description of the Arab media, some researchers have criticized it. For example, Hamada (2001) pointed out that Rugh's study includes generalities which do not reflect the variety and complexity of the Arab media, particularly in terms of their performance and association with public opinion. In the same vein, Idris pointed out that:

> The Egyptian government allows nowadays some kind of political and press diversity. The Egyptian intellectuals call the press which is owned by government the national press, while they call the rest of the press diverse, opposition, independent press (Idris, 1998: 63).

Furthermore, McPhail (2006) criticized Rugh's classification. He suggested that it is difficult to 'categorize media in different countries with various social orders into four categories, namely mobilization, loyalist, transitional and diverse' (p. 202). One of the criticisms raised by McPhail against Rugh's taxonomy is the focus on only one variable, 'the relationship to government and not the type of news and editorial comments those media make' (McPhail, 2006: 202).

With the advent of the 1952 July revolution, the political authority realized the great importance of journalism. Law No. 156 of 1960 was issued to organize and nationalize the newspapers in Egypt. Thus, the ownership of the newspapers of *Dar al-Ahram, Dar Akbar al-Yom, Dar-Roseal-Yusuf and Dar al-Hilal* was transferred to the Socialist Union, which was the only political party at that time (Amin and Napoli, 2000; Abd El-Magid, 2001). In the light of nationalization, journalism fell prey to bureaucracy and, at the same time, became a chattel of the political system, a tool to justify and support government action (Hafez, 1990).

Press systems under Sadat's rule (1970–81)

Hopwood (1982) concluded that Sadat was more open than Nasser, because he claimed to keep no secrets from the people and to let them have a greater share in government. He changed most things except the presidency. In place of power centres, he tried to set up less personal institutions such as the People's Assembly, the press and the multiparty system, although Egypt remained basically a one-party state – that of the centre party which was very much an extension of Sadat's personality. According to Amin (2006), Sadat's regime, 'in theory . . . adopted an open attitude towards the press, but in practice his press policies were ambivalent' (p. 126). In Amin's view, Sadat's political regime eliminated censorship to a large degree but retained state control of the media (Amin, 2002). The Presidency of Anwar Al-Sadat witnessed political, economic, social and media orientations which were radically different from those of the preceding period. Al-Sadat adopted a multiparty system under the 1977 Parties' Law, establishing three political leagues, which became political parties. Those parties were allowed to produce their own newspapers.

Although some controversy existed regarding the issue of the relationship between journalism and political authority, President Sadat ended the debate by announcing that journalism must follow the directives of the authority. Even though political plurality was a fact at the time, the political authority in power imposed organizational restrictions on journalism. These restrictions were enforced when the Socialist Union established the Supreme Press Council (11 March 1975), primarily to create a code of ethics for journalism, and organizational laws that would require journalistic institutions to support political authority. Then in 1980, the Law of Journalism Authority No. 148 transferred the ownership of national newspapers from the Socialist Union to the state, so the Al-Shura Council could supervise and organize the press. According to this law, individuals were not allowed to own newspapers; rather, only joint-stock companies comprised of public or private legal entities, corporate bodies, or political parties were allowed to establish publishing companies. Although Al-Sadat opened the door to the establishment of political parties (which were given the right to issue newspapers) and theoretically ended censorship, the government's control of the media remained (Amin and Napoli, 2000).

Press systems under Mubarak's rule

Under Mubarak, who became president upon Sadat's assassination in 1981, Egypt has been under an emergency law which 'authorizes prepublication censorship, confiscation of newspapers, and closing down of publications' (Amin, 2002: 127). However, President Mubarak's policy towards journalism and journalists has been characterized from the beginning with calmness, rationalism and tolerance. As was the case before, no newspapers have been confiscated or banned (Hafez, 1990).

Mubarak moved Egypt's media system towards more freedom of the press and expression than his two predecessors (Al-Sadat and Nasser) and, as a result, Egyptian journalism has experienced more freedom than the majority of third world countries. Furthermore, Mubarak has allowed the opposition's newspapers to criticize the government. In 2004, *Al-Masri Al-Youm* (Egyptian today) was issued as a private-owned daily newspaper. *Al-Masri Al-Youm* is one of the most successful newspapers in Egypt at the current time. It was unlike anything that had been seen in Egypt for a long time. It used to criticize the regime, and publish hard-hitting investigative journalism against the political regime. Alongside *Al-Masri Al-Youm*, the Egyptian press environment also witnessed the birth of many small, independent and opposition newspapers. Examples of these newspapers are *Al-Badeel, Al-dostour, Elaosboa, Nahdat Misr, Al-Fagr, Sout Al-Umma, Al- Karam,* and *Alyoum Alsabea.* These new newspapers represented a wide array of various views. Moreover, some of these newspapers such as *Al-Fagr, Sout Al-Umma* and *Al-dostour,* crossed some of the red lines and criticized the president himself (Khamis, 2008). They also, have helped to create a more competitive press environment and to increase the freedom of the press.

The development of the political system's relationship with journalism does not guarantee that the press will transform into a powerful force for affecting political decision-making, or for setting the public agenda in Egypt. Further, the government in Egypt, as in other Arab countries, has set the media agenda. As observed by Amin, 'Historically, governments have set the media agenda; radio and television have served as a means to promote their political, religious, cultural, and economic programmes and filter what Egyptians receive, hear and see' (Amin, 2002: 126). Although the Egyptian constitution provides for freedom of speech and the press and substantiates that the press shall perform its mission with freedom and independence, it shall visualize preparing a free atmosphere for the growth of society and its promotion by enlightened knowledge and contributing to reaching the best solutions in all matters connected with the good and interest of the nation and citizens.[2] The current government, in practice, places many restrictions on these freedoms. For example, as Sakr (2005) concluded that:

In Egypt, Law No. 40 of 1977 had reintroduced political parties and, with them, political party newspapers, published under strict control. To all intents and purposes, even after so-called independent papers started to be allowed in the in the mid-1990s, a dualism persisted between government-owned newspapers on one hand and *al-sahafa al mu'arda* (the 'opposition press') on the other. Journalists in both camps, however, worked under tight restrictions. In non-government press they were denied equal access to source or equal representation on the sole legally recognized national journalists' union. Journalists writing for government organs meanwhile worked to pre-set agenda that hardly required any proactive newsgathering at all. (p. 145)

Further, the Press Law, the Publication Law, the Panel Code, strict libel laws and a long-standing state of emergency restrict freedom of expression. Nowadays, many Egyptian journalists are facing iprison sentence. The new press law that passed its first reading in Egypt's people Assembly in July 2006 was so unwelcome to journalists. A number of journalists and opposition leaders protested against this law (Sakr, 2007). As Amin (2000) pointed out 'in theory, there is no press censorship, but in fact censorship permeates every aspect of expression in Egypt- not just newspapers, but broadcasting, theatre, movies, magazines, and books' (p. 186).

In 2007 five chief-editors from the independent and opposition newspapers were sentenced between one and two years in prison for criticizing President Mubarak and his Prime Minister. In 2007, jail sentences for journalists continued in Egypt. For example, Ibrahim Essa, editor of *Al-Dostour* newspaper had been charged with 'endangering national stability'. In 2008, Essa was sentenced to six months in prison for a series of articles published about the health of President Mubarak (Black, 2007).

Furthermore, Adel Hamouda, editor of *Al-fajr newspaper,* along with Abel Halim Quandeil, and Wael Ibrashi, editor *of Sout AL-Umma*, were all given jail sentences, subject to appeal, for 'insulting the president'.

As mentioned elsewhere, the political regime in Egypt holds many instruments to control freedom of the press such as the Supreme Press Council, which owns the state newspapers and has the right to provide licenses for the opposition and private newspapers. Because of difficulties in obtaining licenses many publishers have been required to own licenses in foreign countries such as Cyprus. These kinds of publications must be authorized by the Ministry of Information. However, the department of censorship in the Ministry of Information has the right to ban such newspapers. Further, the political regime dominates the national press and the Egyptian president appoints their editors-in chief. Moreover, the government has monopolistic control of the printing and distribution of newspapers, even those of opposition parties, allowing the government to limit the production of such newspapers. Despite the evidence of change, the Mubarak regime has continued to use many tools to stifle political expression for political opponents. For instance, he used the law of shame and the emergency law to censor and dominate opposing opinions (Elmasry, 2011).

Despite the existence of all these obstacles and restrictions against freedom of press, it is fair to say that over the last four years of Mubarak's term, Egyptian journalists – more than at any time in recent history – began to feel at liberty to openly criticize the regime and its personages. This new-found liberty as confirmed by Black (2007) 'has accelerated in parallel with the recent stop-go political liberalization project in Egypt, which began with a public outpouring of discontent as the United States invaded Iraq in 2003' (Black, 2007: 2).

The significance of the Egyptian newspapers among the other media

The Egyptian press is considered one of the most developed press in the Arab world. In the past, the Egyptian press was very careful in criticizing and libelling the government. Today journalists enjoy a wide range of freedom to express their views without fear of being jailed or reprimanded (Lahlali, 2011). Thus, the Egyptian newspapers have a considerable potential to influence agenda-setting and opinion formation in the current days. The next section deals with the significance of newspapers alongside the electronic media through the following factors:

1   The greatest merit of the Egyptian newspapers over the other media is that it draws a wider readership from among the elite, the intellectual class and the opinion leaders in the society. The other media, on the other hand, are heavily relied on by members of the community who are generally less educated and complete illiterate. The class of people who read the newspapers are able to articulate their views in a more powerful way so as to influence the thinking and perceptions of the less educated (Mohammed, 2008).

2   Media pluralism in Egypt is currently more effective and vivid with newspapers than the electronic media. While the electronic media are still largely under strict state control, the newspaper industry has become relatively open, allowing for more participation and involvement of opposition parties and people with dissenting views from the government-controlled media. This development has become more pronounced within the last 5 years (Mohammed, 2008).

3   It is known that electronic media (radio and TV) in Egypt as in most Arab countries are under government supervision particularly after

the Egyptian revolution 1952. As mentioned earlier, president Nasser was responsible for nationalizing all the Egyptian media organizations, including the electronic media (see Amin, 1998; Amin and Boyd, 1993; Amin and Napoli, 1997; Rugh, 2004). However, in the last few years an attempt to inject private ownership of TV in Egypt has not changed the media environment as far as pluralism is concerned. The two private TV (Dream and Al-Mehwar) stations are owned by Egyptian businessmen[3] who are known to be staunch members of the ruling party. They do not therefore encourage views that are distasteful to the government. Furthermore, their airtimes are allotted for entertainment programmes, such as movies, songs, video clips and also advertising.[4] The programmes of these two TV channels are not even easily available to the majority of the people, because they require satellite decoders to be able to receive programmes. Yet, the Egyptian economy does not make it easy for people within the low income group to afford decoders.

4   While the law allows opposition parties to establish their own newspapers, the law denies them the right to own TV stations. It is important to state that though the current regime provides the Egyptian press in general more freedom than the electronic media however, the broadcasting system is still under a harsh control from the state. It is known that the political regime has begun implementing a plan to decentralize the electronic media by introducing local radio stations and TV channels, nevertheless, as Rugh stated 'the media system is still under the direct control of the government and operates under the mobilization type of broadcasting which views broadcasting as primarily a means of economic and political motivation' (Rugh, 1989; cited in Curran and Park, 2000: 181). This makes the newspapers more accessible to all than electronic media and hence more important a tool for political communication for the wider majority of the population (Mohammed, 2008).

5   The newspaper industry started in Egypt in 1798, long before the formation of political parties. For example, Mustafa Kamil, a famous campaigner for liberation of Egypt against British occupation established, and used his own newspaper, 'Al-Lwaa', for his campaign. The newspaper was followed by the establishment of The Egyptian National Democratic Party (Showman, 2002). As mentioned earlier, the Egyptian press had played a crucial role for independence of Egypt against British occupation. Hafez (1990) pointed out that all the Egyptian press (party and individual) have agreed to work toward achieving that goal. Because

of the absence of an efficient broadcasting system before and even after the 1952 July revolution, the Egyptian press was a politically powerful voice. TV broadcasting in Egypt did not come to be until 1960. Although radio was available, its influence was relatively insignificant (Mohammed, 2008).

For all the above reasons one confidently can say that the Egyptian newspapers are more accessible to all than other mass media and for this reason more important a medium for conveying political information to the Egyptian society. Hence, the Egyptian newspapers are the most influential on the Egyptian public compared with the other media.

The status of Egyptian media under Military Council's rule

The Supreme Council of Armed Forces (SCAF), which came to power after Mubarak stepped down on 11 February 2011, and still in power now, spoke strongly in the early days of his rule about the need for Egypt to embrace freedom and democracy, confirming that a free press was a necessary component in the machinery of democracy. At the beginning, the SCAF attitude toward the press and freedom of speech was tolerance (Egypt State Information Service, 2011). The post-January 25 revolution brought many significant changes in the Egyptian media scene. The Military Council started its rule by granting a wider margin of freedom to the media and permitted a more plural system in both the political and media domains.

The most salient example of this pluralistic media scene was that the SCAF allowed one of the more popular organizations, the Islamist Muslim Brotherhood, to participate in the political life. Moreover, the SCAF has recognized Muslim Brotherhood as a political party. Furthermore, the SCAF began granting private publishing licenses and gave many political groups licenses to establish a new political party (Egyptian State Information Service, 2011).

Even though the media landscape has progressed positively in Egypt, the Military Council still places restrictions on freedom of speech. The SCAF used a number of methods to stifle political expression for political opponents. For instance, in September 2011, many journalists and political bloggers were sent to the military trials after reporting and criticizing the SCAF, for example, Hossam el-Hamalawy, Reem Maged and Nabil Sharaf al-Din were summoned to appear before military judges in relation to what the military perceived as criticisms of the SCAF. In addition, Maikel Nabil, the political blogger was sentenced to three years after he criticized the army for not being transparent in its decision-making.

In 28 October 2011, Mahmoud al-Daba, a journalist at the independent weekly newspaper *Sout Al-Omma* was summoned to the military prosecutor. After criticizing a member of the ruling SCAF (www.almasryalyoum.com/en/node/retrieved, 28 October 2011). According to the constitutional declaration released by the SCAF after the 25 January 2011 Revolution, all Egyptian people became entitled to trial by their natural judge. Since the SCAF took power dozens of activists, bloggers and journalists, however, were sent to military courts. Further, the Military Council extended the Emergency Law (http://egyptelections.carnegieendowment.org/retrieved, 18 November 2011). This law affirms that journalists accused of spreading news that is deemed to be damaging to the president or heads of state can be imprisoned for up to five years. The Emergency Law grants the president the right to hang basic freedoms: fines and punishments like those listed above can be implemented without fair trial and news organizations can be censored or closed in the name of national security (Mohamed, 2011).

The Arabic Network for Human Rights Information (ANHRI) and the Egyptian Organization for Human Rights in a joint report in September 2011 on freedom of the press in Egypt after the 25 January revolution, confirmed that the Egyptian local press coverage of government activities has continued to be editorially partial, driven by the same pre-revolution biases (www.anhri.net/en/, retrieved 25 October 2011). The report investigated the media coverage of the SCAF, covering the period between 10 July and 30 July. It analysed newspapers, news websites and TV channels that were both state-run and privately owned. The report pointed out that the state-media has dealt with the news and issues of the SCAF the same way they used to deal with the ousted president Mubarak (www.anhri.net/en/, retrieved 25 October 2011).

According to the report, the state-owned media replaced the picture of Mubarak and his son Gamal with SCAF members and Prime Minster Essam Sharaf. The SCAF members and Egyptian Prime Minister were more frequent actors in the state-owned media coverage. Further, the state media generally demonstrated support for the SCAF, whereas the privately owned newspapers criticized the military council's performance. The report explained that the lack of change in the state-media coverage could be due to two factors. First, the people who used to work in most of the state-media during Mubarak's rule did not change after the revolution, despite the change in the top leaders. Second, it is difficult for any media institution suddenly to change its decades-old mechanisms and instill new methodologies in a short period of time (www.anhri.net/en/, retrieved 25 October 2011).

Hence, some commentators such as Saeed Shoeib, Huweida Mustafa and Nabil Abel-Fatah, have criticized the Military Council's performance of pursuing the same policy adopted by Mubarak's regime and aimed at impeding the freedom of media. For instance, Saeed Shoeib, the Egyptian journalist, pointed out that the laws and pressures imposed on the media have not changed since Mubarak's resignation. After the 25 January 2011 revolution, there has been much debate about restructuring the state-media, but little has changed in practical terms. The lack of change may be due to two reasons. First, all the state-media are still under the direct control of the state. Second, the existence of laws that allow the political regime to exercise the right to dominate, interfere and close any channel at any time, while allowing other channels to break these same laws when they so wish. (http://arabic.youm7.com/ retrieved, 25 October 2011).

In the same direction, Huweida Mustafa, the Egyptian Journalist and media expert indicated that official media, is still the main voice of Military Council and part of national security (www.almasryalyoum.com/en/node/511139, retrieved 18 November 2011).The ties of loyalty are still strong, and official media still take their orders from the the SCAF. The Military Council dominates the Egyptian media and uses media as tools to portray their viewpoint to the public. According to Nabil Abel-Fatah, state-media is still closely tied to the political power and will not be changed overnight. (www.almasryalyoum.com/, retrieved 18 November 2011).

In conclusion, despite the significant changes in the media landscape after the 25 January 2011 revolution, there is an ambivalent official attitude towards the media. As with many previous political regimes in Egypt (Gamal Abdel-Nasser, Anwar Al-Sadat and most recently Hosni Mubarak), the Military Council that took power after the revolution, 'in theory' adopted an open attitude towards the media, but in practice still places rigid restrictions on journalists. Finally, it can be said that compared to Mubarak's regime, freedom of expression in Egypt under the Military Council did not change a lot and the Military Council failed to present a true democratic environment in Egypt till now (www.anhri.net/en/, retrieved 29 October 2011).

The development of the Egyptian radio

At all stages of mass media development in the Arab world, Egypt has maintained a reputation as a leader, especially in the production of media content (Abdulla, 2003). Since the early 1950s, when the country gained independence from the United Kingdom, Egyptian presidents (Gamal Abdel-Nasser,

Anwar Al-Sadat and most recently Hosni Mubarak) have realized the importance of the mass media for achieving national development (Abdulla, 2003).The beginning of Egyptian radio dates back to the start of the twentieth century, but it did not officially begin until May 1934 when the government, under British occupation, started an official Egyptian radio service run by the Marconi Company of the United Kingdom. Egyptian radio broadcasting was initially started as a private industry by individuals such as Ahmed Sadek Al-Gawahergi, who began the wireless stations. During the 1920s and 1930s there were over 100 private stations, which were owned by groups of businessmen (Boyd, 1999). The history of Egyptian radio can be divided into the following phases.

Stage I (1934–47): This stage was categorized by a ten-year contract between the Egyptian government and the Marconi Company of the United Kingdom to provide a broadcasting service for Egypt. During this period, radio was under the direct control of the Ministry of Transportation. In 1939, radio's control was transferred from the Ministry of Transportation to the Ministry of Social Affairs with the cooperation of the Marconi Company (Dabbous, 1994; Boyd, 1999).

Stage II (1947–52): This period witnessed the end of the Marconi contract. It was ended by the Egyptian government on 4 March 4 1949, two years before its expiration date, in response to the nationalist movement after World War II. The main characteristic of this period was Law 98 of 1949, which stated the rights, and duties of Egyptian radio to include: monitoring of all broadcast stations, permitting new studios to open and encouraging programme exchange among stations. The Ministry of Social Affairs was responsible for radio until the end of World II, when it was moved to the Ministry of Internal Affairs. Until the 1952 revolution, Egyptian radio was moved many times between the Ministries of Social affairs and that of the Interior (Boyd, 1999).

Stage III (1952–81): After the 1952 revolution, radio, like a lot of other projects and services, was nationalized and Egyptianized. Nasser and his regime recognized the potential role of the mass media in the development of Egypt, particularly radio, which became the official voice of the government. He used radio to mobilize the Arab public, and also to support the Arab nationalists' ideas. *Sawt Al-Arab* (Voice of the Arabs) radio station, was the official mouthpiece of Nasser's political regime and the main tool for spreading his objectives. Nasser used *Sawt Al-Arab* to achieve two main objectives, the first of which was to rise against imperialism, and the second to inform the Arab people of its 'own governments" faults (Lahlali, 2011). For this reason radio came under the strict ownership and tight control of the government, which used it to by-pass the literacy barrier to contact the public. Also, most radio services and programmes focused on entertainment and development, and were exported to the rest of the Arab countries (Saleh, 2000; Abdulla, 2003; Rugh, 2004).

Stage IV (1981–90): A new stage started in April 1981 with the application of a particular new system called the Broadcasting Network System. During this period, the radio broadcasting services were divided into seven radio networks: The Principle Network, the Commercial Network, the Voice of Arabs Network, the Local Network, the Sport Network, the Religion Network, and the Cultural Network (Dabbous, 1994; ERTU, 2002).

Stage V (the post-1990 era): After 1990 a huge changes in the Arab media landscape, particularly in Egypt. This era witnessed as Khamis (2008) pointed out the emergence of media privatization, and the opening of private satellite television channels. At present, the Egyptian radio consists of nine networks that broadcast 117,106 hours. These networks are the General Programme, the Middle East, the Voice of the Arabs, the Local Service, the Youth and Sport, the Holy Quran, the Cultural Service, the Specialized Service, and the Beamed Service (see Dabbous, 1994; ERTU, 2002, Abdualla, 2003; Farag, 2003). Moreover, Egyptian radio has also maintained an 'Overseas Service,' broadcasting to foreign countries in 38 languages (Abdulla, 2003; Farag, 2003). Despite, the relative, gradual atmosphere of freedom that is currently prevailing in Egypt after the 25 January revolution, the Egyptian is still under the direct control of the Ministry of Information, which administers broadcasting activity, appoints staff, and determines the work policies of radio and television (Saleh, 2000; Rugh, 2004; Mohamed, 2011).

The development of Egyptian TV

After the 1952 revolution, President Nasser became interested in establishing TV in Egypt. Nasser was quick to realize the potential power in positioning Egypt as a leader, both culturally and politically, in the Arab world. For this reason, the government issued a presidential decree, which established a series of goals for television and radio broadcasting. Among the goals were: evolving the standards of arts and culture through sophisticated programming, spreading culture among masses, and informing the public about national and international news. The policy of the government was to make radio and television available to as many people as possible (Abdulla, 2003).

The history of Egyptian TV stretches back to 1959, when the Egyptian government signed a contract with the Radio Corporation of America (RCA) to provide a complete TV service for Egypt. Egyptian TV started broadcasting on 21 July 1960, on the eighth anniversary of the 1952 revolution

(Saleh, 2000). After 1974, the year when the door was formally opened to the West, the number of Western programmes on Egyptian TV increased again (Boyd, 1999). Unlike other Arab countries, Egypt was able to start TV production without importing engineering equipment from abroad. This was due to the well-financed radio services and film industry, which were in existence at the time. Egyptian TV initially began broadcasting its programmes on two channels. A third channel that was added was soon banned after the 1967 war (Saleh, 2000).

The main goals of the first channel were to provide a mixture of popular programmes, news and programmes concerned with developmental and educational objectives. The second channel, which began broadcasting in July 1961, was designed originally to present cultural, informational and instructional programmes including programmes about foreign cultures and civilizations (Ayad, 2001). A great deal of the early TV programmes was done live and some were taped on the RCA machines supplied as part of the TV contract.

During the earlier years, TV broadcast a great deal of foreign programmes, mostly American and British. Immediately after the 1967 war, there was a decrease in the amount of foreign programmes that was shown on TV. British and American programmes became unacceptable due to the break in diplomatic relations with Great Britain and the United states. After 1974, the year when the door was formally opened to the West, the number of Western programmes on Egyptian television increased again (Boyd, 1982, 1999).

At the start of the 1990s, Egyptian TV began implementing a plan to decentralize the system by introducing local TV channels. The local channels covered specific regions in Egypt. Today, broadcasting activity in Egypt is organized by the law of Broadcasting Media No. 13 (1979), which was modified by law No. 223 in 1989. According to this law, broadcasting affairs are the concern of a public agency known as the Egyptian Radio and TV Union (ERTU). Although administratively autonomous, this agency follows the direction of the state and is under its dominance. The Broadcasting Media law states that the Union aims to convey the message of radio and TV within the framework of the general policies of society and its informative requirements (El-Halawani, 1987). This law and its modifications are intended mainly to directly ensure that all programmes and broadcasting activities both serve authority by creating public support for the political system, and manage public opinion. Furthermore, ERTU is accountable to the Minister of Information. The structure of the broadcast media is highly centralized, partly because it reflects the country's centralized system of supervision and partly because the main philosophy leading media structure supports the use of broadcast media as tools for social and political control (Farag, 2003).

Broadcasting systems and political authority

The radio and TV companies of almost all the Arab world are subject to stricter control from the government than the press, especially since they transcend the obstacles of illiteracy and reach wider audiences. Thus, governments in the Arab world monopolize the ownership, operation and supervision of broadcast institutions (Amin, 2002). Rugh (2004) presented various reasons for the control of the government-owned broadcasting systems in the Arab world. He affirmed that because radio and TV have the ability to overcome borders and literacy obstacles, all the political regimes in the Arab world have a much greater interest in dominating them and keeping them as a tool to mobilize the masses and propagate the official line. In addition, the cost of establishing radio or TV is higher than the cost of establishing print media. Consequently, unlike the print media, TV production is beyond the financial reach of all but a few in these developing countries (Rugh, 2004). In fact, from the beginning, broadcasting systems in the Arab world were under harsh supervision and control from the British and French colonial powers. They used them as instruments of the colonial regime to achieve their objectives. After colonialism, broadcasting systems turned to the newly independent states that were content to keep them as governmental institutions. According to Ayish (2002):

> Arab governments in newly independent states instituted television as a governmental monopoly. The television monopoly model traditionally derives from the notion of broadcasting as a government operation harnessed mainly to serve national development goals. Drawing on public service and centralized broadcast systems dominant in former colonial nations, strong government leverage over television organizations virtually stripped broadcasters of much of their editorial autonomy. Operating within ministries of information, television organizations, for the most part, were funded exclusively from national budgetary allocations and their employees were viewed as part of public sector bureaucracy. (p. 138)

In Egypt, revolutionaries realized the importance of radio from its inception and

> sought to control it. They devoted a great interest to radio and used it as a political tool to direct the masses and propagate their regime's ideology. The broadcasting system had been controlled through the political authority of the Ministry of Information which administered broadcasting activity,

appointed staff, and determined the work policies of radio and television. (Hamada, 1993, 1995)

The new Egyptian leadership in 1952 recognized the significant role of radio as a political propaganda tool. Through stations like 'The Arab Voice', President Nasser broadcast his revolutionist, pan-Arab messages to the rest of the Arab countries, which were mostly still under British and French occupation. As mentioned earlier, when Nasser came to power the mass media he established became among the most influential in the Arab world. Through *Sout Al Arab* 'The Arab Voice', the best known Radio station in Egypt at that time, Nasser mobilized not only Egyptian but also Arab public opinion (Boyd, 1999; Abdulla, 2003). Nasser used 'The Arab Voice' to help the Arab countries gain their independence and to serve other 'nationalist' causes (Boyd, 1999).

In this context, radio helped Egypt speak to the Arab nations, and became a political and cultural tool in the hands of the government. After Sadat's 1979 peace agreement with Israel, when the Arab countries boycotted Egypt, radio was used to counter attacks from these countries (Boyd, 1999). Although the print media under presidents Sadat and Mubarak have witnessed many changes, both towards and away from greater diversity and freedom of expression as mentioned earlier, the broadcasting system (radio and TV) did not see any change under their rules. This may be as Rugh (2004) suggested:

Anyone with a printing press has the technical capability of reaching the literate elite, and while this is seen by the government as a potential threat, it is not nearly as great a political threat as radio or television station broadcasting to millions. (p. 181)

New media and regime response in Egypt

In his book, *Understanding Media*, McLuhan (1964) argued that 'the "content" of any medium is always another medium' (p. 8). He added 'new media are not completely new phenomena. They grow out of old media through complex process of "repurposing" and "incorporation"' (p. 8). In this same sense, Bolter and Grusin (1999) called that process of representing one medium in the form of another – 'remediation'. They argued that '"remediation" is a defining characteristic of the new digital media' (Bolter and Grusin, 1999: 64). The structure of the internet has shifted from a medium which, like traditional media, failed to provide users with interactive opportunities to a more dynamic technology that enables engagement in the content creation process.

The internet has quickly cemented itself as *the* communication medium of the early twenty-first century. The proliferation of new media has intensified competition for audiences causing a destabilization of the established media order (McQuail et al., 1998). These new forms of media in Egypt, in particular, have revolutionized Egyptian society and radically altered its media landscape. It has brought about a new era of diversity of opinions and dynamic public debates which shifted the focus away from the highly direct state ownership, domination and control. The American journalist Thomas Friedman, noticed that the internet, blogs, online social networks such as Facebook, YouTube and text messaging via mobile phones, particularly among young men '. . . is giving Middle Easterners cheep tools to communicate horizontally to mobilize politically and criticize their leaders harshly, outside of the state control' (*The New York Times*, 14 June 2009).

In the same direction, Khamis (2008) added that these changes in the media arena encouraged the birth of new political debates and discussions, the formation of new media effects, as well as an increasing wave of 'liberalization' and 'democratization' in the Arab region. Furthermore, Lynch (2005) explained how the new media in the Arab world have acted as motors of change which have the ability not just to set the public agenda, but also to encourage citizens to protest against autocratic Arab regimes. In addition, Faris (2010) noted that 'while states, including Egypt, have become more a adept at surveillance and filtering of online activities, social media networks make it impossible for authoritarian countries to control their media environments in the way that such regimes have typically in the past' (p. viii). The next section discusses, briefly, the development of new media in Egypt followed by debating the relationship between the Egyptian political regime under Mubarak and social media network till the 25 January Egyptian revolution.

The first use of internet services in Egypt date back to October 1993, taking the form of a link between the Egyptian Universities Network (EUN) and European Academic and research Network. The user community at that time was estimated at about 2000 to 3000 users (Abdulla, 2003). Government officials believed that internet had the capacity to stimulate socio-economic development, private sector growth and expansion of the internet economy (Farag, 2003).They supported the use of the internet to transfer Egypt into a knowledge-based society, enabling it to draw closer to Western countries in social and economic dimensions, and securing Egypt's leading position in the Arab counties. Among these competing values and uses, the economic and business priorities have gained the upper hand (Farag, 2003).

After 1994, the internet in Egypt became a public service, not only for the educational sector, but also for the commercial community in Egypt. As a result, the number of users increased from 2000 in 1994 to more than 25,000 in early

1997 (Abdulla, 2003). In 1996, the free internet access policy was replaced by an open access policy, where internet access offered to the commercial domain was privatized, and more than 12 private internet Service Providers started operation for the first time. After a series of negative articles in the state press claiming that the internet was being used to spread revolutionary materials, an official body, the internet Society of Egypt (ISE), was formed to act as regulatory body concerning internet matters (Abdulla, 2003).

In 2000, the number of the internet users in Egypt was estimated at 220,000, most of them located in Cairo, followed by Alexandria, with only limited accessibility outside of these cities. In 2002 the user community was estimated at about one million users, with one of the largest growth rates of internet connectivity in the Middle East. Between early 2008 and the first quarter of 2009, the number of internet users in Egypt increased from just under 11 million to 13 million, which equated to more than 17 per cent of the population, representing an annual growth rate of 20 to 30 per cent (Faris, 2010; Mohamed, 2011). At this level, some media scholars have argued that this number of users would qualify the internet to be classified as a mass medium that can impact the society (Morris and Ogan, 1996). The Egyptian government responded to the increase of internet use by implementing legislation to observe users.

- In June 2006, The Egyptian High Administration Court confirmed that the Information Ministry and the Ministry of Communication and Information Technology had the authority to block, suspend or shut down web sites that they considered a threat to 'national security' (Mohamed, 2011). In consequence, the security police selectively concealed specific a number of web sites, blogs and cybercafés and various kind of online journalism.

In one example of such action, Abel-Karim Amer, a 22-year-old Egyptian, became the first blogger to be jailed (for four years beginning in 2007), after being convicted on several counts of offending President Mubarak. The Abel-Karim story shows the strong link between blogging and censorship in Egypt. In addition, many bloggers were illegally arrested for days or months by orders of Minister of the Interior. Hence, many organizations such as 'Reporters without Borders' and 'The Committee to Protect Journalism' considered Egypt to be one of the worst countries for allowing freedom to electronic publishing and for observing international conventions that prevent the censorship of electronic websites (Mohamed, 2011).

Despite the censorship of online publishing under the Mubarak political regime, Egyptian blogs have begun to form a significant virtual society that is having a political, social and cultural impact on the public agenda. Egyptian blogs have attracted a new generation of political activists. At the beginning, the most important Egyptian bloggers posted comments in English such as the Arabist, Baheyya, Big Pharaoh and others. No country in the region has experienced a bigger impact from blogging and other types of internet activism than Egypt. In contrast to other countries in the Middle East such as Saudi Arabia, Egypt has no strict method to control or filter internet connections. In 2008, Mubarak's political regime arrested more than 100 bloggers (Faris, 2010; Mohamed, 2011).

It is also important to note that the relationship between the bloggers and newspapers was actually toxic because of competition between them, with some bloggers viewing themselves the 'new journalists'. But this relationship it slowly developed into a cooperation between them (Faris, 2010). The impact of bloggers in Egypt is not limited only to people who have access to internet. It can also reach out to those people who do not have internet access (Mohamed, 2011).

Mohamed (2011) argued that Egyptian political bloggers depend on sources that are associated with independent newspapers, satellite TV programmes and the information quoted from human rights organizations' websites. These sources frequently provide critical and oppositional views to the Egyptian government. For instance, some of these criticisms have included statements denouncing the governing regime's corruption, lack of respect for the rule of law, abuse of power, restrictions on demonstrations and industrial action, and its crackdown on internet activists.

Bloggers rarely incorporated links to the Egyptian state-media. They can enjoy greater freedom to speak out online because the Egyptian government has limited powers to control their online access. For example, political bloggers typically used internet cafes to collect news and reports from other activists and protesters about arrests and protests. Further, once they had posted their messages on a web site it was instantaneously transmitted to large potential readerships. Even if some of their number were arrested, others would still blog about the arrests and reach a wide audience, circumventing the restrictive gatekeeper practices of government-controlled mainstream media organizations (Faris, 2010; Mohamed, 2011). According to one commentator, 'nothing will stop bloggers from blogging or reading what they want to read on the Internet: as long as there is an Internet, there is a way to go around censorship and around barriers; they can block a Website, but you can establish another one' (Mohamed, 2011: 190).

Egyptian political bloggers have brought issues to public interest that the traditional media have long ignored. This fact has been evident in regard to stories about sexual harassment and torture of government detainees, exploitation of power, thuggery in the streets, failure to recognize workers' civil rights or their protests to improve their financial living conditions and calls for political reform. Within the Egyptian context, bloggers have set the agenda about other important issues ignored by mainstream news media, and have helped to uncover silent truths not covered by the state-media. They have also provided platforms for the Egyptian people to speak out on political matters and have their voices heard (Mohamed, 2011).

In addition, Egyptian political bloggers have played an important role in providing story ideas and information for the traditional media to develop and follow. This means there is an inter-media agenda, between the bloggers and the traditional media. As such, blogs have become part of the competitive sphere of news gathering and reporting, often providing alternative content to what is presented in the traditional media. It can be concluded that Egyptian political bloggers have succeeded in setting the agenda of many issues which the traditional media rarely cover. They represent an alternative media or citizen's media.

The second generation internet in the form of blogging and social networks provided protected channels that governing authorities were not able to silence (Howard and Hussain, 2012). The beginning of the Egyptian revolution was catalysed through online social media before the physical activism commenced on 25 January 2011. Because of online social media, the revolution moved from the virtual world to the real world. And people themselves after thirty years of an oppressive regime and in 18 days of peaceful revolution forced Mubarak to resign.

Notes

1 Mohamed Ali (1805–48) is the founder of modern Egypt.
2 Article 3, Law no. 96 of the year 1996 (*Official Journal*, issue no. 25, 30 June 1996).
3 The first private TV channel 'Dream' was established on November 2001. This channel is owned and sponsored by the Famous Egyptian businessman Ahamed Bahgat. The second TV channel 'Al-Mehwar TV' was established in 2002, this Channel was owned and operated by the businessman Hassan Ratib and the Egyptian Radio and TV Union.
4 The main target of 'Dream TV' is to create a sort of useful precautions and advertise for the all audience and a kind of free cooperation and also entertaining through the last songs and video clips and meeting with the most famous super stars in all scopes.

References

Abdulla, R. (2003) *The Uses and Gratifications of the Internet Among Arab Students in Egypt*. Unpublished thesis. University of Miami, Miami.

— (2006) An overview of media developments in Egypt: Does the internet make a difference?, *Global Media Journal (GMJ), Mediterranean Edition*, 1, 88–100.

Abd El-Magid, L. (2001) *Communication Legislations in Egypt,* in Arabic. Cairo: Dar Al-Arabi Linasher Wa Al-Tawzea.

Abu-Zeid, F. (1977) *Crisis of Democracy in the Egyptian Press*, in Arabic. Cairo: Maktabat Madboly.

— (2000) Problems of political communication in Egypt: Workshop on 26 June 2000. *The Egyptian Journal of Public Opinion Research*, in Arabic. Cairo: Cairo University.

Amin, H. (1998) American programmes on Egyptian television. In Y. Kamalipour (ed.), *US Images Around the World*. New York: SUNY Press, pp. 319–34.

— (2002) Freedom as a value in Arab media: perceptions and attitudes among Journalists. *Political Communication*, 19(2), 125–35.

Amin, H., and Boyd, D. (1993) The impact of home video cassette recorders on the Egyptian film and television consumption patterns. *European Journal of Communication*, 18(1), 2–7.

Amin, H., and Napoli, J. (1997) De-Westernizing' of media studies: The Middle East experience, paper presented at the workshop on *De-Westernizing Media Studies*. Seoul, Korea, 16–20 November.

— (2000) Media and power in Egypt. In James Curran and Myung-Jin Park (eds), *De-Westernizing Media Studies*. London: Routledge, pp. 178–88.

Ayad, K. (2001) *The Developmental Dimensions of the Egyptian Media Role in the Peace Process: A Content Analysis Study with a Future Perspective*. Unpublished doctoral thesis. University of Leicester, Leicester.

Ayish, M. (2002) Political communication on Arab world television: evolving patterns. *Political Communication*, 19, 137–54.

Black, J. (2007) Egypt's press: More free, still fettered. In *Arab Media and Society*. Cairo: The American University. Available at: www.arabmediasociety. com/articles/downloads/2008011423035_ams4_jeff_black (accessed 4 march 2013).

Bolter, J., and Grusin, R. (1999) *Remediation: Understanding New Media*. Cambridge: Mitt Press.

Boyd, D. (1999) *Broadcasting in the Arab World: A Survey of the Electronic Mediain the Middle East*, 3rd edn. Ames, IA: Iowa State University Press.

Dabbous, S. (1994) Mass media in Egypt. In Y. Kamalibour and H. Mowlana (eds), *Mass Media in the Middle East: A Comprehensive Handbook*. London: Greenwood Press, pp. 60–73.

Egyptian State Information Service. Available at: www.egypt.gov.eg/ (accessed 10 July 2011).

El-Halawani, M. (1987) *The Broadcasting System in the Arab World*, in Arabic. Cairo: Dar El Fiker Al-Arabi.

Elmasry, M. (2011) Producing news in Mubarak's Egypt: An analysis of Egyptian newspaper production during the late Hosni Mubark era. *Journal of Arab & Muslim Media Research*, 4(2 and 3), 121–44.

Farag, A. M. (2003) The internet in Egyptian society and its use as a news medium. Unpublished doctoral thesis. Faculty of Graduate Studies and Research, McGill University.

Faris, D. (2010) Revolutions without revolutionaries? Social media networks and regime response in Egypt. Unpublished dissertation. Faculty of Graduate Studies and Research, University of Pennsylvania.

Hafez, S. (1990) The political files of the Egyptian press. (in Arabic). *Communication Studies*. Cairo, Egypt, (4) 60–72.

Hamada, B. (1993) *The Role of Mass Media and Political Decision Making in the Arab World* (in Arabic). Centre for Arab Unity Studies, Beirut: Lebanon.

Hamdy, N. (2008) Building capabilities of Egyptian journalists in preparation for a media in transition. *Journal of Arab and Muslim Media Research*, 1(3), 215–37.

— (2001) The Arab image in the minds of western image-makers. *The Journal of International Communication*, 7, 7–35.

Hopwood, D. (1982) *Egypt: Politics and Society, 1945–1981*. London: George Allen and Unwind.

Howard, P. N., and Hussain, M. M. (2012) Egypt and Tunisia: The role of digital media. In L. Diamond and M. F. Plattner (eds), *Liberation Technology; Social Media and the Struggle for Democracy*. Baltimore: Johns Hopkins University Press, pp. 110–23.

Ibrahim, H. (1994) The press and political authority in the Arabic world. Unpublished doctoral thesis. Cairo University, Cairo.

Idris, F. (1998) The nature and role of the Arab press in the Arab foreign policy. Unpublished doctoral thesis. University of Leicester, Leicester.

Iskandar, A. (July 2006) *Paradox of the Free Press in Egypt*. USEF Expert Panel Discussion Notes, Washington, DC.

Khamis, S. (2008) Modern Egyptian media: Transformations, paradoxes, debates and comparative perspectives. *Journal of Arab and Muslim Media Research*, 1(3), 259–77.

Lahlali, M. (2011) *Contemporary Arab Broadcast Media*. Edinburgh: Edinburgh University Press.

Lynch, M. (2005), Assessing the democratizing power of Arab satellite TV. *Transnational Broadcasting Studies Journal (TBS)*, 1, 150–5.

McLuhan, M. (1964) *Understanding Media: The Extensions of Man*, New York: McGraw Hill Book Co.

McPhail, T. (2006) *Global Communication, Theories, stakeholders, and Trends*, 2nd edn. Blackwell publishing.

McQuail, D. (2005) *Mass Communication Theory*, 5th edn, London: Sage.

McQuail, D., Graber, D., and Norris, P. (1998), Conclusion: Challenges for public policy. In Graber, D. McQuail and P. Norris (eds), *The Politics of the News: The News of Politics*. Washington, DC: Congressional Quarterly Press, pp 251–57.

Mellor, N. (2005) *The Making of Arab News*. Lanham, MD: Rowman and Littlefield.

Mohamed, A. S. (2011) Between the hammer and the anvil: Blogs, bloggers, and the public sphere in Egypt. Unpublished dissertation. Faculty of Graduate Studies and Research, McGill University.

Mohammed, H. (2008) Political communication and agenda-setting, a case study of the Egyptian newspapers. Unpublished dissertation. University of Leicester.

Morris, M., and Ogan, C. (1996)The Internet as a mass medium. *Journal of Communication*, 46(1), 39–50.

Negida, S. (1988) Journalism and political life in Egypt in the period from December 1953 to 1945. Unpublished doctoral thesis. Faculty of Mass Communication, Cairo University.

Rugh, W. (2000) The Arab Press: News media and political process in the Arab world. In J. Curran and M. Park (eds), *De-Westernizing Media Studies*. London: Routledge, p. 181.

— (2004) Arab Mass Media Newspapers, Radio, and Television in Arab Politics. Praeger Publisher.

Sakr, N. (2005) The changing dynamics of Arab journalism. In Hugo De Burah (ed.), *Making Journalists*. London: Rutledge, pp. 142–56.

— (2007) *Arab Television Today*. London: I.B. Tauris.

Saleh, M. (2000) Private broadcasting in Egypt: Prospects and concern a case study. Unpublished MA dissertation. The American University, Cairo.

Severin, W. J., and Tankard, J. W. (1992) Communication Theories: Origins, Methods and Uses in the Mass Media, 3rd edn, New York: Longman.

— (2001) Communication Theories: Origins, Methods and Uses in the Mass Media, 5th edn, New York: Longman.

Showman, M. (2002) *The History of the Egyptian Media*, in Arabic. Cairo: Dar Al-Arabi Linasher Wa Al-Tawzea.

Vatikiotis, P. (1991) *The History of Modern Egypt, from Mohamed Ali to Mubarak* (4th edn). London: Weidenfeld and Nicholson.

Zayani, M. (2008) The challenges and limits of universalist concepts: Problematizing public opinion and a mediated Arab public sphere. *Middle East Journal of Culture and Communication*, 1, 60–79.

6

The Changing News Landscape of Libya

Mokhtar Elareshi and Julian Matthews

Introduction

The past decade has witnessed significant changes in the provision of news around the world. News flow has increased dramatically during this period, while technological developments have changed the media landscape. The emergence of the internet has provided a new platform for news provision for established news suppliers, and opened up new access paths to audiences for new news providers, including private citizens (The Pew Research Center for the People and the Press, 2000; Allan, 2006; Gunter et al., 2009).

The digitization of mainstream media, such as television (TV), has also increased the overall volume of news. Increased channel capacity has spawned many new TV news channels (Ghareeb, 2000). These changes have created a much more competitive news marketplace and many established news operators have experienced difficulties in maintaining their customer bases, which has had knock-on financial effects. Many print newspapers have had to cut their staff numbers, while radio and television news rooms have also curtailed their operations to cut costs. Many news providers in the print and broadcast media have established new services on the internet (Althaus and Tewksbury, 2000; Saleh, 2007). They compete with each other on the same news platform. They also face competition from new news providers that operate only online (Vyas et al., 2007).

These changes have begun to affect the news landscape in Libya. For many years, news coverage in Libya was almost entirely dependent upon local news services. This led to a provision of a news diet of limited diversity (Al-Asfar, 2002; Saleh, 2007). With the introduction of satellite TV broadcasting, TV audiences in Libya had exposure to news uplinked from outside its national boundaries (Al-Asfar, 2002; Rugh, 2004). These international news services were better resourced than local Libyan news providers (Al-Shaqsi, 2000; Al-Asfar, 2002) and presented a much extended news menu, news from different perspectives and a higher quality of production (Rugh, 2004; Miladi, 2006; Fahmy and Johnson, 2007). This new provision triggered previously untapped appetites for news among Libyan people, and especially among younger members of the population.

Not everyone, including the Libyan government, has welcomed the development of news stations that are based outside Libya (El-Nawawy and Iskander, 2002; Zayani, 2005; Fahmy and Johnson, 2007; Mellor, 2007). For the Libyan broadcasting industry, the popularity of international TV news services such as *Al Arabiya* and *Al-Jazeera* has posed a threat to the audience shares of local TV news services. Whether local news services can survive this onslaught and what steps they might need to take to do so remain important questions. This chapter reports findings from an original study of TV news audiences in Libya that attempts to track and profile the news consumption habits of young Libyans, who now represent a significant proportion of the population. This chapter examines news consumption and the Libyan media system in 2009 and does not reflect any of the more recent political changes that have taken place in the country. It explores whether greater viewing of new international TV news services is linked to diminished viewing of local TV services and the public perception of the qualities of local and non-local news suppliers to determine why some services are popular and why others are less so.

The Libyan TV news scene

Historically, the Libyan media system has undergone dramatic changes from the first US forces television station broadcast in 1956 (Al-Asfar, 2002) and later developments of local radio and TV programmes during the 1960s (El-Zilitni, 1981). Broadcast news provides a useful example of this recent transformation, where beforehand its programmes were limited in number and characterized by an established news presentational style and news content that was shaped to avoid criticisms of the foreign or domestic policy of the government in accordance with tight political control in the country (Rugh, 1979, 2004; Menassat, 2011).

In line with growth in the Arab world generally, the Libyan media industry has recently migrated news outputs onto digital terrestrial and satellite platforms and the internet, creating strong demands from the Libyan public for increased access to satellite TV channels in particular. Government policy-makers, in responding to such demand and wider economic and technological changes, have helped to widen access to satellite dish technology beyond the preserve of Libyan elites and the wealthy.

During the 1990s, the spread of satellite dishes was limited to elites or wealthy Libyans who could afford dishes and the mandatory electronic devices needed to decode incoming signals. The lower cost of satellite dishes (now less than £150) has initiated their greater uptake and sparked a continuing growth in audience numbers for satellite television coinciding with a marked decrease in those watching local channels. As a result, greater numbers of Libyans have the opportunity to view a greatly increased variety of satellite programming from both government and non-government services – a development which is important to be reviewed here.

At the present time, the developing news scene includes both government and non-government services. *Al Jamahiriya TV Satellite Channel*, for example, is state-owned and reproduces, due largely to financial constraints, all of the programmes from its *Al Jamahiriya* terrestrial channel (Al-Asfar, 2002). The service offers five main newscasts per day, broadcasting two different news programmes for foreign language speakers including a newscast in English that airs at 12:00 and another in French at 16:00. Generally, the news coverage reflects an international appeal, with programmes providing greater space and prominence to international affairs than local ones.

Al Libiya TV Satellite Channel, by contrast, is a non-governmental channel owned by the firm Al-Ghad Group for Media Services (IREX, 2006; Reporters without Borders, 13 February 2008) and was, until the 2011 uprisings against the *Gadhafi* regime, supported by *Al Gadhafi's* son, Saif al-Islam (Menassat, 2011). It was the first satellite channel to offer professional news and entertainment programmes departed from a general broadcasting taboo of addressing issues related to the Libyan regime (IREX, 2006) amidst strong opposition from the state and powerful circles within Libya as well as other neighbour countries, such as Egypt. Such difficulties pushed the channel to broadcast from other countries such as Jordan and the United Kingdom (Cherian, 2011).

Several additional Libyan satellite TV services characterize the news scene in combination with those mentioned above, including a free of charge service called *Al Manawa TV* that broadcasts news about local events, sport and cultural activities including contemporary and traditional Arab music and children's programmes (Al-Asfar, 2002). *Al Hedaya TV* is an Islamic channel that provides alternative programmes, current affairs and entertainment programming from an Islamic perspective in a similar way to the output of *Al Tawasul TV* (Networking). Further, *Al Badeel TV*, which is owned by Libya's Revolutionary Committees Movement, broadcasts programmes on ideological ideas about *Al Gadhafi's* ideological treatise, *The Green Book*. *Al Nadi TV* carries breaking news from local and world sport, including sports matches and player news in a similar way to the other sports-based news channel *Al Jamahiriya Sport 1 TV*. Other channels such as *Al Shbabiya TV* and *Libya Educational 1 TV* focus on young adults with the latter offering programmes on new technologies, animals, cultures, research and new science to meet their perceived educational needs. *Al Mutawassit TV* is a non-governmental channel also owned by the Al-Ghad Group that broadcasts programmes of social nature and comedy yet its signal has been jammed since its launch (Al-Tawil, 2010).

Internationally, *Al-Jazeera TV* and *Al Arabiya TV* are two further channels received by the Libyan publics but broadcast from outside the region. *Al-Jazeera* is a Qatari-government-owned satellite television service that provides independent Arab news broadcasting (Sakr, 2007) on issues confronting the Arab world (Zayani and Ayish, 2006). It includes high-quality production value reflected in the rhythm and style of its news presentation (Lynch, 2006; Jamal and Melkote, 2008) and uses news presenters who have trained or worked for famous TV channels (Auter et al., 2005; Zayani, 2005).

A range of commentators, from regional Arab and Islamic governments to Western governments (Zayani and Ayish, 2006), have criticized *Al-Jazeera TV* coverage from time to time. The second channel is *Al Arabiya TV*. This is owned and funded by the Saudi royal family (Zayani, 2005; Lynch, 2006; Fandy, 2007) and broadcasts 24 hours a day, carrying news, current affairs, business and financial market reports, sports news and documentaries. It claims to offer news that is not inflected with sensationalism or deliberate provocation which thus provides a 'responsible' alternative to the programming of *Al-Jazeera* (Lynch, 2006).

In summary, the use and impact of new satellite TV news services characterized the rapidly evolving Libyan news scene up to 2011. Representing a range of dramatically different news formats from those used traditionally by indigenous national news operators, satellite TV channels have changed the way information and entertainment is being received (Ghareeb, 2000; Rugh, 2004), even, it is claimed, redrawing lines between the Libyan regime and citizens on the one hand and mass media on the other (Rugh, 2004; Menassat, 2011). Such services improved the amount and extent of news circulation and presented the Libyan public with richer and more varied perspectives (Barker, 1999; Menassat, 2011). Their glossier forms of news presentation

(Rugh, 2004), in the cases of *Al-Jazeera* and *Al Arabiya*, contrasted sharply with older, local, terrestrial channels and raised questions about the continued relevance of established local TV news services to an audience whose news appetites were being re-conditioned by new international news operations. Research has shown that the viewing figures for local Libyan TV news channels, such as *Al Jamahiriya* for example, dwindled over the 1990s and 2000s (Al-Asfar, 2002) at a time when the numbers of people watching international TV channels grew, especially for *Al-Jazeera* TV (Zayani, 2005; Zayani and Ayish, 2006; Karam, 2007b). Hence, we should ask: Which news TV services are being widely consumed by Libyan news consumers and what factors, including notions of credibility and information quality (Wanta and Hu, 1994) inform their choices?

Researching Libyan news consumption

The research reported in this chapter was based on a self-completion questionnaire survey of undergraduate students, aged 17–24 years, recruited from across different parts of the University of Al-Fateh, Tripoli – the largest university in Libya. The survey was conducted in December 2009 with a sample of 400 undergraduate students, following a stratified random sampling approach of 14 university faculties, with sampling strata set by gender and faculty. The questionnaire[1] was administered in the university with either the first author or an assistant as moderator and each student in the sample was randomly selected from the student population of each faculty. The survey recorded data on respondents' news media exposure patterns and credibility perceptions associated with a range of news media. Much of the focus was placed on television as a news platform and the audience's reception of new satellite TV services – *Al Jamahiriya*, *Al Libiya*, *Al-Jazeera* and *Al Arabiya*. The study indicated the new sources that were most used and trusted by young, well-educated people in Libya.[2]

Patterns of news consumption

The survey asked respondents to specify the televised news services they consumed. These services were listed by name and respondents were provided with a frequency scale (spanning seven points from 'never consumed' to 'daily consumption'[3]) to estimate their viewing of each service. These data enabled comparisons to be made of reported use of new and old TV news services and revealed that TV news channels are consumed in the following order: the *Middle East Broadcasting Centre* (*MBC*) (67%), *Al-Jazeera* (59.5%), *Al Shbabiya* (56.8%), *Al Arabiya* (50.2%), *Al Libiya* (41%), *Al Jamahiriya* (34%), *Al Hurra* (16.5%), *BBC* (*Arabic*) (14.8%), *ATA* (13%); *ANN News* (9.8%), *France 24* (*Arabic*) (7.5%) and *RTA* (4.2%). Here, respondents reveal their preferences for television channels through their frequent consumption of *MBC*, an entertainment channel that targets programmes to women and young people (Ghareeb, 2000; Al-Asfar, 2002; Jamal and Melkote, 2008). Of the specific news-based channels, respondents report their frequent consumption of the pan-Arab satellite channels *Al-Jazeera* and *Al Arabiya* and diminishing consumption of the two local TV news channels, *Al Libiya* and *Al Jamahiriya*.

This analysis of news consumption patterns in Libya began by examining demographic differences. Some significant variations in the reported consumption of specific news suppliers occurred that were linked to gender, family size and faculty. In terms of gender, differences appeared in the reported consumption of specific TV channels, including: *Al-Jazeera*, *MBC*, *Al Hurra*, *BBC* (*Arabic*) and *RTA*. More specifically, male students were more likely than female students to watch news via *Al-Jazeera* (68.5% vs 53%) and slightly more likely to view *Al Hurra* (17.3% vs 15.9%) and fairly more likely to watch news through *BBC* (*Arabic*) (18.5% vs 12.1%). Nonetheless, female students were more likely than male students to watch news via *MBC* (74.1% vs 57.1%) and slightly more likely to watch *RTA* (4.3% vs 4.2%). These findings are consistent with previous studies that suggest males, rather than females, are more likely to watch, and be heavy viewers of, *Al-Jazeera* users (Johnson and Fahmy 2005; Jamal and Melkote 2008). Similarly, the reported preference for *MBC* is explained by channels programming which in this case is targeted to female audiences in the age range of those participating in the study.

In a similar way, the analysis (using the Kruskal–Wallis *H* test) showed that the faculty in which the respondents studied appeared significant at times in shaping respondents' consumption of the six named TV news channels: *Al Jamahiriya*, *Al Libiya*, *Al Jamahiriya* (Terrestrial TV), *Al Shbabiya*, *MBC* and *ATA*. While SSAL students were more likely to watch news on *Al Jamahiriya* (Terrestrial TV) (SSAL 68% vs NST 57% vs AVM 56%), *Al Shbabiya TV* (SSAL 85% vs AVM 82% vs NST 71%), *MBC TV* (SSAL 87% vs NST 84% vs AVM 77%) and the *Iranian TV ATA* (SSAL 52% vs AVM 51% vs NST 43%) than the other two groups, AVM students consumed more news via *Al Jamahiriya TV* (AVM 78% vs SSAL 74% vs NST 68%) and *Al Libiya TV*. It seems that SSAL respondents have more free time to watch news on local and international TV news services than do NST and AVM respondents. In addition, SSAL respondents increased interest in these programmes' subject matter and particular topics may explain the level of their consumption as higher than those respondents studying science (NST and AVM).[4]

Adding to the differentiated picture of the respondents news consumption was the finding that there were only two significant family size differences in watching the news TV channels, *Al Jamahiriya* (Terrestrial) and *BBC TV* (*Arabic*).[5] Those who lived in small-sized family households (71%) were more likely to consume news via terrestrial TV compared to those who lived in large-sized families (68%), those who lived by themselves (67%) and those who lived in medium-sized families (61%). Further, those who lived in small-sized families watched more news on BBC (*Arabic*) than did all the other family size groups. Despite the assumption that *Al Arabiya TV* would compete with international TV channels such as *Al-Jazeera TV*, the analysis showed that there was no significant difference among demographic groups, with respondents having similar responses and attitudes to these channels.

This analysis of respondent's news consumption also included the endorsements they give to news services. A factor analysis was conducted to investigate which news channel factors were given the strongest endorsements by respondents.[6] Table 6.1 lists the news TV channels for each of the four factors (non-Arabic channels, local TV channels, Arabic News TV channels and Arabic Entertainment channel) with the corresponding factor loadings.

The factor analysis produced clear results, showing that the respondents could easily be clustered into local families of TV channels: non-Arabic TV channel consumers, local Libyan TV channel consumers, Arabic news TV channel consumers and Arabic entertainment TV channel consumers. Further its Eigenvalue scores[7] revealed strong interrelationships between the different non-Arabic TV channels[8] and demonstrated quite strong interrelationships between local TV channels and Arabic news TV channels.[9] Nevertheless, the entertainment channel *MBC* was strongly loaded on a separate factor in contrast to assumptions that it would load on Factor 3 (with Arabic news TV channels). Thus, in the minds of respondents these TV channels were apparently closely connected. In addition to the endorsements given to programmes, the study also examined the motives behind respondents' news consumption.

Motives behind news consumption

Previous research (see, e.g. Henningham, 1982; Henke, 1985; Kayany and Yelsma, 2000; Al-Obaidi et al., 2004; Ofcom, 2007a, b) suggests that individuals consume different news media platforms for different purposes and have different rationales for choosing news from different media sources.

TABLE 6.1 Factor loadings for consuming news on different news TV channels

TV channels		Factors			
	M	1	2	3	4
Factor 1: Non-Arabic TV channels	**1.44**				
– France 24 TV (Arabic)	1.28	0.758			
– ANN News TV	1.44	0.718			
– BBC TV (Arabic)	1.60	0.694			
– Russia Today TV (Arabic)	1.23	0.658			
– Al Hurra TV	1.64	0.559			
– Al Alam Today TV (Arabic)	1.49	0.538			
Factor 2: Local TV channels	**2.21**				
– Al Libiya TV	2.27		0.790		
– Al Jamahiriya TV	2.20		0.781		
– Terrestrial TV	1.92		0.704		
– Al Shbabiya TV	2.45		0.697		
Factor 3: Arabic news TV channels	**2.41**				
– Al-Jazeera TV	2.47			0.860	
– Al Arabiya TV	2.35			0.836	
Factor 4: Arabic entertainment TV channel	**2.56**				
– MBC TV	2.56				0.906
Eigenvalue		3.39	1.96	1.54	1.06

TABLE 6.1 *Continued*

TV channels	Factors				
	M	1	2	3	4
% variance explained		26.08	15.04	11.82	8.18
Cronbach's alpha (reliability score %)		0.76	0.74	0.74	

Notes: News items measured on a three-point scale (1= never and 3 = daily). Extraction method: Principal Component Analysis; rotation method: Varimax (eigenvalue > 1).

The motivational factors outlined in previous work were included in this survey to capture the reasons that informed respondents' consumption of news sources. Respondents were required to indicate these, on a four-point scale ('1' not at all important to '4' very important) across 13 general motivational reasons[10] included in the survey. Later, a factor analysis was completed to determine the interrelationships among these reasons and derive a smaller number of factor variables for subsequent multivariate data analysis.[11] Table 6.2 shows the results of a multivariate factor analysis on lists of the motivational items clustered into three groupings.

The principal components analysis with varimax rotation was applied to the 13 general motivational items and yielded a four-factor solution that explained 50.1 per cent of the total variance. Factor 1, called Information and Interest comprised four items (eigenvalue = 2.43; percentage variance = 20.2%). Factor 2, called Surveillance Needs included three items (eigenvalue = 1.5; percentage variance = 12.3%). Factor 3, called Entertainment and Conversational Currency also comprised three items (eigenvalue = 1.09; percentage variance = 9.1%). Factor 4, called Others, included just one item 'for other reasons' (0.793) (eigenvalue = 1; percentage variance = 8.5%). The fourth factor was excluded for failing to add significantly to the factor solution.

The above findings also show that respondents recognized that basic surveillance needs, information needs and their general interests inform their decision to consume news. Also revealed are the specific intentions behind their consumption of news which resonate with the findings from previous research studies. First-year students, for example, were more likely to explain 'entertainment' as a main motivation to watch news programmes than final-year students, which reflects the conclusions reached by Huang

TABLE 6.2 News motivation factors

Items		Factors		
	M	1	2	3
Factor 1: Information and interest	**2.86**			
– For information about daily life, e.g. travel, health, education	3.46	0.731		
– For personal interest	3.20	0.659		
– As a duty of responsibility to keep up-to-date	2.08	0.595		
– To get a different perspective from another country/ countries	2.73	0.486		
Factor 2: Surveillance needs	**3.40**			
– To know what's going on across the country	3.61		0.669	
– To know what's going on in the world	3.41		0.662	
– To be able to form my own opinions about issues	3.17		0.556	
Factor 3: Entertainment and conversational currency	**2.43**			
– For entertainment	2.12			0.748
– Through habit	1.97			0.664
– To join in conversations with friends, family, or colleagues	3.21			0.467
Cronbach's alpha (reliability score %)		0.56	0.44	0.42

Notes: Extraction method: Principal Component Analysis; rotation method: Varimax with Kaiser normalization (eigenvalue > 1). M = mean scores for items on a four-point scale (1= not at all important and 4= very important).

(2009) and Karam (2007a). Likewise, the desire to keep up with the latest news that is reported by SSAL respondents is consistent with Rubin (1983) and Huang (2009) conclusions that some students tend to pick up and then value the habit of watching news routinely. Overall, the survey results make clear that news is important to respondents for information and surveillance purposes but it is also seen as a source of entertainment. The gratifications that respondents seek from TV news were another aspect of the analysis to which we will now turn.

Gratifications sought from specific TV news services

In order to examine the role that news plays in the lives of those regular consumers of TV news, the survey asked respondents to provide the reasons behind their consumption of specific news programmes on specific TV channels, and to explain the perceived gratifications derived from them. Table 6.3 presents the reasons for gratifications obtained from watching the following specific newscasts: (1) *News 18:00* on *Al-Jazeera TV*, (2) *News 18:00* on *Al Arabiya TV*, (3) *News 21:30* on *Al Jamahiriya TV* and (4) *News 22:00* on *Al Libiya TV*.

The findings from the table reveal that respondents share similar opinions about consuming news information from pan-Arab TV news services. A majority (more than 80%) of respondents said they watched *News 18:00* on *Al-Jazeera* news, for example, because it summarizes relevant news events, keeping them up to date with current affairs and teaching them new things. Likewise, the programme was described as a credible and trustworthy news source that considers important issues and provides its audience with support for their own viewpoints and interesting things to talk about. Only a minority of the respondents agreed that they used the service because it is uncensored. Similarly, most of the respondents (more than 75%) reacted positively to *News 18:00* on *Al Arabiya* for similar reasons as those outlined for *Al-Jazeera* and respondents also showed the lowest agreement on the view that the uncensored content of the programme motivated their consumption.

In the same way, respondents expressed similar views over the factors that influence their consumption of the two local TV stations, agreeing extensively with most of the listed items when discussing *News 22:00* on *Al Libiya*. They value the programme for its coverage of world issues, ability to teach and its information that helps make up their minds on important issues and support their viewpoints on others. Few respondents stated that they consumed the news service because it is uncensored. The reasons offered for watching *News 21:30* on *Al Jamahiriya* were similar to those expressed for *Al Libiya*. This study also examined the differences in respondents' rating of TV news services.

TABLE 6.3 Gratifications associated with each newscast programme

Gratifications items	1*	2*	3*	4*
– It gives a summary of what's happening around the world	86.8	81	68.1	63.4
– It keeps up with current affairs and events	86.0	81.5	67.9	68.0
– I learn how to do things I haven't done before	84.0	81.5	68.1	73.3
– It is a credible source of news	83.5	82.8	64.9	64.4
– It helps me make up my mind about the important issues of the day	83.5	76.7	74.2	77.6
– It supports my own viewpoints to other people	82.3	78.9	73.4	67.5
– It gives me interesting things to talk about	81.9	82.3	68.1	68.4
– I can trust the information they give me	80.7	75.9	64.4	64.8
– I can pass the information on to other people	73.7	66.8	61.2	55.9
– To watch news presented from different perspectives	73.3	74.1	58.8	55.7
– The newscasters give a human quality to the news	75.7	75.9	56.4	46.2
– The news presenters are better on this channel	70.7	65.1	51.3	40.8
– I can compare my own ideas to what the commentators say	64.2	63.8	60.1	55.1
– It is uncensored	40.1	32.3	27.7	28.0

Notes: Percentages indicate those who agreed strongly or agreed with each item.
*1 – Al-Jazeera (n = 243); 2 – Al Arabiya (n = 232); 3 – Al Libiya (n = 188); 4 – Al Jamahiriya (n = 247).

Differences between TV news services in the motivational profiles

Once the general motivations that inform news consumption were established, the analysis examined the differences between respondents' rating of TV news services on specific gratification measures. Table 6.4 shows the mean differences between motivational profiles and TV news services and Bonferroni tests conducted on these mean scores uncovered no significant differences between the two local TV channels or between the two international TV channels.[12] However, differences emerged in the motivational profiles between the following news services: *Al Jamahiriya* and *Al-Jazeera*; *Al Jamahiriya* and *Al Arabiya*; *Al Libiya* and *Al-Jazeera*; *Al Libiya* and *Al Arabiya*.

The findings show that the two local TV news services (*Al Jamahiriya* and *Al Libiya*) and the two Arab satellite TV news services (*Al-Jazeera* and *Al Arabiya*) deliver similarly on a range of gratifications. Nonetheless, in the latter comparison, *Al-Jazeera* received higher scores on two gratification measures – a finding denoting that the respondents rate this news service over *Al Arabiya* as providing a better quality news service all-round. Additionally, *Al-Jazeera* received a universally higher rating when compared with the two local TV news services (*Al Jamahiriya* and *Al Libiya*). *Al Arabiya* was also rated higher than the local TV stations, yet by contrast did not differ significantly from *Al Jamahiriya* on four gratification measures ('I learn how to do things that I haven't done before,' 'it is uncensored,' 'I can pass the information on to other people,' 'it helps me make up my mind about important issues of the day') and similarly with *Al Libiya* on four measures ('it is uncensored,' 'I can pass the information on to other people,' 'it helps me make up my mind about important issues of the day' and 'I can compare my own ideas with what the commentators say').

Finally, the analysis sought to examine the particular gratifications news consumers obtained from viewing the following specific TV news sources: *News 18:00* on *Al-Jazeera*, *News 18:00* on *Al Arabiya*, *News 21:30* on *Al Jamahiriya* and *News 22:00* on *Al Libiya*. The comparison showed that respondents shared similar opinions about their consumption of pan-Arab TV news services. In terms of watching *News 18:00* on *Al-Jazeera*, a majority (more than 80%) provided the following reasons: the service was credible, trustworthy, provided quality information and different perspectives and supported learning about important issues and interactions with others. Only a minority of the respondents, however, agreed that they used the service because it is uncensored. Similar answers were provided by majority of respondents

TABLE 6.4 Differences between TV news services in motivational profiles

Gratifications items	1†	2†	3†	4†	F-value
– The newscasters give a human quality to the news	3.35[a]	3.56[b]	4.10[ab]	4.00[ab]	26.25***
– The news presenters are better on this channel	3.18[a]	3.45[b]	4.05[ab]	3.81[ab]	24.43***
– It keeps up with current affairs and events	3.77[a]	3.82[b]	4.32[ab]	4.14[ab]	17.61***
– It gives a summary of what's happening around the world	3.77[a]	3.77[b]	4.32[ab]	4.14[ab]	17.14***
– It is a credible source of news	3.80[a]	3.82[b]	4.29[ab]	4.19[ab]	15.89***
– I can trust the information they give me	3.77[a]	3.76[b]	4.24[ab]	4.02[ab]	13.24***
– It gives me interesting things to talk about	3.70[a]	3.72[b]	4.13[ab]	4.07[ab]	12.41***
– To watch news presented from different perspectives	3.60[a]	3.62[b]	3.98[ab]	3.93[ab]	9.26***
– I learn how to do things I haven't done before	3.94[a]	3.78[b]	4.24[ab]	4.12[b]	8.27***
– It is uncensored	2.96[a]	3.03[b]	3.41[ab]	3.15	6.85***
– It supports my own viewpoints to other people	3.77[a]	3.85[b]	4.09[abc]	4.04[abc]	6.54***
– I can pass the information on to other people	3.49[a]	3.57[b]	3.85[ab]	3.75	5.45**
– I can compare my own ideas to what the commentators say	3.49[a]	3.56	3.77[a]	3.76[a]	4.44**
– It helps me make up my mind about the important issues of the day	4.02[a]	3.98[b]	4.24[abc]	4.02[c]	3.18*

Notes: Means with uncommon superscripts differ significantly at the 0.05 level. Scores ranged from 1 to 5.
* $p < 0.05$; ** $p < 0.01$; *** $p < 0.001$.
†1 – Al JamahiriyaTV ($n = 247$); 2 – Al Libiya TV ($n = 188$); 3 – Al-Jazeera TV ($n = 243$); 4 – Al Arabiya TV ($n = 232$).

(more than 75%) for their viewing of *News 18:00* on *Al Arabiya*, including a minority agreeing that they watched because 'it is uncensored'.

Equally, comparable opinions were offered for respondents' consumption of pan-Arab TV news services. Responses tended to agree extensively with most items (almost 70%) when detailing the reasons behind respondents' consumption of *News 22:00* on *Al Libiya*, providing most agreement with the following in decreasing order: the service helped to form opinions, support viewpoints on issues, provide interesting things to talk about, summarizes what is going on in the world and provides learning on how to do things. The lowest agreement was measured on the item that 'it is uncensored'. Additionally, the analysis demonstrated that respondents indicated parallel reasons for watching *News 21:30* on *Al Jamahiriya* as they did for *Al Libiya* at the same levels of agreement (almost 70%).

Motivations for viewing specific TV news services

In addition, this analysis examined the specific variables that informed the respondents' viewing of the four TV news services: *Al Jamahiriya*, *Al Libiya*, *Al-Jazeera* and *Al Arabiya*. A stepwise multiple regression analyses was undertaken, in which several independent variables (including motivational factors) were introduced as predictor variables in order to understand and forecast the effects of different variables of certain TV channel consumption. Table 6.5 lists the predictor factors set against the news service and the results of a stepwise multiple regression analyses.

The results show evidence of the different reasons that respondents provide for their viewing of each of the four TV news services. The viewing of local TV news services such as *Al Jamahiriya* and *Al Libiya TV* were closely linked to respondents' consumption of other local news media. For *Al Libiya*, respondents reported as important to their viewing the following variables, including entertainment, sport and the quality of news anchors. The latter variables were unrelated to claimed viewing of *Al Jamahiriya* whereas viewing of the two international satellite TV channels was explained by respondents' consumption of other pan-Arab TV news services, the quality of news anchors and was negatively associated with reliance on word of mouth for news information. Trust and interest in sport also emerged as important to viewing of *Al-Jazeera*. What is more, the study also explored the importance of respondents' perceptions of the credibility of these news programmes.

TABLE 6.5 Final squares models predicting reported watching of specific TV channels

Items	Jamahiriya TV	Libiya TV	Jazeera TV	Arabiya TV
– Credibility of news source	0.19**			
– Watch news from different perspectives	0.12*			
– News from Libyan TV channels	0.24***	0.25***		
– News from local radio	0.13*			
– Celebrity behaviour news (important issue)	−0.17**	−0.15*		
– News from local magazines	0.15*			
– Talk to friends	0.15*			
– Makes up mind about the important issues of the day		0.20**		
– The anchors are better		0.16*	0.13*	0.15*
– Entertainment (important issue)		0.19**		
– Sports news (interest issue)		0.15*	0.13*	
– News from pan-Arab TV channels			0.37***	0.35***
– Word of mouth			−0.12*	−0.16*
– Trust of news			0.17**	
Variance explained (adjusted R^2)	0.26	0.28	0.26	0.17
R^2	0.29	0.30	0.27	0.18

Notes: Stepwise regression: $*p < 0.05$; $**p < 0.01$; $***p < 0.001$. Scores for news question were collapsed and reversed to 4 = daily and 1 = don't use. The positive scores indicated more consumption/use of these channels, while negative scores indicated less frequent use of these channels.

Credibility and news consumption

Individuals' perceptions of the news programmes' credibility and trustworthiness are important to their consumption. Previous studies explain that these evaluations and perceptions (Tsfati, 2003) inform individuals discussions about news when interacting with others (Uslaner, 2002; Gunter, 2005) and ultimately their news consumption choices. In order to understand how the respondents judged the credibility of news coverage, the analysis compared the overall credibility ratings of the four TV news services.[13] In general, the findings uncovered noticeable differences between the credibility profiles of pan-Arab TV news services and those that originated within Libya in line with previous research.[14] The pan-Arab TV news services, *Al-Jazeera* and *Al Arabiya*, were generally more highly regarded than even the new local TV news operations in terms of their credibility (see Table 6.6).

The observed contrast between the credibility value given to international TV news services over local TV news services confirm findings from previous research that suggests international news channels create different perceptions among their audiences than do local media (Choi et al., 2006). More specifically the findings show that pan-Arab TV services are rated as more credible news sources than local TV news services on a wide range of items, despite local TV services being judged similar in terms of their credibility. Nevertheless, the two pan-Arab TV services were not equally well received with *Al-Jazeera*, for instance, being rated as the better service in terms of the quality of its credibility.

TABLE 6.6 Overall credibility scores

TV channels	Mean	SD	Possible range	n
– *Al-Jazeera TV* news credibility index	3.90	1.34	1–5	398
– *Al Arabiya TV* news credibility index	3.71	1.33	1–5	398
– *Al Libiya TV* news credibility index	3.38	1.39	1–5	397
– *Al Jamahiriya TV* news credibility index	3.18	1.49	1–5	400

Note: Higher scores indicate higher levels of perception of credibility.

Further comparisons undertaken on the credibility indexes of different TV news channels[15] revealed significant variation between the TV news services. Respondents reported pan-Arab TV services as providing fairer coverage than the local TV services (*Al Jamahiriya* and *Al Libiya*), showing their perception of the latter's services as less credible and less relevant to their lives. Moreover, respondents rated *Al-Jazeera* news coverage as significantly more likely to 'tell the whole story' than news reported by *Al Arabiya*, *Al Libiya* or *Al Jamahiriya* – a finding consistent with the conclusions of Fahmy and Johnson (2007).[16] Together with *Al Arabiya*, *Al-Jazeera* was also commended on account of its well-trained reporters.[17] Additionally, there were observable distinctions between respondents' views on the local TV services also, with respondents reporting the coverage of the new TV service, *Al Libiya*, as more credible and likely to separate fact from opinion than the long-established service, *Al Jamahiriya*.

Discussion and conclusion

This chapter has explained that the emergence of pan-Arab satellite TV news services is an important contextual development for understanding young adults' news consumption in Libya. Given that previous research findings (Ghareeb, 2000; Al-Asfar, 2002; Harb and Bessaiso, 2006; Miladi, 2006) have outlined the continuing significance of such services for the news scene in the Arab world generally, this chapter has sought to examine their place in the consumption patterns of a sample of young adults in Libya. Reporting on a survey-based research project, this has outlined how young people consume news from pan-Arab satellite TV news services rather than local Arab TV news services and have introduced respondents' motivations to explain these patterns of news consumption.

As has been recognized by previous research studies conducted in Libya and elsewhere in the Arab world (Abdel Rahman, 1998; Marghalani et al., 1998; Al-Shaqsi, 2000; Al-Asfar, 2002; Auter et al., 2005; Ofcom, 2007a) and confirmed by this chapter, news consumers watch TV news services to fulfil a complex mix of surveillance needs, information needs and to satisfy their general interest. From the study's findings, we learn that consumption choices appeared congruent with respondents' previous experience of viewing and their positive perceptions of that TV service. Past viewing of local Libyan services combined with a view that these reflect Libyan opinions and interest informed viewers' choice to consume local TV services for instance, whereas previous consumption of pan-Arab TV channels linked with preferences for factual rather than entertainment news informed the selection of pan-Arab

TV services. Likewise, the notions of news programme's production values informed the news consumption of different news services. In contrast to the other local TV channel, *Al Libiya TV* was rated by respondents as the better local service on account of its news value – a finding which may explain how this new local TV source has altered young Libyans' opinions on the value of local media production. Certainly, its presence may be central to the process of reducing trust and the consumption of the other long-established TV stations while concurrently enhancing consumption of other TV news services such as *Al-Jazeera*.

More significantly, the research has confirmed findings from elsewhere that Libyans like other Arab viewers seek a refuge in watching news on the new Arab satellite TV channels (see, e.g. Sakr, 2001; Al-Asfar, 2002; Auter et al., 2005; Karam, 2007a; Jamal, 2009) and introduced views on programme quality and credibility as important explanations for their consumption choices. Perceptions of programme quality, professionalism and usefulness ensured that the pan-Arab news services, *Al-Jazeera* and *Al Arabiya*, were rated above the new local TV services operations. The survey showed that the two pan-Arab news services were perceived to be more credible than the local TV services – a finding consistent with conclusions from previous research that indicate that pan-Arab TV news services tended to attract distinctive opinions in contrast to those associated with local news media (Choi et al., 2006). Further, *Al-Jazeera* was seen as more credible than the other pan-Arab TV news service *Al Arabiya*, confirming the view that *Al-Jazeera* is most watched and perceived to be the most credible source of news in the Arab world (e.g. Ayish, 2004b; Johnson and Fahmy, 2005; Fahmy and Johnson, 2007).

In conclusion, this discussion has revealed the importance of perceptions of the credibility of news sources for news consumers and their news consumption. News consumers discuss those news services rated as more credible as important to them, revealing how their perceptions of quality informs their relationship with the various news sources available to them. Perceived as important to the news consumer, the reputation of a news source is connected to news consumers' views of their personal credibility understood in terms of their knowledge and understanding of salient issues. This observation provides a subtle and yet powerful way of assessing the importance of news source credibility in the process of consumption – that is, that such sources are used by individuals in constructing their identities and feature prominently in their interactions with others. More research on these observations is required.

Finally, since this research was carried out, there have been fundamental changes to Libyan society with the ousting and replacement of the *Gadhafi* regime after 42 years in power. Questions could therefore be asked about the relevance and validity of this research now that these political changes have occurred. At the time of writing, Libya remains in a state of flux. Nevertheless, assuming that its society returns to some semblance of normality and that news services continue to operate and expand as before, the lessons learned about Libyan news appetites and consumption from this research can be expected to have some relevance in helping us to understand the implications for the public and news providers of future media developments in the country.

Notes

1 The survey questionnaire was structured into a number of distinct sections that asked questions of importance attached to news topics, news consumption habits, respondents' perceptions of a number of local and non-local TV news services and personal details. The focus was placed on the use of new satellite TV channels, including two that are pan-Arab (*Al-Jazeera* and *Al Arabiya*) and two that are local (*Al Jamahiriya* and *Al Libiya*). Respondents were asked to state how often they used different news sources for news and how much they consumed different news media from a list of news platforms. The list contained (a) news on the main Libyan TV channels including *Al Jamahiriya*, *Al Libiya*, terrestrial and *Al Shbabiya*; (b) news on channels from Arabic countries consisting of *Al-Jazeera*, *Al Arabiya*, *ANN News* and MBC; (c) news on channels broadcast from non-Arabic channels comprising *Al Hurra*, BBC (*Arabic*), *France 24* (*Arabic*), *Russia Today* (*Arabic*) (RTA) and *Al Alam Today* (*Arabic*) *News* (*ATA*); (d) news in newspapers containing *Al Jamahiriya*, *Al Shams*, *Al Fajr Al Jadeed*, *Al Shat Oea* and *Quryna*; (e) news on local radio including *Allibiya FM*, *Tripoli FM* and *Voice of Africa*. Respondents also indicated their agreement with 13 general motivational items associated with news consumption on a four-point ('very important' to 'not at all important') scale. These items were adapted from relevant previous studies (R. B. Rubin et al., 1994; Al-Shaqsi, 2000; Ofcom, 2007a). Further respondents were asked to indicate their reasons for watching four satellite TV services (*Al Jamahiriya*, *Al Libiya*, *Al-Jazeera* and *Al Arabiya*) and endorse a number of possible gratifications derived from each programme. Respondents were finally required to provide details about their gender, age, faculty, family members and family monthly incomes. With regard to news credibility measurement, the survey included a news credibility scale adapted from Gaziano and McGrath (1986) and others. Respondents were asked to evaluate the 11 credibility items of these TV news services on a series of five-point bipolar scales (fair or unfair). Items were coded or recoded so that they were scaled in the same direction with five as the highest possible rating (positive rating) and one the lowest possible rating (negative rating).

2 More than half the final sample was female (58%) and under half was male (42%). The average age of the sample was 21. Nearly two out of three

respondents (57%) reportedly lived in medium-sized families, while 30.5 per cent lived in large-sized families. Around three in four respondents (74%) lived in low-income families earning less than £500 pounds sterling (about US$800) a month and one in eight (12%) lived in middle-income families earning from £501 to £1,000 pounds sterling (about US$801 to US$1,600) a month.

3   After initial frequency distributions were computed, this scale was collapsed to a three-point scale (with scoring reversed), by combining 'daily', '4–6 days per week' to become 'daily' (3) and combining '1–3 days per week' and 'less than once a week' to become 'occasionally' (2) while keeping the 'never' (1) point intact. Collapsing the scale helped to equalize the distribution of respondents across frequency options and avoid the use of data that derived from very small cell sizes.

4   Faculty variable was clustered into three common faculties: (1) Faculties of Social Sciences, Arts and Law (SSAL) included Faculties of Arts and Media, Arts, Education (Tripoli), Education (*Janzour*), Education (*Bengasheer*), Languages, Physical Education, Economics and Political Sciences and Law. (2) Faculties of Natural Sciences and Technologies (NST) including Faculties of Sciences, Engineering and Information Technology. (3) Faculties of Agriculture and Veterinary and Medicine (AVM) including Faculties of Agriculture and Veterinary and Medicine.

5   Small-sized family means less than four members, medium-sized family means between four and eight members and large-sized family means more than eight members.

6   Factoring criteria were: (a) minimum primary loading ≤ 0.40 on a factor; (b) a factor eigenvalue ≤ 1; and (c) each item has a loading ≤ 0.40. The average mean scores were computed for each factor and rankings produced from these data. The averaged mean ranking revealed that the most watched TV channels were Arabic entertainment TV channels, followed by Arabic TV channels, local TV channels and non-Arabic TV channels. Internal reliability of factors was tested by Cronbach's alpha (0.75), the Bartlett's test of sphericity was [(1,240.75) ($p < 0.01$)] and the KMO (Kaiser-Meyer-Olkin measure of sampling adequacy) value was 0.75, $p < 0.01$.

7   Internal consistency for this scale was high – Cronbach's alpha = 0.76.

8   This was the case despite the very strong correlations that *ANN News TV*, an Arabic TV channel based in Syria, displayed with non-Arabic TV channels.

9   With the same reliability scale scores, Cronbach's alpha = 0.74.

10 These harvested from relevant research studies (Rubin and Perse, 1987; Marghalani et al., 1998; Jamal and Melkote, 2008).

11 In doing so, the factoring criteria were: a factor eigenvalue ≤ 1, a minimum primary loading ≤ 0.40 on factor and each item has a loading of ≤ 0.40. Further statistics were applied, for example, the reliability of the measurement was tested by using a common reliability test of Cronbach's alpha (0.63). Further tests were run using Bartlett's test of sphericity [(428.490) ($p < 0.000$)], followed by the KMO value, which was 0.704 ($p < 0.000$), which signalled that

the data were suitable for factor analysis. Brace et al. (2009) stated that for a measure of factorability, a KMO value of more than 0.60 is acceptable.

12 The table shows that an analysis of variance revealed a number of significant differences in evaluations. Bonferroni tests on these means.

13 Cronbach's alphas for news coverage on *Al Jamahiriya*, *Al Libiya*, *Al-Jazeera* and *Al Arabiya* credibility indexes were 0.78, 0.75, 0.70 and 0.72 respectively.

14 Jamal (2009) found that *Al-Jazeera* was preferred by more Arab viewers than any other channel. Al-Asfar (2002) found that *Al-Jazeera* was the most popular TV channel with Libyan audiences, and was seen as the most credible source of news (Ayish, 2004a; Gentzkow and Shapiro, 2004; Johnson and Fahmy, 2005; Fahmy and Johnson, 2007), a finding that could support earlier studies that the more individuals rely on a source the more credible they judge it to be (Greenberg, 1966; Wanta and Hu, 1994).

15 An analysis was carried out on the bipolar-type items using a repeated measures analysis of variance (ANOVA) test.

16 They pointed out that news on *Al-Jazeera* successfully managed to separate fact and opinion, offer accurate, factual and thorough reporting over that of *Al Arabiya* and the rest of the news services.

17 These findings are consistent with prior research that found perceptions of news credibility could be affected by the content of news reports (Austin and Dong, 1994) and even by the news anchors delivering the report (Markham, 1968).

References

Abdel Rahman, H. (1998) Uses and gratifications of satellite TV in Egypt. *Transnational Broadcasting Studies*, (1). Available at: www.tbsjournal.com/Archives/Fall98/Documents1/Uses/uses_table.html.

Al-Asfar, M. (2002) Direct satellite broadcasting its impact on the audiences for local television channels in Tripoli Libya. Unpublished PhD thesis. University of Manchester, UK.

Allan, S. (2006). *Online News: Journalism and the Internet*. Maidenhead: Open University Press.

Al-Obaidi, J. A., Lamb-Williams, C. and Mordas, V. (2004). The king of all mediums: A field study of college students use of mediums for news. *International Journal of Instructional Media*, 31(3), 239–56.

Al-Shaqsi, O. S. (2000). The influence of satellite and terrestrial television viewing on young adults in Oman: Uses, gratifications and cultivation. Unpublished PhD thesis. University of Wales Cardiff, Wales.

Al-Tawil, K. (31 December 2010) TV channel linked to Al-Qadhafi's son accuse Libyan intelligence of jamming it. *Al-Hayah Online*. Available at: www.biyokulule.com/view_content.php?articleid=3184. (accessed 4 March 2013).

Althaus, S., and Tewksbury, D. (2000) Patterns of internet and traditional news media use in a networked community. *Political Communication*, 17, 21–45.

Austin, E., and Dong, Q. (1994) Source v. content effects of judgments of news believability. *Journalism Quarterly*, 71(4), 973–83.

Auter, P., Arafa, M. and Al-Jaber, K. (2005). Identifying with Arabic journalists: How Al-Jazeera tapped parasocial interaction gratifications in the Arab world. *International Communication Gazette*, 67(2), 189–204.

Ayish, M. (2004a) News credibility during the 2003 Iraq War: A survey of UAE Students. In R. D. Berenger (ed.), *Global Media Go to War: Role of News and Entertainment Media during the 2003 Iraq War*. University of Michigan: Marquette Books, pp. 321–32.

— (2004b) News credibility during the Iraq War: A survey of UAE students. *Transnational Broadcasting Studies*, 12 (Spring). Available at: www.tbsjournal. com/ayish.htm.

Barker, C. (1999) *Television, Globalization and Cultural Identities*. Buckingham: Open University Press.

Brace, N., Kemp, R. and Snelgar, R. (2009) *SPSS for Psychologists*, 4th edn. Basingstoke: Palgrave Macmillan.

Cherian, V. (2011) *Controversial Libyan TV Station Heads to London*. Available at: www.digitalproductionme.com/article-1253-controversial_libyan_tv_station_heads_to_london/ (accessed 12 January 2011).

Choi, J., Watt, J. and Lynch, M. (2006) Perceptions of news credibility about the war in Iraq: Why war opponents perceived the Internet as the most credible medium. *Journal of Computer-Mediate Communication*, 12(1), 209–29.

El-Nawawy, M., and Iskander, A. (2002). *Al-Jazeera: How the Free Arab News Network Scooped the World and Changed the Middle East*. Boulder, CO: Westview Press.

El-Zilitni, A. (1981) Mass media for literacy in Libya: A feasibility study. Unpublished PhD thesis. University of Ohio State, OH.

Fahmy, S., and Johnson, T. J. (2007) Show the truth and let the audience decide: A web-based survey showing support among viewers of Al-Jazeera for use of graphic imagery. *Journal of Broadcasting and Electronic Media*, 51(2), 245–64.

Fandy, M. (2007) *(UN) Civil War of Words: Media and Politics in the Arab World*. London: Praeger.

Gaziano, C., and McGrath, K. (1986). Measuring the concept of credibility. *Journalism Quarterly*, 63(3), 451–62.

Gentzkow, M., and Shapiro, J. (2004) Media, education and anti-Americanism in the Muslim world. *The Journal of Economic Perspectives*, 18(3), 117–33.

Ghareeb, E. (2000) New media and the information revolution in the Arab world: An assessment. *The Middle East Journal*, 54(3), 395–418.

Greenberg, B. S. (1966) Media use and believability: Some multiple correlates. *Journalism Quarterly*, 43(4), 667–70.

Gunter, B. (2005). Trust in the news on television. *Aslib Proceedings: New Information Perspectives*, 57(5), 384–97.

Gunter, B., Campbell, V., Touri, M. and Gibson, R. (2009) Blogs, news and credibility. *Aslib Proceedings: New Information Perspectives*, 61(2), 185–204.

Harb, Z., and Bessaiso, E. (2006) British Arab Muslim audiences and television after September 11. *Journal of Ethnic and Migration Studies*, 32(6), 1063–76.

Henke, L. (1985) Perceptions and use of news media by college students. *Journal of Broadcasting and Electronic Media*, 29(4), 431–6.

Henningham, J. (1982) How TV news meets people's needs. *Journal of Sociology*, 18(3), 417–27.

Huang, E. (2009) The causes of youths' low news consumption and strategies for making youths happy news consumers. *Convergence: The International Journal of Research into New Media Technologies*, 15(1), 105–22.

IREX (2006) *Media Sustainability Index 2005: The Development of Sustainable Independent Media in the Middle East and North Africa*. Available at: www. irex.org/programmes/MSI_MENA/2006/MSIMENA06_Libya.asp (accessed 24 March 2009).

Jamal, A. (2009) Media culture as counter-hegemonic strategy: The communicative action of the Arab minority in Israel. *Media, Culture and Society*, 31(4), 559–77.

Jamal, A., and Melkote, S. (2008) Viewing and avoidance of the Al-Jazeera satellite television channel in Kuwait: A uses and gratifications perspective. *Asian Journal of Communication*, 18(1), 1–15.

Johnson, T. J., and Fahmy, S. S. (2005) The CNN of the Arab world or a shill for terrorists? How support for press freedom and political ideology predict credibility of Al-Jazeera among its audience. The Annual Meeting of the International Communication Association, Sheraton New York, NY.

Karam, I. (2007a) Arab satellite broadcasting, identity and Arab youth. Unpublished PhD thesis. City University London, UK.

— (2007b) Satellite television: A breathing space for Arab youth? In N. Sakr (ed.), *Arab Media and Political Renewal: Community, Legitimacy and Public Life*. London: I.B. Tauris and Co Ltd, pp. 80–95.

Kayany, J., and Yelsma, P. (2000) Displacement effects of online media in the socio-technical contexts of households. *Journal of Broadcasting and Electronic Media*, 44(2), 215–29.

Lynch, M. (2006) *Voices of the New Arab Public: Iraq, Al-Jazeera, and Middle East Politics Today*. New York: Columbia University Press.

Marghalani, K., Palmgreen, P., and Boyd, D. (1998) The utilization of direct satellite broadcasting (DBS) in Saudi Arabia. *Journal of Broadcasting and Electronic Media*, 42(3), 297–314.

Markham, D. (1968) The dimensions of source credibility of television newscasters. *Journal of Communication*, 18(1), 57–64.

Mellor, N. (2007) *Modern Arab Journalism: Problems and Prospects*. Edinburgh: Edinburgh University Press.

Menassat (2011) *State of the Media*. Available at: www.menassat.com/?q=en/media-landscape/state-media-7 (accessed on 28 June2011).

Miladi, N. (2006) Satellite TV news and the Arab diaspora in Britain: Comparing Al-Jazeera, the BBC and CNN. *Journal of Ethnic and Migration Studies*, 32(6), 947–60.

Ofcom (2007a) *Annexes to New News, Future News Research and Evidence Base*. Available at: http://bit.ly/alKj93 (accessed on 24 August 2009).

— (2007b) *New News, Future News: The Challenges for Television News after the Digital Switch-Over.* Available at: http://bit.ly/aYxH9d (accessed on 11 February 2010).

Reporters without Borders (13 February 2008) *Annual Report 2008 – Libya.* Available at: www.unhcr.org/refworld/docid/47b418d82c.html (accessed on 24 April 2009).

Rubin, A. M. (1983) Television uses and gratifications: The interactions of viewing patterns and motivations. *Journal of Broadcasting*, 27(1), 37–51.

Rubin, A. M., & Perse, E. M. (1987). Audience activity and television news gratifications. Communication Research. 14(1): 58–84

Rubin, R. B., Palmgreen, P. and Sypher, H. E. (eds) (1994) *Communication Research Measures. A Sourcebook.* New York London: The Guilford Press.

Rugh, W. A. (1979) *The Arab Press: News Media and Political Process in the Arab World.* New York: Syracuse University Press.

— (2004) *Arab Mass Media: Newspapers, Radio, and Television in Arab Politics.* London: Praeger.

Sakr, N. (2001) *Satellite Realms: Transnational Television, Globalization and the Middle East.* London: I.B. Tauris and Co Ltd.

— (2007) *Arab Media and Political Renewal: Community, Legitimacy and Public Life.* London: I.B. Tauris and Co Ltd.

Saleh, I. (2007) The Arab search for a global identity: Breaking out of the mainstream media cocoon. In P. Seib (ed.), *New Media and the New Middle East.* New York: Palgrave Macmillan, pp. 19–37.

The Pew Research Center for the People and the Press (2000) *Internet Sapping Broadcast News Audience: Investors Now Go Online for Quotes, Advice.* Available at: http://bit.ly/aEOdn9 (accessed 4 March 2010).

Tsfati, Y. (2003) Does audience skepticism of the media matter in agenda setting? *Journal of Broadcasting and Electronic Media*, 47(2), 157–76.

Uslaner, E. M. (2002) *The Moral Foundations of Trust.* Cambridge: Cambridge University Press.

Vyas, R. S., Singh, N. and Bhabhra, S. (2007) Media displacement effect: Investigating the impact of internet on newspaper reading habits of consumers. *The Journal of Business*, 11(2), 29–40.

Wanta, W., and Hu, Y. (1994) The effects of credibility, reliance, and exposure on media agenda setting: A path analysis model. *Journalism Quarterly*, 71(1), 90–8.

Zayani, M. (2005) *The Al-Jazeera Phenomenon: Critical Perspectives on New Arab Media.* London: Pluto Press.

Zayani, M., and Ayish, M. (2006) Arab satellite television and crisis reporting. *International Communication Gazette*, 68(5–6), 473–97.

7

News Developments and Changes to News Consumption Patterns in the Arab World

Khalid Al-Jaber and Barrie Gunter

Earlier chapters in this book have already indicated that the Arab news media landscape evolved dramatically in the late twentieth and early twenty-first centuries. New satellite television news services have transformed the news broadcasting menus and appetites of Arab audiences. The growing reach of the broadband internet has opened up new channels of communication through which news can enter and leave the Arab world. These developments have created new demands for news provision among news consumers in the region. They also pose significant challenges to indigenous news providers that must compete with services often uplinked from outside national borders that can operate without the constraints imposed upon local broadcasters by governments and their regulators. These changes have also presented challenges to Arab governments accustomed to having significant degrees of control over the media.

News provision in the Arab world has been transformed by the rise of satellite television broadcasting since 2000. This platform carries a number of news-oriented television services that provide an Arab perspective on news issues relevant to the Arab world. Some of these broadcasters are beginning to compete with major broadcast news services owned and operated in the West for audience interest. Perhaps the highest profile pan-Arab world news operation is *Al-Jazeera*. This service serves a potential audience across and beyond the Arab world that numbers in the hundreds of millions (Sakr, 2005).

The supporters of *Al-Jazeera* identified its success as stemming from the quality of its journalism and the freshness of its approach to news presentation (Al-Sayeq, 2000; Rasheed, 2001). It opened up a new style of news provision to Arab audiences that seemed to be less constrained than any provided by government-controlled news services (Rampal, 2007). It learned from Western styles of journalism and at the same time produced news that covered Arab issues from relevant Arab perspectives.

There are many important questions that need to be answered for us to understand more systematically how local media and their audiences have responded to communications technology developments and the new sources of news they can convey. Have local audiences changed their news consumption habits? Do new news suppliers pose a threat to established local suppliers by capturing their audiences? What do local national Arab audiences think about the new news providers? How do they compare, in their minds, with the local services to which they have long become accustomed? Is there room for both pan-Arab and local news services? Can they each cater to distinct niche markets? This chapter will present findings from new research carried out in three Cooperation for the Arab States of the Gulf (GCC) countries, Bahrain, Qatar and Saudi Arabia, which explored the use of new satellite television news services. On the issue of niche markets, the study investigated whether viewing of local and non-local news services is mutually exclusive and whether news consumers articulate distinctive motivational profiles in relation to them.

Audiences motives and TV news consumption

Interest in audiences' motives for media consumption has spanned several decades and variously examined the 'functions of media' (Wright, 1960) and 'uses and gratifications' of mass communication (Katz and Foulkes, 1963). Over subsequent decades, researchers have continued to endorse the importance of understanding what drives media consumers towards specific communications platforms and types of content (Blumler and Katz, 1974; Levy, 1983; Rosengren et al., 1985; Rubin and Perse, 1987; Lin, 1990, 1993). The concept of audience motivation has formed one persistent aspect of ongoing debates about audience activity versus passivity in media consumption (Biocca, 1987).

The notion that audiences are active comprises a multi-stage concept. 'Activity' can be manifest in respect of the initial selection of media or media content to consume, in relation to the level of involvement with it once selected, and finally in the way it is used by audience members through being incorporated into existing knowledge systems, behavioural scripts or future decision making (Blumler, 1979; Levy, 1983). Each of these stages is not conceived to work in isolation, but to be causally linked (Levy and Windahl, 1984). Further distinctions have been made in relation to specific stages of audience activity. For example, the last-stage application of media content can be differentiated into usage that is designed to attain specified goals ('instrumental usage') and that which is simply performed out of habit as an end in itself ('ritualistic usage'). These different gratification orientations can result in selection of different types of media content in the first stage (Rubin et al., 1985; Rubin and Perse, 1987).

Audience motives have been linked to watching of news on television (Levy, 1978). The nature of active selection of news is important in determining whether motivated viewers simply watch more of all kinds of news or are selective in what they choose to view from within the genre (Levy, 1983). Evidence has emerged that audience motives do not simply play a part in determining how much news is consumed but also the types of news that are targeted by news consumers. Henningham (1985) examined gratifications people derive from TV news in relation to their preferences for different types of news. The results revealed that people who watch TV news for information tend to prefer serious and high-impact news stories, while those seeking entertainment prefer human interest news stories and stories about conflict or human tragedy.

The reasons people display for consuming or avoiding media content in the Arab world has come in for closer attention in recent years. Several studies revealed that key motivations underpinning the media choices of viewers in Arab world, particularly in Saudi Arabia, included surveillance, diversion, relaxation, companionship, passing time and social utility (Abouzinada, 1988; Al-Attibi, 1986; Al-Amoudi, 1990; Al-Habib, 1995; Al-Oofy, 1990; Al-Heezan, 1993; Merdad, 1993). Despite its recent popularity, in its early days, satellite television services were roundly rejected by audiences in Saudi Arabia for being politically and culturally 'anti-Islamic' (Marghalani et al., 1998).

A study of Egyptian viewers' motivations linked to news watching showed that an overwhelming majority (89%) reported that they watched news on satellite television to understand what is going on in the world, while clear majorities also claimed to watch to learn things happening in the world (81%), to obtain useful information for daily life (79%), observe foreign cultures and traditions (79%) and to obtain information about foreign lifestyles (76%). The study found that understanding was the most important cognitive need reported by all respondents in satellite TV households and diversity was the most important affective need reported (Rahman, 1998).

Yousef (1999) reported that Kuwaitis watched television for relaxation, companionship, habit, passing time, entertainment, social interaction, information seeking and escape. He also found that more than half of Kuwaitis spend one to three hours daily from Saturday to Wednesday watching television. News and drama were the two most watched types of programmes. Kuwaiti viewers changed channel frequently and the researcher speculated that higher levels of channel changing might signal avoidance of programmes that do not fulfil important sought gratifications.

Al-Shaqsi (2000) applied the uses and gratifications model to investigate the uses of satellite TV channels and found that they were mostly used to satisfy goal-directed needs, specifically cognitive needs such as surveillance and avoiding censored news. Later research has indicated that some Arab markets (in one instance in Kuwait) have begun to embrace satellite TV news services such as *Al-Jazeera* particularly when they have a strong interest in politics coupled with a distrust in government (Jamal and Melkote, 2008).

Audience motives represent characteristics than can be used to differentiate between audience sub-groups. At the same time, motivational profiles of news consumers can themselves vary between different demographic groups. Under exceptional circumstances, however, these variances can temporarily dissipate signalling stronger shared needs across different sectors of the audience. Abduljaleel (1994) conducted a study using the uses and gratifications model to investigate the impact of the Iraqi invasion of Kuwait upon the communication habits and media usage of Kuwaiti civilians under occupation. The findings indicated that crisis situations seem to level out former usage differences associated with gender, age and education. Furthermore, the study found that people tend to reject media that presents an ideological bias that differs greatly from their own or whose interpretation of events differs from the people's direct experiences.

The reasons people display for consuming or avoiding media content in the Arab world has come in for closer attention. Despite its recent popularity, in its early days, satellite television services were roundly rejected by audiences in Saudi Arabic for being politically and culturally 'anti-Islamic' (Marghalani et al., 1998). One particular motivational factor that has been examined in the context of satellite TV news provision is the Arab world is parasocial interaction. This concept has a long history in relation to the study of audiences' engagement with mass media (Horton and Wohl, 1956). It posits that members of the audience can forge virtual social relationships (or 'para'-social relations) with on-screen actors, performers and presenters. Despite not being able to engage in direct interpersonal communication with them, audience members can develop feelings for or about on-screen actors over time and following repeat exposure. In doing so they make many interpretations about the character of on-screen actors just as they would in developing opinions about people they might meet in their everyday lives (Auter, 1992; Auter and Palmgreen, 2000).

Parasocial relationships can become established between audience members, news presenters and reporters (Levy, 1979; Perse, 1990; Rubin and Step, 2000). A positive impression of a newscaster, for instance, can form part of the core reasons for tuning into a news bulletin and also enhances the perceived credibility of that broadcast as a news source (Perse, 1990). The perceive personality of a presenter, their appearance and on-screen competence at performing are critical factors that drive impression formation. Regardless of the substantive content of the news itself, these presentational elements can determine whether a newscast and the news provider behind it attract and retain loyal followers (Auletta, 1991; Kearns, 1999; Kerbel, 2001).

This chapter presents some findings from a survey study conducted online with news consumers from Bahrain, Qatar and Saudi Arabia. This study had a wide scope and examined news interests, the distribution of news consumption across different news sources, the use of new versus old televised news services, the motivations associated with consumption of satellite television news services and perceptions of the qualities of news delivered by specific news providers.

Exploring news consumption in Bahrain, Qatar and Saudi Arabia

A self-completion, online questionnaire survey was carried out with Arabic-speaking respondents in Bahrain, Qatar and Saudi Arabia. For this chapter, the main focus is placed on the use of news on satellite TV channels with services that traversed national boundaries. How did use of these channels fit within wider news consumption habits and which factors relating to viewers' personal characteristics and sought gratifications from news services were significant as mediators of these viewing behaviours?

From an initial contact sample of 2,146 respondents, filters were deployed to block out responses from respondents living outside these three countries, yielding a final sample of 1,752 participants. These comprised 568 respondents from Bahrain, 553 from Qatar and 631 from Saudi Arabia. Data were collected between 10 December 2009 and 12 March 2010.

A pre-structured questionnaire included questions about news media consumption; general news interests, gratifications and expectations about journalistic standards; opinions about five televised news services; motivations for watching each of the five televised news services; perceptions of the quality of news on these televised news services; and personal details. Our focus here is placed on consumption habits and gratifications associated with news.

The news consumption questions asked about the frequency with which respondents used each of eight different categories of news sources: local TV channels (that included *Saudi Arabia TV, Kuwait TV, Bahrain TV, Qatar TV, UAE TV, Oman TV*), Arabic news satellite TV channels (e.g. *Al-Jazeera, Al-Arabiya, BBC (Arabic), Al-Hurra, France 24*), non-Arabic satellite TV news services (e.g., *CNN, BBC World News*), the internet, radio, newspapers, magazines and mobile devices. A frequency scale was supplied for each source: daily, most days, a few times a week, once a week, a few times a month, less than once a month, never. A further question focused named the specific TV news channels and probed further for reported frequencies of viewing (daily, 4–6 days per week, 1–3 days per week, less than once a week, never). The news source categories question had been used in earlier research about Arab news media consumption (Al-Shaqsi, 2000). The named TV news source frequency of viewing questions had also been used in previous research (Marghalani et al., 1998)

Respondents were provided with a list of 29 news topics and were asked to indicate along a five-point agree–disagree scale the extent to which they agreed it was important for news services to report on each of these topics. The topic list was informed by the work of Rahman (1998) and comprised: (1) human interest stories, (2) politics in Arab world, (3) worldwide politics and current events, (4) city, business and financial issues, (5) current events in your country, (6) entertainment, (7) crime news, (8) consumer affairs, (9) sports news, (10) travel news, (11) weather news, (12) human rights issues, (13) minority issues, (14) youth issues, (15) Iranian nuclear weapon, (16) Israel/Palestine conflict, (17) rerrorism issues, (18) Sunnis and Shias, (19) Arab–Arab conflict, (20) the Iraq conflict, (21) the Afghani conflict, (22) Darfur conflict, (23) financial crisis, (24) Europe issues, (25) American issues, (26) Latin American issues, (27) Asia issues and (28) Africa issues.

Seventeen gratifications statements were presented to respondents grouped under four headings: opinion leadership, free marketplace of information, surveillance and parasocial interaction. Some of these items had been used in previous studies (Palmgreen et al., 1980; Levy and Windahl, 1984; Gaziano and McGrath, 1986; Ganahl, 1994; Jamal and Melkote, 2008). Responses to each item were provided along five-point scales: agree strongly (5), agree (4), no opinion (3), disagree (2) and disagree strongly (1).

A principal components analysis with varimax rotation was computed on the news gratification statements and produced four clusters that were labelled 'free marketplace of news', 'parasocial interaction and surveillance', 'discussion and judgements' and 'trustworthy source'. Table 7.1 presents the constituent items of each gratification factor and the percentages of respondents who agree strongly or agreed that it was important for news services today to satisfy these gratifications.

In a further section of the questionnaire, the same gratifications items were used to indicate motives for watching each of five satellite TV news channels: *Al-Jazeera*, *Al-Arabiya*, *BBC* (*Arabic*), *France 24* (*Arabic*) and *Al-Hurra*. Finally personal details were obtained from respondents that included their age, gender, highest level of education, gross annual household income, occupational status, marital status and political orientation (extremely liberal, liberal, neutral, conservative, extremely conservative).

The self-completion questionnaire was posted online, using the SurveyMonkey (www.surveymonkey.com/) service. Respondents could gain access to the survey instrument via the internet from different locations such as at home, work, or other public spaces offering online interfaces. Links to the survey were placed on the websites of a number of local and national Arabic newspapers in the three countries. The survey website allowed respondents to input their own data that were automatically stored electronically.

News gratifications profiles

News gratifications clustered into four factors called 'free marketplace of news', 'parasocial interaction and surveillance', 'discussion and judgements' and 'trustworthy source'. As Table 7.1 indicates, the first of these factors was defined by perceptions that it is important for news services to give coverage to a range of political points of view, to display the work of Arab governments, including activities governments might not necessarily wish to have exposed. The second factor was characterized by the provision of diverse and comprehensive coverage of events presented by competent news professionals that respondents enjoyed watching. The third factor indicated that Arab news audiences seek news that has utility for them in helping to develop informed opinions about their governments and ongoing political issues. The final factor indicated the importance of having access to credible sources of up-to-date information.

The findings here resonated well with previous studies of public opinion about Arab news media. Marghalani et al. (1998) applied a gratifications scale to explore patterns of use and avoidance of satellite TV services in Saudi Arabia. This study found that a mix of technological, free marketplace of information, political, economical, cultural and religious forces were associated with the adoption of news satellite TV channels.

TABLE 7.1 Endorsement of news gratifications

News gratifications	Saudi Arabia (%)	Bahrain (%)	Qatar (%)
Free marketplace of news			
It gives different political points of views the chance to exist	91	89	92
It shows the real work of Arab political rulers and governments, including their misconduct	91	88	89
It covers news and issues those Arab political leaders and governments try to hide	90	90	90
It shows the real work of Arab political leaders	91	88	89
The channel is free to discuss any political issue	86	85	84
It provides me with uncensored information	86	88	90
Parasocial interaction and surveillance			
It provides me with good visual coverage of events	95	94	94
It presents news events with thorough, in-depth analysis	92	87	93
It has the best news reporters	89	88	88
I compare my ideas with what commentators say	71	69	75
It discusses issues in exciting ways	73	71	68
I enjoy watching their news anchors	53	47	53
Discussion and judgements			
It helps me judge Arab governments	87	84	87
Helps me make up my mind about important issues	83	82	84
I use its discussions of issues	82	75	84

TABLE 7.1 *Continued*

News gratifications	Saudi Arabia (%)	Bahrain (%)	Qatar (%)
Trustworthy source			
It provides me with up-to-date information	99	98	99
It is a credible source	99	97	98

Parasocial motives emerged here as having some importance, but were endorsed far less than other gratifications. Previous research has shown that in relation to Al-Jazeera, viewers did engage with the station through its presenters and that this was more important to audiences living locally than for those living away from the Arab world (Auter et al., 2005). The findings here indicated that for news consumers in Bahrain, Qatar and Saudi Arabia the perceived competence of news reporters was important, while the sheer enjoyment of seeing them was much less widespread.

News consumption and gratifications

When the respondents from across Bahrain, Qatar and Saudi Arabia were asked to report on their general news consumption habits, the internet received the most widespread endorsement as the news source used 'daily or almost daily' (see Table 7.2). The second most popular news sources on average across these three GCC countries, and the most popular overall in Saudi Arabia, were Arab TV news services. Together these two news services dominated the news sources named by this three-nation sample. All other news sources, including newspapers and local or national TV services followed far behind. One other significant finding here was the more widespread endorsement of mobile communications as a news source than radio. This source, of course, represents an alternative platform for reception of internet news.

Correlation coefficients were computed to establish whether there were significant relationships between reported use of news sources and the four news-related gratification factors. These coefficients were computed separately for each national sample in Bahrain, Qatar and Saudi Arabia. Reported use of the internet as a news source was significantly correlated with the 'discussion and judgement' factor ($r = 0.16$, $p < 0.01$) among the Saudi sample

TABLE 7.2 Use of different news sources

News sources	N	Saudi Arabia (%)	Bahrain (%)	Qatar (%)	All (%)
Internet	1,686	72	69	74	72
Arabic News TV	1,685	76	64	69	70
Newspapers	1,592	23	27	30	27
Local and National TV	1,532	18	16	18	17
Mobile	1,515	15	20	14	16
Radio	1,502	12	16	13	14
Non- Arabic News TV	1,531	5	8	8	7
Magazines	1,489	2	4	4	3

Note: Percentages say they used news sources 'daily/almost daily'.

and with the 'trustworthy source' factor ($r = 0.12$, $p < 0.01$) for the Qatari sample. In both cases, a stronger endorsement of these gratification factors was associated with greater claimed use of the internet for news. Thus, among Saudi Arabian respondents, the use of the internet was linked to a need for information that enables opinion formation about the government and current political issues. In Qatar use of the internet for news was linked to the importance attached to finding a credible news source.

The use of the second most popular news source overall, pan-Arab TV news services, was significantly correlated with the 'parasocial and surveillance' factor ($r = 0.16$, $p < 0.01$) in Saudi Arabia, with the 'free marketplace of news' ($r = 0.15$, $p < 0.01$) and 'parasocial interaction and surveillance' ($r = 0.25$, $p < 0.001$) factors in Bahrain, and with the latter two factors ($r = 0.20$, $p < 0.01$; $r = 0.10$, $p < 0.05$) plus the 'discussion and judgement' factor ($r = 0.10$, $p < 0.05$) in Qatar. All these correlation coefficients indicated that the greater the importance attached to each of these gratifications factors, the more the respondents claimed to watch pan-Arab TV news services.

Further significant correlation coefficients emerged between claimed use of local and national TV services for news and the 'free marketplace of news' factor in Saudi Arabia ($r = -0.12$, $p < 0.01$) and also in Qatar ($r = -0.15$, $p < 0.01$), and with the 'parasocial interaction and surveillance' factor in Bahrain ($r = 0.12$, $p < 0.01$). These findings revealed that weaker adherence to the opinion that news services should provide news from a range of political perspectives and challenge the political status quo was linked to greater claimed viewing of local and national (largely government-controlled) TV channels among respondents from Saudi Arabia and Qatar. In Bahrain, greater claimed viewing of local and national TV services was associated with seeking effective and comprehensive news coverage by familiar presenters.

Predictors of viewing of pan-Arab TV news services

Having examined reported use of general categories of news services, further analyses were computed to investigate predictors of reported use of the two most widely used pan-Arab TV news services, *Al-Jazeera* and *BBC* (*Arabic*). In a multiple regression analysis, four sets of variables were entered as predictor variables and regressed against claimed viewing of these two pan-Arab TV services. Separate regression analyses were computed for each national sample – Bahrain, Qatar and Saud Arabia.

One block of predictor variables comprised questions asked about the frequency with which respondents used each of eight different news sources: local TV channels, Arabic news satellite TV channels (e.g. *Al-Jazeera* and *Al-Arabiya*), non-Arabic satellite TV news services (e.g. *CNN*, *Fox*), the internet, radio, newspapers, magazines and mobile devices. A frequency scale was supplied for each source: daily, most days, a few times a week, once a week, a few times a month, less than once a month, never.

The frequency with which respondents said they watched the news on local TV channels (*Saudi Arabia TV, Kuwait TV, Bahrain TV, Qatar TV, UAE TV, Oman TV*), Arabic satellite TV news channels (*Al-Jazeera, Al-Arabiya, BBC* (Arabic), *Al-Hurra, France 24*) and non-Arabic TV channels (*CNN, BBC News, Euro News*) represented another block of predictor variables. The frequency scale used here was: daily, 4–6 days per week, 1–3 days per week, less than once a week, never.

Each of the 17 gratification items was entered, along with 29 news interest items. The news interest items comprised a list of news topics for each of which respondents indicated an opinion about how important it was for a high-quality news service to cover such issues. Finally, each analysis included personal details variables concerning respondents' age, gender, highest level of education, gross annual household income and political orientation.

All six regression analyses yielded statistically significant predictor models for claimed viewing of *Al-Jazeera* and *BBC* (*Arabic*) for the samples from Saudi Arabia, Bahrain and Qatar.[1] The analyses accounted for a considerable proportion of the variance in claimed viewing of Al-Jazeera in Bahrain (46%)

and Qatar (57%), but much less in Saudi Arabia (26%). On average, these analyses accounted for smaller amounts of variance in reported viewing of BBC (Arabic) across these three national markets (26%, 30% and 35% respectively).

Predictors of viewing Al-Jazeera

Claimed viewing of *Al-Jazeera* was predicted in Saudi Arabia by claimed viewing of pan-Arab TV news channels in general (beta = 0.21, $p < 0.001$); importance of covering the Israel–Palestine conflict (beta = 0.17, $p < 0.01$) and any conflicts between Arab nations (beta = 0.13, $p < 0.01$); the importance of news source credibility (beta = 0.17, $p < 0.01$); less frequent reading of magazines (beta = −0.15, $p < 0.01$); and claimed viewing of *Al-Arabiya* (beta = 0.11, $p < 0.01$).

In Bahrain, claimed viewing of *Al-Jazeera* was predicted by greater general watching of pan-Arab TV news channels (beta = 0.54, $p < 0.001$); the importance of news services as providers of up-to-date information (beta = 0.19, $p < 0.001$); and the importance attached to news services providing coverage of politics in the Arab world (beta = 0.11, $p < 0.05$).

In Qatar, claimed watching of *Al-Jazeera* was predicted by greater general watching of pan-Arab TV news channels (beta = 0.54, $p < 0.001$); the importance of up-to-date information (beta = 0.13, $p < 0.05$); the importance of coverage of politics in the Arab world (beta = 0.13, $p < 0.05$); and the importance of credible news sources (beta = 0.12, $p < 0.05$).

Predictors of viewing BBC (*Arabic*)

Claimed viewing of BBC (*Arabic*) was predicted in Saudi Arabia by five variables: the importance attached to coverage of events in own country (beta = 0.32, $p < 0.01$); rejection of news as entertainment (beta = −0.25, $p < 0.01$); claimed viewing of *Al-Arabiya* (beta = 0.24, $p < 0.01$); claimed viewing of *France 24 (Arabic)* (beta = 0.24, $p < 0.01$); and the importance attached to showing the real work of Arab governments (beta = 0.21, $p < 0.01$).

In Bahrain, claimed viewing of BBC (*Arabic*) was predicted by three variables: claimed viewing of *France 24 (Arabic)* (beta = 0.29, $p < 0.001$); the importance of news services that help viewers to judge Arab governments (beta = 0.20, $p < 0.05$); and the importance of receiving coverage of worldwide politics and current events (beta = 0.20, $p < 0.05$).

In Qatar, reported watching of *BBC* (*Arabic*) was predicted by three variables: the importance attached to good visual coverage of events (beta = 0.27, $p < 0.01$); greater viewing of non-Arab news TV channels (beta = 0.26, $p < 0.01$); and greater viewing of *Al-Arabiya* (beta = 0.25, $p < 0.05$).

Discussion

An online survey of adult news consumers in Bahrain, Qatar and Saudi Arabia found that despite having an expanded range of news sources available to them, most depended on two major sources – the internet and pan-Arabic satellite TV news services. The popularity of Arabic TV news services far outstripped reported use of local and national TV services. It is also significant to note the emergence of the internet. Given that the survey was restricted to respondents who were able to complete an online survey, however, it seems likely that this survey tapped into a news consumer population that was already internet savvy. The popularity of television compared with newspapers has been explained in terms of literacy levels across Arab states. The gap between nominations of the internet versus offline newspapers observed here, however, indicates that literacy was less of an issue than a preference for online delivery.

Claimed viewing of pan-Arab TV news services was not predicted by reduced viewing of more local TV news services. In this respect, the findings did not confirm research emerging from Libya (Elareshi and Gunter, 2011; see also Chapter 6). In the latter case, young and well-educated adult news consumers who watched pan-Arab TV services such as *Al-Jazeera* and *Al-Arabiya* more often, also reported watching local Libyan TV news services (even those on broadcast on a satellite TV platform) less often. The difference in results here may say something about the relative standing of local TV news services in these different Arab countries. This result also indicates that despite earlier rejection of satellite TV services by Gulf countries (see Marghalani et al., 1998), they seem now to have been accepted.

While overall news gratification profiles did not differ greatly between these countries, gratification variables were associated with or predictive of news consumption patterns in different ways among respondents from these countries. Arab news consumers value news services that provide open political discussion and challenge or at least ask searching questions about government polices and performance. They said that they sought well-presented and thorough analysis of events and issues. They also widely valued news that can provide information they can utilize to develop better informed opinions about their governments and important issues of the day. They also sought up-to-date and credible news.

Respondents from all three countries indicated that attaching importance to the free flow of political ideas, well-presented news and access to information to help formulate well-rounded opinions about current issues leads them to turn to pan-Arab TV news services rather than local and national (government-controlled) TV news. Despite the widespread popularity of the internet as a news source, this was used more often only by respondents in Saudi Arabia who sought information to help them judge governments and to take decisions on important issues or by respondents in Qatar for whom news credibility was important. Greater reported use of the internet was also closely associated with the need to be able to judge Arab governments. This finding is consistent with Jamal and Melkote (2008) who observed that acceptance of new satellite TV news services in Kuwait was associated with being able to assess how much to trust the incumbent government.

Despite earlier evidence that parasocial interaction was linked to watching Al-Jazeera (Auter et al., 2005), the current research indicated that this interpersonal level of engagement was defined mostly in terms of perceived competence of news presenters rather than any other intrinsic qualities they might have.

What is apparent from the regression analyses is that viewing of *Al-Jazeera* and *BBC* (*Arabic*) channels is associated in all three countries with a tendency to watch other non-local Arab and non-Arab TV news services. News interests were also linked to watching these channels, but these were primary drivers of viewing *Al-Jazeera* only in Saudi Arabia among respondents who sought good quality information about the Israel–Palestine conflict and any Arab–Arab conflicts. It is interesting to note that seeking quality coverage of current events in their own country led Saudi respondents to watch *BBC* (*Arabic*) more often, but not *Al-Jazeera*.

News gratifications were associated with claimed viewing of *Al-Jazeera* and *BBC* (*Arabic*) in all three countries, but not in the same ways. Past research has indicated that source credibility is an important factor for viewers in determining their loyalty to specific news broadcasters (Auter et al., 2005). In Saudi Arabia and Qatar, the importance of new source credibility predicted greater reported viewing of *Al-Jazeera*, while in Bahrain, greater viewing of this channel was linked to the need for up-to-date information. Greater viewing of *BBC* (*Arabic*) was predicted by needing the news to show the real work of Arab governments among Saudi respondents and for the new to help to judge Arab governments by respondents in Bahrain. In Qatar, watching more of this channel was predicted by the need for good visual coverage of events.

Pan-Arab world satellite TV news services have established a firm foothold in the region. Broadcasters such as *Al-Jazeera* have led the way in creating Arab news platforms that extend beyond single national boundaries and that can compete with services delivered by Western broadcasters. The delivery of services that gratifies the core news needs of indigenous audiences in a credible fashion has attracted large followings that remain loyal. Variances still exist between Arab countries, however, in the degree to which specific gratifications explain why people view specific satellite TV news services. The data presented here provide no direct explanation for these differences between national Arab TV markets. They could indicate a greater disconnect between specific gratifications sought and delivered in respect of these services in the opinions of different national Arab audiences. More fundamentally they could signal greater disconnect between the type of political system encouraged by these new privately owned news services and the political system that remains in place.

Note

1 Saudi Arabia analyses: *Al-Jazeera* – $F[6,351] = 20.5$, $p < 0.001$; adjusted multiple $R^2 = 0.26$; *BBC (Arabic)* – $F[5,89] = 9.9$, $p < 0.001$; adjusted multiple $R^2 = 0.35$.
Bahrain analyses: *Al-Jazeera* – $F[3,317] = 89.7$, $p < 0.001$; adjusted multiple $R^2 = 0.46$; *BBC (Arabic)* – $F[3,127] = 15.3$, $p < 0.001$); adjusted multiple $R^2 = 0.26$.
Qatar analyses: *Al-Jazeera* – $F[4,327] = 106.5$, $p < 0.001$; adjusted multiple $R^2 = 0.57$; *BBC (Arabic)* – $F[3,105] = 15.3$, $p < 0.001$; adjusted multiple $R^2 = 0.30$.

References

Abduljaleel, M. (1994) The uses of mass communication under a crisis situation: A comparative study of Kuwaiti's utilization of information sources before and during the Iraq occupation of Kuwait. Unpublished doctoral dissertation. University of Oregon.

Abouzinada, Z. A. (1988) The diffusion and use of videocassette recorders among adult members of an extended community in the kingdom of Saudi Arabia. Unpublished doctoral dissertation. Ohio State University.

Al-Amoudi, K. A. (1990) Expectations, values and norms as predictors of uses and gratification of mass media in Saudi Arabia. Unpublished doctoral dissertation. Florida State University.

Al-Attibi, A. A. (1986) Interpersonal communication competence and media consumption and needs among young adults in Saudi Arabia. Unpublished doctoral dissertation. Ohio State University.

Al-Habib, S. A. (1995) The perception of Jordan and Saudi elites on national and international radio services. Unpublished doctoral dissertation. University of Oklahoma.

Al-Heezan, M. (1993) Comparative analysis of audience exposure to the first channel (Arabic) and to the second channel (English) in the kingdom of Saudi Arabia. Unpublished doctoral dissertation. Bowling Green State University.

Al-Oofy, A. D. (1990) The uses, status, and effects of video cassette recorders on other media, audiences, and the new Islamic awareness in Saudi Arabia. Unpublished doctoral dissertation. The Ohio University.

Al-Sayeq, A. (2000) In a free witnessing, Al-Jazeera speaks to itself. *Al-Amen*, 38.

Al-Shaqsi, O. (2000) The influence of satellite and Terrestrial TV viewing on young adults in Oman: Uses, gratifications and cultivation. Unpublished doctoral dissertation. Cardiff University.

Auletta, K. (1991) *Three Blind Mice: How the TV Networks Lost Their Way*. New York: Random House.

Auter, P. (1992) TV that talks back: An experimental validation of a parasocial interaction scale. *Journal of Broadcasting and Electronic Media*, 36(2), 173–82.

Auter, P., Arafa, M. and Al-Jaber, K. (2005) Identifying with Arabic journalists: How Al-Jazeera tapped parasocial interaction gratifications in the Arab world. *Gazette: The International Journal for Communication Studies*, 67(2), 189–204.

Auter, P., and Palmgreen, P. (2000) Development and validation of a new parasocial interaction measure: The Audience-Persona Interaction Scale. *Communication Research Reports*, 17(1), 79–89.

Biocca, F. (1987) Opposing conceptions of the audience: The active and passive hemispheres of mass communication theory. In J. Anderson (ed.), *Communication Yearbook 11*. Newbury Park, CA: Sage, pp. 51–80.

Blumler, J. G. (1979) The role of theory in uses and gratifications studies. *Communication Research*, 6, 9–36.

Blumler, J. G., and Katz, E. (1974) *The Uses of Mass Communication: Current Perspectives on Gratifications Research*. Beverly Hills, CA: Sage.

Elareshi, M., and Gunter, B. (2011) News consumption among young Libyan adults: Are new satellite TV news services displacing local TV news? *Journal of African Media Studies*, 4(2), 173–91.

Ganahl, R. (1994) Newspaper readership and credibility: An application of media uses and gratification theory. Unpublished doctoral dissertation. University of Missouri.

Gaziano, C., and McGrath, K. (1986) Measuring the concept of credibility. *Journalism Quarterly*, 63(3), 451–62.

Henningham, J. (1985) Relations between television news gratifications and content preferences. *International Communication Gazette*, 35(3), 197–207.

Horton, D., and Wohl, R. R. (1956) Mass communication and para-social interaction. *Psychiatry*, 19, 215–29.

Jamal, A., and Melkote, S. R. (2008) Viewing and avoidance of the Al-Jazeera satellite television channel in Kuwait: A uses and gratifications perspective. *Asian Journal of Communication,* 18(1), 1–15.

Katz, E., and Foulkes, D. (1963) On the use of the mass media as "escape": clarification of a concept. *Public Opinion Quarterly*, 27, 377–88.

Kearns, B. (1999) *Tabloid Baby*. Nashville, TN: Celebrity Books.

Kerbel, M. R. (2001) *If It Bleeds, It Leads: An Anatomy of Television News*. Boulder, CO: Westview Press.

Levy, M. R. (1978) The audience experience with TV news. *Journalism Monographs*, 55, 1–29.

— (1979) Watching TV news: Para-social interaction. *Journal of Broadcasting*, 23, 69–80.

— (1983) Conceptualising and measuring aspects of audience activity. *Journalism Quarterly*, 60, 109–14.

Levy, M., and Windahl, S. (1984) Audience activity and gratifications: A conceptual clarification and exploration. *Communication Research*, 11, 51–77.

Lin, C. A. (1990) Audience activity and VCR use. In J. Dobrow (ed.), *Social and Cultural Aspects of VCR Use*. Hillsdale, NJ: Lawrence Erlbaum, pp. 75–92.

— (1993) Modelling the gratification-seeking process of television viewing. *Human Communication Research*, 20(2), 224–44.

Marghalani, K., Palmgreen, P. and Boyd, D. A. (1998) The utilization of direct satellite broadcasting (DBS) in Saudi Arabia. *Journal of Broadcasting and Electronic Media*, 42(3), 297–314.

Merdad, A. S. (1993) Foreign television programmes and their sources: An empirical analysis of media usage and perceptions of its effects by young viewers in the kingdom of Saudi Arabia. Unpublished doctoral dissertation. Wayne State University.

Palmgreen, P., Wenner, L. A. and Rayburn, J. D. (1980) Relations between gratifications sought and obtained: A study of television news. *Communication Research*, 7, 161–92.

Perse, E. M. (1990) Media involvement and local news effects. *Journal of Broadcasting and Electronic Media*, 34, 17–36.

Rahman, A. H. (1998) Uses and gratifications of satellite TV in Egypt. *Transnational Broadcasting Journal*, (1). Available at: www.tbsjournal.com/Archive/Fall98/Documents1/Uses.

Rampal, K. R. (2007) Global news and information flow in the internet age. In R. Y. Kamalipour (ed.), *Global Communication* (2nd edn). Belmont, CA: Wadsworth/Thomson Learning, pp. 105–32.

Rasheed, A. (8 April 2001) Khadeegah Ben Qanah: Al-Jazeera embarrassed the Arab satellite channels. *Al-Etihad*.

Rosengren, K. E., Wenner, L. A. and Palmgreen, P. (1985) *Media Gratifications Research: Current Perspectives*. Beverly Hills, CA: Sage.

Rubin, A., and Perse, E. (1987) Audience activity and television news gratifications. *Communication Research*, 14, 246–68.

Rubin, A., Perse, E. and Powell, R. (1985) Loneliness, parasocial interaction, and local television news viewing. *Human Communication Research*, 12, 155–80.

Rubin, A., and Step, M. M. (2000) Impact of motivation: Attraction and parasocial interaction on talk radio listening. *Journal of Broadcasting and Electronic Media*, 44(4), 635–54.

Sakr, N. (2005) Maverick or model? Al-Jazeera's impact on Arab satellite television. In J. K. Chalabi (ed.), *Transational Television Worldwide: Towards a New Media Order.* London: J. B. Tauris, pp. 66–95.

Wright, C. R. (1960) Functional analysis and mass communication. *Public Opinion Quarterly,* 24, 605–20.

Yousef, M. (1999) Kuwait television audiences: Motivation and behaviors. Unpublished doctoral dissertation. University of South Carolina.

8

News Media and Political Socialization of Young People: The Case of Bahrain

Ebrahim Abdulrahman Al-Shaikh and Vincent Campbell

Introduction

The so-called Arab Spring of 2011 saw a number of countries across the Arab world experiencing political turmoil. One of the interesting debates to emerge from these events concerned the extent of the role of media, both online social media such as Facebook and Twitter (Beaumont, 2011), and television news channels, still a relatively new phenomenon in the Arab world (Hasan, 2011). The role of the media in Arab countries has only relatively recently become a subject of academic analysis and scrutiny. What research has been done acknowledges the dearth of empirical evidence supporting claims of significant influence of the media (old and new) on political change in those countries. For instance, one recent collection looking at the role of the media in the Arab world highlights problems with assertions of media influence in the region:

> Bold assessments of a causal link between television content and public opinion would be more convincing if backed by evidence that opinion polls alone are unable to capture – about how diverse groups in Arab countries

really regard such matters as pluralism, legitimacy, political reform and media representations of dissent. (Sakr, 2007: 5)

This acknowledgement of a limited body of research evidence concerning the role of the media in Arab countries, combined with strident assertions about the Arab Spring, demonstrates the need for serious empirical investigation, in particular in terms of the relationship between Arab peoples' usage and attitudes towards media, as well as their political attitudes, in a period of both political and media change.

Bahrain serves as a particularly good focal point for such empirical analysis for a number of reasons. Even prior to the unrest of 2011, it had undergone a period of political and media change for some years, such as the so-called Manāma Spring of 2000–1 (Sakr, 2001), as well as having experienced political unrest since the mid-1990s linked to long-standing problems with sectarianism. Instead of trying to identify strong media effects in isolated incidents or tightly time-bound events like those of the Arab Spring in some countries, in Bahrain it is possible to consider questions about possible media influences on political attitudes and social structures in a more conceptually and empirically grounded manner. In particular, Bahrain offers the opportunity to explore the possible role of the media in *political socialization*, defined broadly as 'the way society transmits its political culture from generation to generation' (Langton, 1969: 4).

Theories of political socialization tend to centre on the importance of social institutions (the family, education, the media, etc.) as having particular influence on people's political attitudes (Rosamund, 2002), so examining the patterns of media usage and political attitudes among young people in a society undergoing political and media change, such as Bahrain, offers the potential for identifying core sites of political socialization possibly contributing to societal change. This chapter explores these issues of the role of media in political socialization through a case study of secondary school students in Bahrain. The study involved comparative empirical analysis of patterns of students' media consumption, as well as their political awareness, attitudes and engagement, in the context of patterns of sectarianism. The chapter begins by providing some background regarding the Bahraini political and media context. It then proceeds to a discussion of theories and models of political socialization, before turning to the empirical work conducted, which is the central focus of the chapter.

Bahrain

Bahrain is a small island state, situated in the Arabian Gulf, near the east coast of the Kingdom of Saudi Arabia. For many centuries Bahrain was subject to claims of control by neighbouring countries, particularly Iran, and also subject to European colonialism, being under British control for much of the twentieth century before achieving independence in 1971. The roots of the sectarian divide in Bahrain, however, stretch back to the historical and on-going Iranian interference (Sick, 1995). After a failed initial attempt at a form of representative government soon after independence from Britain, Bahrain became an Emirate in 1975 (Al-Eid, 2006: 33–6). Since the death of the Emir, in 1999, significant political reform has been introduced, with a popular vote of 98.4 per cent in 2001 supporting a transition from an Emirate to a Kingdom with additional political reforms. In 2002, the first steps on this path were taken when the Emirate became a Kingdom, further steps towards political reform followed in subsequent years – all of which significantly pre-date the Arab Spring.

Despite being, arguably, the poorest in natural resources among the Gulf States (Alqasimi and Albeaini, 1999: 53), by the mid-2000s Bahrain had become the fastest growing economy in the Arab world and, according to the US-based Heritage Foundation, had the most free economy in the Middle East. Bahrain was the first Gulf State to start exporting oil (in 1934) and a further factor in this success has been that the country is also a centre of financial and banking activity in the Arabic Gulf region (Alqasimi and Albeaini, 1999: 53).

As a result of these dominant economic activities, socioculturally, the composition of the population of Bahrain is highly diverse. Out of a population around 1.2 million, according to the official Census of 2010, more than half consists of non-nationals who are mostly transient workers in the major industries of Bahrain, and come from across the Globe. The presence of non-nationals, reflecting a diverse range of ethnic and religious groups, on top of the existing ethnic and religious groups among nationals, means Bahrain has become a multi-religious, multi-confessional and multi-cultural society and one where the nature of economic activity places these diverse groups into regular close contact with one another. Interestingly, one important demographic factor not addressed by the 2010 census, demonstrating its continued political sensitivity in the country, is the distribution of Sunni and Shia in Bahrain. Thus, while Bahrain can be seen as comparatively open politically, economically, and socioculturally, it has found itself in a constant state of flux facing continuous challenges which have made it difficult to merge its two positions: an open society and also a conservative one. It is also, in a sense, a young society in that the young represent the majority of the population.[1] This makes research into young people's socialization particularly relevant in the case of Bahrain.

Media and communication in Bahrain

A distinctive feature of Bahrain is a long-established system of public education, the country being one of the first Gulf States to establish systemic public schooling, beginning in 1919. Education and literacy levels are comparatively high compared to other Arab states (UNESCO, 2005). By 2002, some 97.1 per cent of eligible children were entering primary education (UNESCO, 2005: 312) and 95.6 per cent were entering secondary education (UNESCO, 2005: 337). While overall adult literacy levels stood at around 87.7 per cent (UNESCO, 2005: 280), youth literacy, defined by UNESCO as literacy for people between the ages of 15 and 24, stood at 99.3 per cent as of 2002 (UNESCO, 2005: 281) the highest of all Arab states for which data were available.

In spite of the comparatively high levels of literacy, the newspaper sector in Bahrain has struggled to develop. The first newspaper in Bahrain (*Jahredat Al-Bahrain – The Bahrain Newspaper*) was established in 1939 by Abdullah Al Zayed. However, the efforts of Al Zayed, and others, to create a Bahraini press were regularly thwarted by British colonial rulers who closed down as many as ten newspapers between the 1930s and 1960s, either because they adopted an anti-colonialist view during the Second World War or because they advocated nationalism. Post-independence there was little structural change to the newspaper industry, with print media still largely under the control of the political authorities, and as recently as the beginning of 2002 there were just two Arabic and two English newspapers in circulation. Since the 2002 political reforms, however, there has been a significant expansion of newspapers, with 17 titles at the time of writing (August 2012). These include five dailies and three weeklies, two of which are English language newspapers; ten of these titles are online publications.[2]

The pattern in broadcast media is similar to that of print media. Access to broadcast media in Bahrain is extensive, with 99 per cent of households having access to radio by 1999 (UNESCO, 2005: 289), and some 95 per cent with access to television as of 2002 (UNESCO, 2005). Bahrain was among the first Gulf States to start radio broadcasting in the early 1940s (Al-Eid, 2006: 67; Abu Raad, 2004: 102–4), with the television service begun in 1973 by RTV being the first colour TV broadcast in the Arab world (Al-Eid, 2006: 72). In January 1993 Bahrain Radio and Television became a public corporation and currently the Bahraini Government 'undertakes the control of the media sector', including radio, television and the national news agency (Al-Rumaihi, 2002: 119). Domestic private broadcasting channels are not currently available, but are anticipated in the future, so currently Bahraini broadcasting is government-controlled with a variety of other channels provided by international broadcasters (such as *Al-Jazeera*, *Al-Arabia*, *MBC*, *CNN* and the *BBC*).

The most significant development in Bahrain media to date has been the emergence and expansion of new media, particularly the internet. Some of this is due to governmental activity. For instance, in the 2010

UN e-Government Development Report (United Nations Department of Economic and Social Affairs, 2010), the Bahraini e-Government ranked first in the Middle East, third in Asia and thirteenth worldwide. According to the Bahraini Telecommunications Regulatory Authority[3] by the end of 2010, there were 188,000 internet subscribers, all of whom were broadband subscribers, while this figure had been just 14,956 in 2004. The UN report states that the number of broadband subscribers increased by 19 per cent between 2009 and 2010 and indicates that about 85 per cent of households in Bahrain now had fixed broadband (United Nations Department of Economic and Social Affairs, 2010: 30). The combination of high levels of internet access and literacy has seen a significant growth in the use of social networks among Bahraini citizens particularly with the growth in the use of internet-capable mobile phones. For example, according to the official Facebook website, the number of Bahraini people using this social network had reached 289,680 by August 2011, an increase of 30.9 per cent on the previous year.[4] Mourtada and Salem (2011: 16) reported 61,896 Twitter users in Bahrain between January and March 2011. This positions Bahrain among the top performing Arab countries in terms of Twitter user penetration with a figure of 5.01 per cent (Mourtada and Salem, 2011: 17).

Aside from these international social networks, a number of local discussion forums have proved both immensely popular with Bahraini citizens and highly contentious to the political authorities. The Media Affairs Authority (MAA) blocked a number of forums on the grounds of their alleged role in recruitment and mobilization of opposition to the authorities, their call to violence, vandalism and property damage and their advocacy of hatred. In general, these forums have become the mouthpiece of each sect in Bahrain, and each of these forums has members belonging to same sect; for example, one of the largest and most well-known forums for Sunni people is the Bahrain Portal Forum, and similarly, the Sanabis Cultural Forum is one of the largest and most well-known forums for Shia people, and both have attracted around a 100,000 members at the time of writing.

Other forums have fewer members than these, however, the general structure of the majority of these relates to Shia villages in Bahrain, often using village names as the forum names, and many of these have been among those blocked by the MAA. These membership and participation figures are high compared to the size of the population. The focus of discussions on these forums is predominantly on local political issues, and many contain sectarian hatred and incitement to violence against the other group, whether from Shia to Sunni or from Sunni to Shia. In the protests of 2011, a key difference was how the focus of these already existing disputes became directed towards the entire Bahrain state.

People using new media technologies for political and sectarian activities is not determined by the technologies themselves, however, rather it is a product of a number of contributing factors over time in this particular context. The presence of this kind of highly charged, sectarian material in online social networks involving large proportions of the population in Bahrain, at least in part, may reflect a context in which a young, highly literate population are growing up in a period of political reform, with a relatively limited and government-controlled mainstream media lagging behind in terms of its development and enabling of public discussion and participation. Understanding the relationship between these patterns of media use, political attitudes and the role of sectarianism within that relationship, requires examining these aspects within a clear theoretical and analytical framework relating to the role of the media in political socialization.

Political socialization

A fundamental starting point in thinking about political socialization is the position that 'we do not begin our lives with an in-built sense of political tradition' (Rosamund, 2002: 58). Similar to the view that media technologies do not innately determine how they are used, political attitudes and behaviour are regarded as not innate but acquired over time. Theories of political socialization are thus concerned with 'those development processes through which persons acquire political orientation and patterns of behaviour' (Dennis et al., 1969: 7).

Scholars in this field have argued that 'political socialisation processes operate at both the individual and community levels' (Dawson and Prewitt, 1969: 13). Hence, research has examined the ways in which individuals and communities acquire political awareness, attitudes and behaviour (Hyman, 1959; Hess and Torney, 1967; Langton, 1969; Atkin and Gantz, 1978). Jaros usefully explains that "political socialisation is the study of political *learning*' (1973: 23, emphasis added). So, rather than focusing on short-term political behaviour, as much commentary on the role of new media in the Arab Spring has done, which is problematic in terms of isolating and measuring causal effects, the concerns of the study whose findings are discussed below are on 'the process mediated through various agencies of society, by which an individual learns politically relevant attitudinal disposition and behaviour patterns' (Langton, 1969: 5).

Political socialization researchers have operationally defined the analysis of political learning into a series of areas of investigation, focusing on who learns, what is learned, from whom it is learned, the circumstances in which learning takes place, at what level of awareness learning takes place and the effects of learning (following Greenstein, 1965). This set of questions has become the typical approach for many scholars (e.g. Dennis et al., 1969; Langton, 1969; Greenberg 1970; Jaros, 1973). These questions are addressed through researching individuals and communities in terms of attributes such as levels of political knowledge, interest, participation, involvement, cynicism, efficacy and so on (e.g. Hyman, 1959; Greenstein, 1965; Hess and Torney, 1967; Dennis et al., 1969).

One of the areas of continued debate in political socialization research is the question of when in people's lives political socialization occurs. Essentially, there are two positions within the debate, usefully categorized as the 'primacy' and 'recency' positions (Rosamund, 2002: 66; see also Kavanagh, 1983). The primacy position focuses on 'the centrality of the early years to individual development' (Rosamund, 2002: 67), while the recency position argues that 'political learning is an on-going process related to changing experiences throughout the life cycle' (Rosamund, 2002: 68). These different positions have contributed to the investigation of a variety of potential 'agents of social-ization', 'those individuals, groups or institutions, which are responsible for the transmission of the information through which people acquire their sociali-sation' (Rosamund, 2002: 73). Potential agents of socialization have been considered to include 'the family, peer group, school, adult organisations, and the mass media' (Langton, 1969: 5), as well as social class (e.g. Campbell et al. 1960; Flanigan, 1968) and religion (e.g. Al-Salem, 1981; Dhaher, 1982).

Previous Western studies have suggested that parents and family and the mass media are among the most important sources of information and opin-ions in the development of political knowledge, efficacy, participation and party identification (Hyman, 1959; Dawson and Prewitt, 1969; Greenstein, 1969; Chaffee et al., 1973; Jennings and Neimi, 1974; Conway et al., 1981; Quéniart, 2008). Other authors have argued that school is another important agent of political socialization (Hyman, 1959; Hess and Torney, 1967; Jaros, 1973).

In terms of the media, numerous studies have identified strong correlations between media use, political awareness, interest, knowledge and participa-tion in relation to a variety of media, including television news (Garramone and Atkin, 1986; Chaffee and Kanihan, 1997; Pasek et al., 2006), broadcast news (e.g. Johnson, 1973; Atkin and Gantz, 1978), newspapers (Culbertson and Stempel, 1986; Chaffee and Kanihan, 1997; Pasek et al., 2006) and the internet (Davis and Owen, 1998; LaPlante, 1998; Shah et al., 2001; Weber and Bergman, 2001; Liao, 2003; Johnson and Kaye, 2003; Tolbert and McNeal, 2003; Kenski and Stroud, 2006; Pasek et al., 2006).

Few studies of political socialization have been carried out in the Arab world, indeed the concept of socialization is typically more closely associated with religious, specifically Islamic, socialization than politics (e.g. Suleiman, 1985; Altuwaijri, 2001; Ganem, 2006). Where studies have looked at socialization in the wider sense, the central importance of religion and the family have been identified in Arab societies (Al-Salem, 1977, 1981; Dhaher, 1981, 1982). Some studies have examined political awareness, attitudes, interest and engagement in a variety of Arab countries such as Egypt (Hamada, 1995; Al-Sakran, 2001), Kuwait (Al-Salem and Farah, 1977; Farah, 1979), Morocco (Suleiman, 1985), Tunisia (Tessler and Hawkins, 1979), the UAE (Khaleq and Omran, 1997; Al-Mashat, 1988) and Palestine (Kuroda and Kuroda, 1972; Sayigh, 1977; Farah, 1980). Some older studies, explicitly incorporating Bahrain in their analyses, found evidence of higher levels of political engagement and awareness among Bahrainis compared to those living in other Gulf States as far back as the early 1980s (Al-Salem, 1981; Dhaher, 1981, 1982), while a more recent study found evidence that religion played an important role in Bahraini citizens' socialization (Abu Raad, 2004: 137).

Political socialization in Bahrain: A new study

Political socialization data from the Arab World is patchy and incomplete. In an era of both media and political change in the region the Middle East and North African theatre is a potentially very useful arena in which to investigate the relationship between the media and political socialization. In particular, Bahrain offers an excellent context in which to explore political socialization due to the combination of the country undergoing a period of significant and recent political change, and parallel significant changes in the media landscape with the expansion of print and online media in particular. In addition, with high levels of education and literacy among a population with a large proportion of young people, there are also opportunities for investigating possible inter-relations between the media and political socialization incorporating elements of both primacy and recency schools of thought. Finally the ongoing presence of a sectarian divide, and its articulation through new media such as online social networks, provides a clear intersection between possible agents of socialization in the Bahraini case and renders it ripe for investigation.

The case study described in this chapter aimed to explore the inter-relation between the media and political socialization by focusing specifically on secondary school students in Bahrain. The data presented are from a larger study looking both quantitatively and qualitatively at political socialization among secondary school students and the focus in this chapter is on the key findings and analysis of a quantitative survey exploring students' political activity, media use, and attitudes towards politics and media. Through such data, possible agents of political socialization among secondary school students in Bahrain may be identifiable, offering both potential insights into political and social changes in Bahrain, as well as contributing to wider theoretical and empirical questions about political socialization.

A survey of young Bahrainis

A survey was conducted among Bahraini secondary school students from April to May 2010. According to the 2010 Bahraini Census, Bahrain's population is distributed across five governorates as follows: Capital (26.7%); Central (26.4%); Northern (22.4%); Muharraq (15.3%); and Southern (8.2%). There are 25 secondary schools in total across the governorates, and students attend these schools according to the subject specialisms selected by the students themselves within five subject areas (Scientific, Literary, Industrial, Commercial and Religious).[5]

A purposive sample of students was drawn aiming to ensure an even balance according to subject specialism and gender, and representation across the five governorates. The survey was completed by 1,178 students from 12 schools, divided equally between governorates. The majority of the respondents were aged between 15 and 17 (74%), with around a quarter (26%) aged between 18 and 22 (including students who were either repeating years, or who began their education later), and there was a reasonable gender balance with slightly more female students (53%) in the sample than male students (47%).

The survey followed the structure and content of previous research studies into political socialization (Hyman, 1959; Greenstein, 1965; Dennis et al., 1969; Chaffee and Yang, 1990). It also incorporated elements from previous studies specifically on political socialization and the media, including studies focused on traditional mass media (Atkin and Gantz, 1978; Conway et al., 1981), as well as more recent studies of new media (Ferguson and Perse, 2000; Pew Center 2010).

The survey consisted of a total of 70 questions organized into nine thematic sections focusing on: students' socio-economic and demographic characteristics; their political attitudes and interests; their political knowledge and awareness; their involvement in politics and political affairs; their perceptions of government/politicians' performance and Bahraini political affairs; their use of traditional and new forms of media (television, newspapers and the internet) and perceptions of the news; their sources of news and political knowledge; their perceptions of and attitudes regarding sectarianism and tolerance; and their religious interests and activities.

Political interests, knowledge and involvement

The findings of the survey presented below concentrate on respondents' political interests, knowledge, and involvement, as well as analysing their attitudes and usage of a range of media sources of political information.

In terms of political interest, participants were asked a series of questions about their feelings about politics and their interest in local, regional and international political issues. In general terms, less than a tenth of the sample described themselves as 'very interested' in politics (7%), compared to almost four-fifths (79%) saying they were 'quite interested', with the remainder (15%) declaring themselves to be 'not interested'. Breaking interest down into local, regional and international political issues, there was slightly more interest in regional issues such as Palestine and Iraq (93% saying 'quite' or 'very' interested), than for local issues (90% saying 'quite' or 'very' interested'), with international politics slightly further behind (86% quite/very interested).

The survey also measured students' religious interests through questions looking at, for instance, how often they attend religious locations, and how frequently they watch religious programmes on television. The data showed that over half (56%) of the school students attend religious locations regularly, while over two-thirds (69%) watch religious programmes regularly on television. Pearson correlation analysis was applied to examine any possible relationship between political and religious interest and found a slight positive correlation ($r = 0.23$, $p < 0.001$) in the sample.

To measure the political knowledge of Bahraini school students, 12 questions were asked addressing international (such as names of world leaders), regional (such as names of regional leaders) and local political information (about the Bahrain government and political system). The mean score of correct answers was 39 per cent indicating variable levels of political knowledge among the students. While almost nine-tenths (89%) of the students knew the president of the United States, and four-fifths (79%) the president of Iran, for instance, only just over half (52%) knew the name of their own MP, and only a fifth (21%) knew the name of the Bahraini foreign minister.

In terms of political involvement, the participants were asked a series of questions about their frequency of involvement in a variety of political activities. The results are shown in Table 8.1.

TABLE 8.1 Political involvement

Practices	Frequency of involvement (%)		
	Quite a lot (%)	Only sometimes (%)	Never (%)
Boycott certain products for political, ethical or environmental reasons	23	59	18
Follow what's going on in government and public affairs	13	60	28
Sign petitions	12	54	35
Picket or march	11	41	48
Discuss current political issues with any of your teachers	8	56	36
Take part in demonstrations	8	34	59
Donate money or pay a membership fee to a political party	7	35	58
Urge someone to get in touch with a local councillor or MP	6	40	56
Take an active part in a political campaign	6	35	60
Present your views to a local councillor or MP	4	28	69
Attend political meetings	4	28	69

Note: Due to rounding percentages may not add exactly to 100.

Table 8.1 shows that few political activities were engaged in regularly by Bahraini school-age students. In particular, the majority of these students expressed non-involvement in party political activities (such as attending political meetings or communicating with/talking to MPs), and there was also evidence of a lack of regular activity in terms of demonstrations and marches. Far greater activity was present in terms of monitoring and discussing public affairs, although even here activity was regarded more often as an occasional activity, 'only sometimes' undertaken. Pearson correlation was used to test the relationship between political knowledge and involvement, and there was evidence of a positive correlation between knowledge and involvement ($r = 0.42$, $p < 0.001$) in this sample.

Of particular interest to issues of political socialization, the students were asked what they regarded as important sources of political information. The results are displayed in Table 8.2.

As mentioned earlier, and indicated from previous studies (Dhaher, 1981; Al-Salem, 1981), the evidence here supports the idea that family and religion continue to play important roles as sources of political information in Bahrain but it is striking to see the significance placed on the internet by school students, with almost three quarters regarding it as 'very important'. This is a distinctive finding when compared to Abu Raad's study of university students in Bahrain which placed the state as the leading source (Abu Raad, 2004: 135). That study used a different categorization of sources, not disaggregating media into their respective forms, so a precise comparison is not possible. Nonetheless, the data here suggest that media, especially new media, may have been more important for school students in 2010 than they were for university students in 2004 as sites of political information, and thus potentially for political socialization.

Television was also regarded as very important by just over half of the school students. Hard copy newspapers were perceived as the next most important media source, but both of these media fell some way behind the

TABLE 8.2 Sources of political information

Source	Source importance		
	Very important (%)	Quite important (%)	Not at all important (%)
Internet	72	26	2
Parents	64	34	3
Television	52	45	3
Religious leaders	46	49	5
Brothers and sisters	45	50	5
Friends	39	56	5
Newspapers	32	64	4
School	22	61	18
Radio	20	64	17
Magazines	16	73	12

Note: Due to rounding percentages may not add exactly to 100.

internet as important sources: fewer than half (47.0%) of the respondents reported regularly reading a newspaper, for example.

One possible reason for the differential importance attributed to different types of media may relate to the preferred modes of political involvement and the suitability of, and attitudes towards different types of media among school students. If we look at school students' usage and attitudes towards television more closely, for instance, the complexity of the situation becomes more apparent. Only a small fraction (4%) of the respondents said they never watched television, with three quarters (75%) saying they watched at least two or more hours of television every day. However, the majority of school students' television viewing was not concentrated on political information or news, with almost three quarters (74%) saying they watched entertainment programmes daily or almost every day compared to only just over a quarter saying the same of local news (28%) and international news (27%). Furthermore, a fifth (21%) of respondents said they never watched local news on television, and a little less than a fifth (19%) said they never watched international news on television.

As previous studies (e.g. Musaiger, 2006) have also indicated, this suggests that television for Bahraini school students is predominantly an entertainment medium. Nonetheless, some four-fifths of school students do watch television news at least on occasion, indicating it remains a potentially important source of political information and potential socialization. Indeed, Pearson correlations conducted on the data gathered in this survey indicated a clear positive correlation between television viewing and political interest ($r = 0.460$, $p < 0.01$), and also between television viewing and political involvement ($r = 0.496$, $p < 0.01$).

Looking specifically at the outlets of television news watched by Bahraini school students and their attitudes towards those outlets offers some interesting additional findings. Table 8.3 displays the main channels used for local and international news by respondents.

The three leading individual TV channels for news in Bahrain were the domestically based *Bahrain Television*, watched every day by just over a fifth of school students for local news, and two regional news channels from outside Bahrain, *Al-Jazeera* and *Al-Arabia*, both watched slightly more frequently for international than local news by school students. A wide range of other channels were watched in small proportions by school students as well, though the data suggest that school students tended to individually watch only one or two channels for news, rather than watching lots of different channels.

Respondents were asked about the extent to which they felt that the television channels were consistent with their own views about Bahrain, and the

TABLE 8.3 Television channel viewing for local/international news

Channel	Type of news	Frequency of viewing			
		Daily/ almost every day (%)	Once or twice a week (%)	Once or twice a month (%)	Never (%)
Others*	Local	45	9	12	35
	International	34	9	14	43
Bahrain TV	Local	22	13	26	38
	International	18	11	25	46
Al-Jazeera	Local	21	13	23	44
	International	22	11	22	45
Al-Arabia	Local	18	13	25	44
	International	19	12	24	46

Notes: Due to rounding percentages may not add exactly to 100.
*Incorporating the suite of seven channels provided by the Middle East Broadcasting Centre (MBC), English-language channels like CNN and the BBC, as well as examples of the 40+ Shiite channels based outside Bahrain such as Al-Manar and Al-Aalam, all watched in very small proportions by participants in this survey.

TABLE 8.4 Television channels' consistency with school students' political views

Channel	Level of consistency			
	Very consistent (%)	Quite consistent (%)	Not very consistent (%)	Not at all consistent (%)
Others	26	27	17	30
Al-Jazeera	22	31	21	25
Al-Arabia	21	30	22	27
Bahrain TV	9	29	27	34

Note: Due to rounding percentages may not add exactly to 100.

results are displayed in Table 8.4. The table shows that no channels enjoyed high levels of perceived consistency with school students' political views, indeed, for all channels considered here greater proportions of respondents regarded the channels' views to be not at all consistent with than to be very consistent with their own views.

Interestingly it was the domestic provider, *Bahrain Television*, which was perceived as the least consistent with Bahraini school students' views, although respondents also indicated a high level of trust in *Bahrain Television*, with around four-fifths (79%) saying they trusted the channel. Trust in *Bahrain Television* compared relatively well in terms of the levels of trust in other media measured in this survey. Results indicated that almost nine in ten school students trust Bahrain newspapers (89%), ahead of Bahraini news websites (86%), followed by *Bahrain Television* and then Bahraini discussion forums (79%).

The relative importance given to different media forms (indicated in Table 8.2) then does not appear to be strongly associated with the levels of trust school students place in different media, as traditional media such as newspapers and television are highly trusted outlets, even where, in the case of television at least, they are not perceived as presenting views consistent with those of school students. The perceived importance of the internet as a source of political information (indicated in Table 8.1) may therefore relate to the different potential uses of the internet when compared to traditional media. Table 8.5 examines the school students' internet usage, breaking it down into the different activities students engage in.

Almost two-thirds of school students reportedly used e-mail, almost half reportedly used Facebook and more than a third said they used discussion forums and chat groups on a daily basis. With the exception of using discussion forums or chat groups focused on international political issues, it is activities where students can contribute that were more frequently utilized than, for instance, news and political websites (and, indeed, traditional news media) where there were few, or no, opportunities to interact. From these data, the importance of the internet to Bahraini school students could be found in the opportunity they provided directly to participate in the production and discussion of political information. Pearson correlations indicated positive and statistically significant links between internet usage and political interest ($r = 0.318$, $p < 0.01$), as well as between internet usage and political involvement ($r = 0.486$, $p < 0.01$). Given the rapid growth and controversial nature of internet usage in Bahrain discussed earlier in the chapter, this empirical evidence of the clear importance of the internet for Bahraini school students in terms of political information and activity highlights the potential significance of the internet as a new agent of political socialization in Bahrain.

TABLE 8.5 Internet usage

Activity	Frequency of use			
	Daily/ almost every day (%)	2–4 days a week (%)	Once a week/ less than once a week (%)	Never (%)
E-mail	64	10	14	11
Facebook	46	8	15	30
Discussion forum/chat group (local political issues)	37	13	21	29
Discussion forum (general issues)	35	16	22	26
Chat group (general issues)	35	11	21	33
News website (general)	28	12	29	29
News website (local political issues)	25	14	33	28
News website (international political news)	20	15	35	30
Political website (general)	17	12	35	36
Discussion forum/chat group (international political issues)	19	9	22	49

Note: Due to rounding percentages may not add exactly to 100.

Conclusion

A new survey indicated that Bahraini school students display varying levels of political interest, knowledge and involvement and that these socialization indicators were statistically related to both their social circumstances and media use. Young Bahrainis regarded religion and family as important sources of political information, supporting previous research in general, as well as that from Bahrain and the Arab world more specifically, that these are significant agents of political socialization (e.g. Hyman, 1959; Dhaher, 1981; Abu Raad, 2004). Whereas previous studies in the Arab World had concentrated solely on religion (e.g. Suleiman, 1985; Altuwaijri, 2001; Ganem, 2006), this study found evidence of the significance of the media in Bahraini school students' political activity. As argued in relation to countries outside the Arab World (e.g. Culbertson and Stempel, 1986; Chaffee and Kanihan, 1997), television appeared similarly to occupy an important space in Bahraini school students' political learning. There was evidence too of the emergence of the internet as a very important space for Bahraini school students' political learning, again supporting research from beyond the region (e.g. Pasek et al., 2006).

This research indicated that the rapidly changing media landscape may have consequences for the political development of Arab countries, particularly as their populations grow up exposed to new forms of media content, especially those forms that enable interaction with, and the production of, political information. Whether those consequences are positive or negative is another matter.

In the context of Bahrain, where concerns about the expression of sectarianism through new media and possible negative social consequences of this are currently very pressing, it is interesting to note the responses from this survey regarding views on the current political institutions. Just over three quarters (77%) of the school students surveyed expressed confidence in the Bahrain government, about the same for confidence in the Bahrain parliament (77%) and just over four-fifths (82%) declared confidence in the judiciary. A smaller proportion, but still a significant majority of over three-fifths (62%) of respondents, expressed satisfaction with government performance. Such data indicated that political socialization is a nuanced and complex process, sensitive to local sociopolitical contexts.

Notes

1 According to the estimated population of the Kingdom of Bahrain by Age Group, Nationality and Sex-Census 2010, the number of Bahraini people aged 10–39 years was 293,837 (Central Information Organization, 2010).

2 Official correspondence with the Press and Publication, Information Affairs Authority, Kingdom of Bahrain, 2011.

3 Bahrain e-Government official site: www.bahrain.bh.

4 According to Mourtada and Salem (2011: 10–11), Bahrain Facebook penetration rates are on par with the top ten countries globally.

5 All five areas are open to male students while female students cannot take the Industrial or Religious specialisms.

References

Abu Raad, M. (2004) The role of media in political socialization, a practical study on universities students in Bahrain. Unpublished master's dissertation. Arab League University, Cairo, Egypt.

Al-Eid, A. (2006) *Mass Media Uses and Gratification in the Kingdom of Bahrain.* Kingdom of Bahrain: Ministry of Information.

Al-Mashat, A. (1988) Political socialization in the United Arab Emirates. *Social Association Journal,* 5(19), 215.

Alqasimi, K., and Albeaini, W. (1999) *Bahrain's History, Present and the Future.* Alexandria, Egypt: The Modern University Office.

Al-Rumaihi, E. (2002) The development of mass media in the Kingdom of Bahrain. Unpublished PhD thesis. University of Exeter: Exeter.

Al-Sakran, M. (2001) *Political and (Social) Socialization.* Cairo, Egypt: House of Culture.

Al-Salem, F. (1981) The issue of identity in selected Arab Gulf States. *Journal of South Asian and Middle Eastern Studies,* 4(4), 3–20.

Al-Salem, F. and Farah, E. (1977) Political efficacy, political trust, and the action orientations of university students in Kuwait. *International Journal of Middle East Studies,* 8(3), 317–28.

Altuwaijri, M. A. (2001) *Family and Socialisation in the Society of the Saudi Arabian.* Riyadh: Obeikan Library.

Atkin, C. K., and Gantz, W. (1978) Television news and political socialization. *Public Opinion Quarterly,* 42, 183–94.

Beaumont, P. (25 February 2011) Friends, followers and countrymen: The uprisings in Libya, Tunisia and Egypt have been called "Twitter Revolutions" – but can Social Networking overthrow a Government? *The Guardian,* G2, 4.

Campbell, A., Converse, P., Miller, W. and Stokes, D. (1960) *The American Voter,* unabridged edn. New York: John Wiley and Sons.

Central Information Organization (2010) Population demographic characteristics in the Kingdom of Bahrain: Research study about sectarian characteristics. Unpublished report. Central Information Organization, Bahrain.

Chaffee, S. H., and Kanihan, S. (1997) Learning about politics from the mass media. *Political Communication,* 14, 421–30.

Chaffee, S. H., McLeod, J. and Wackman, D. (1973) Family communication patterns and adolescent political participation. In J. Dennis (ed.), *Socialization to Politics: Selected Readings.* New York: John Wiley and Sons, pp. 349–64.

Chaffee, S. H., and Yang, S. (1990) Communication and political socialization. In O. Ichilov (ed.), *Political Socialization for Democracy.* New York: Columbia University Teachers College Press, pp. 137–58.

Conway, M. M., Wyckoff, M., Feldbaum, E. and Ahern, D. (1981) The news media in children's political socialization. *Public Opinion Quarterly,* (45), 164–78.

Culbertson, H., and Stempel, G. H. (1986) How media use and reliance affect knowledge level. *Communication Research,* 13(4), 579–602.

Davis, R., and Owen, M. (1998) *New Media and American Politics.* Oxford: Oxford University Press.

Dawson, R. E., and Prewitt, K. (1969) *Political Socialization: An Analytic Study.* Boston: Little, Brown and Co.

Dennis, J., Easton, D. and Easton, S. (1969) *Children in the Political System: Origins of Political Legitimacy.* New York: McGraw-Hill.

Dhaher, J. A. (1981) Culture and politics in the Arab Gulf States. *Levant*, 4(5), 187–207.

Farah, T. E. (1979) Inculcating supportive attitudes in an emerging state: The case of Kuwait. *Journal of Asian and Middle Eastern Studies*, 11(4), 56–68.

— (1980) Learning to support the PLO: Political socialization of Palestinian children in Kuwait. *Comparative Political Studies*, 12(4), 470–84.

Farah, T. E., and Kuroda, Y. (1987) *Political Socialization in the Arab States*. Boulder, CO: Lynne Rienner.

Ferguson, D. A., and Perse, E. M. (2000) The World Wide Web as a functional alternative to television. *Journal of Broadcasting and Electronic Media*, 44(2), 155–74.

Flanigan, W. H. (1968) *Political Behaviour of the American Electorate*, 1st edn. Boston: Allyn and Bacon.

Ganem, M. (2006) *Religious Socialization of the Child*. Alexandria: Egyptian Library.

Garramone, M., and Atkin, K. (1986) Mass communication and political socialization: Specifying the effects. *Public Opinion Quarterly*, 50(1), 76–86.

Greenberg, S. E. (1970) *Political Socialization*. New York: Atherton Press.

Greenstein, F. I. (1965) *Children and Politics*. London: Yale University Press.

— (1969) *Children and Politics*, revised edn. London: Yale University Press.

Hamada, B. (1995) Use of the media and political participation. In *Series of Political Research*, Cairo University, Faculty of Economics and Political Science, Cairo, Egypt.

Hasan, M (7 December 2011) Voice of the Arab Spring. *New Statesman*. Available at: www.newstatesman.com/broadcast/2011/12/arab-channel-jazeera-qatar (accessed 8 December 2011).

Hess, R. D., and Torney, J. V. (1967) *The Development of Political Attitudes in Children*. Chicago: Aldine Publishing Company.

Hyman, H. H. (1959) *Political Socialization: A Study in the Psychology of Political Behavior*. New York: The Free Press.

Jaros, D. (1973) *Socialization to Politics*. New York: Praeger Publishers.

Jennings, K., and Neimi, R. (1974) *The Political Character of Adolescence: The Influence of Families and Schools*. Princeton, NJ: Princeton University Press.

Johnson, N. (1973) Television and politicization: A test of competing models. *Journalism Quarterly*, 51, 447–55.

Johnson, T. J., and Kaye, B. K. (2003) Boost or bust for democracy? How the internet influences political attitudes and behaviors. *Harvard International Journal of Press/Politics*, 8(3), 9–34.

Kavanagh, D. (1983) *Political Science and Political Behaviour*. London: Unwin.

Kenski, K., and Stroud, N. (2006) Connections between internet use and political efficacy, knowledge, and participation. *Journal of Broadcasting and Electronic Media*, 50(2), 173–92.

Khaleq, A., and Omran, A. (1997) The political culture of the Emirates University students' studies. *Journal of the Gulf and Arabian Peninsula Studies*, 22(85), 107–39.

Kuroda, Y., and Kuroda, A. K. (1972) Palestinians and world politics: A social-psychological analysis. *Middle East Forum*, (Spring), 45–58.

Langton, K. P. (1969) *Political Socialization*. Oxford: Oxford University Press.

LaPlante, J. (1998) Political learning in adolescence: A survey of political awareness and attitudes of middle school students in the Heartland. Unpublished PhD dissertation. University of Oklahoma, Norman, OK.

Liao, H. (2003) Communication and political socialization the case of kids' voting in Western New York. Unpublished PhD dissertation. State University of New York, New York, NY.

Mourtada, R., and Salem, F. (2011) Civil movements: The impact of Facebook and Twitter. *Arab Social Media Report*, 1(2), 1–30.

Musaiger, A. (2006) *Surveys in the Bahraini Community*. Abu Dhabi: Pen House for Publishing and Distribution.

Pasek, J., Kenski, K., Romer, D. and Jamieson, K. H. (2006) America's youth and community engagement: How use of mass media is related to civic activity and political awareness in 14- to 22-year-olds. *Communication Research*, 33(3), 115–35.

Pew Center (2010) New media, old media: How blogs and social media agendas relate and differ from traditional press. Available at: http://pewresearch.org/pubs/1602/new-media-review-differences-from-traditional-press (accessed 1 April 2012).

Quéniart, A. (2008) The form and meaning of young people's involvement in community and political work. *Youth and Society*, 40(2), 203–23.

Rosamund, B. (2002) Political socialisation. In B. Axford, G. K. Browning, R. Huggins and B. Rosamond (eds), *Politics: An Introduction*, 2nd edn. Routledge: London, pp. 57–81.

Sakr, N. (2001) Reflections on the Manāma Spring: Research questions arising from the promise of political liberalization in Bahrain. *British Journal of Middle Eastern Studies*, 28(2), 229–31.

— (2007) Approaches to exploring media – Politics connections in the Arab world. In N. Sakr (ed.), *Arab Media and Political Renewal: Community, Legitimacy and Public Life*. London: I.B. Tauris, pp. 1–12.

Sayigh, R. (1977) Source of Palestinian nationalism: A study of a Palestinian camp in Lebanon. *Journal of Palestine Studies*, 6(3), 17–40.

Shah, D. R., Kwak, N. and Hilbert, R. (2001) "Connecting" and "Disconnecting" with civic life: Patterns of internet use and the production of social capital. *Political Communication*, 18(1), 141–62.

Sick, G. (1995) Iran: The adolescent revolution. *Journal of International Affairs*, 49(1), 145–66.

Suleiman, W. M. (1985) Socialization to politics in Morocco: Sex and regional factors. *International Journal of Middle East Studies*, 7(3), 313–27.

Tessler, A., and Hawkins, H. (1979) Acculturation, socioeconomic status, and attitude change in Tunisia: Implications for modernization theory. *Journal of Modern African Studies*, 17(3), 473–95.

Tolbert, C. J., and McNeal, S. R. (2003) Unravelling the effects of the internet on political participation? *Political Research Quarterly*, 56(2), 175–85.

UNESCO (2005) *Education for All Global Monitoring Report: Literacy for Life*. Paris: UNESCO.

United Nations Department of Economic and Social Affairs (2010) *E-Government Survey 2010*. New York: United Nations.

Weber, L. M., and Bergman, J. (2001) Who participates and how? A comparison of citizens "Online" and the mass public. Unpublished paper presented at the Annual Meeting of the Western Political Science Association, 15–17 March, Las Vegas, NV.

9

What Is the Future for News in the Arab World?

Roger Dickinson and Barrie Gunter

In this book we have collected together material with the primary aim of supporting a deeper understanding of the contemporary Arab news media than has been possible so far by drawing on recent empirical research conducted by Arab media scholars in several countries in the Arab world. We are, however, acutely aware at the same time that these media are undergoing profound change and are operating in rapidly evolving political and economic contexts. These are bringing forth new practices and organizational arrangements and challenging existing principles of media regulation, practices of news production and habits of news consumption.

In almost every part of the world news is now being produced on shifting terrain. One of the chief characteristics of the contemporary news industry is its constant and rapid evolution and, in some respects, radical reconfiguration. The forces at play here are political, sociocultural, economic and technological and as we write they are acting in different ways on the news industry around the world as it adapts to the forces of globalization, changes in regulatory regimes and changing audiences.

Detailed discussion of the very latest changes in the Arab world, as we pointed out in Chapter 1, lie outside the remit we have set ourselves for the present volume, but the point about the news industry and its changing nature needs to be borne in mind when reflecting on the various contributions we have been able to draw together here. The use of digital technologies linked to the wired and wireless internet appeared to play an important part in the popular uprisings that occurred from late 2010 through to 2012 in enabling dispersed individuals to establish communications networks and build platforms for lobbying and publicity that lay largely outside government control (see Diamond and Plattner, 2012). So far, scholars who have studied these phenomena have debated the centrality of digital media in driving the events of the Arab Spring. Some have argued that blogs, microblogs and social media sites enabled ordinary people to make their views known in an environment where real political debate was restricted by autocratic rulers and that this, together with actions on the ground, combined to topple the incumbent regimes (Meier, 2012). Others (e.g. Howard and Hussain, 2012) go further to argue that digital media were instrumental in bringing about the political and constitutional changes seen during this period.

There is no doubt that the Arab media landscape has evolved rapidly in the first years of the twenty-first century. Not only has the size of the media sector increased significantly, it has changed in its intrinsic nature. By challenging traditional forms of Arab news presentation and adopting formats that resembled those used by major global news operators based in the West, *Al-Jazeera* has been a powerful motor of change since its launch in 1996. Although much of the Arab media industry remains under government control, growing numbers of news services in many countries across the region have been accorded greater operational freedoms, especially with regard to the styles and formats in which news is reported and presented.

The internet has also opened up new channels for the spread of news and for more open political debate that can evade government censorship (Goldsmith and Wu, 2006). This and the spread and growth of the commercial media sector in the region have created an Arab news industry that on the surface resembles, in some countries, those of the more liberal media systems of the West, apparently operating free of government control. Beneath the surface, however, the reality may be quite different, for governments can rapidly create and invoke regulatory frameworks that place legal restrictions on how new media and old media in new formats are permitted to operate (see Lagerkvist, 2010).

It is evident in each of the preceding chapters that technological change has been accompanied by change at a number of social, socio-structural and cultural levels. The adoption of digital technologies by governments and citizens has diversified the Arab news landscape in terms of ownership, sources of provision and the range of content reported. There is clear evidence that second generation web tools such as blogging, microblogging and social media sites are shifting control over the news agenda from a few elite sources of provision to the wider population. An environment has been created to facilitate open political debate (Al-Saqaf, 2012; Howard and Hussain, 2012). At the same time Arab governments have been aware of changing news appetites whetted by exposure to international sources of news supply and have responded in a number of ways. The initial response in the shape of *Al-Jazeera* further fuelled this appetite for news that was not only diverse, but also represented Arab perspectives on issues and events in a way that did not always toe the line of specific governments. As the research and analysis presented in this book have shown, this public appetite for varied and objective news and open political debate can be detected across the Arab region. It would appear that this does not represent a rejection of established religious or spiritual values and codes or an unconditional acceptance of Western-style democracy. Rather it seems to indicate a desire for the sorts of news services that can inform personal judgments about current events and issues in preference to government propaganda.

In this concluding chapter we draw together what has been learned from the analyses provided in the earlier chapters of the book and revisit specific news developments and news consumption patterns that have been surfacing across the Arab world. We describe what we believe are the most important changes that have occurred and examine their degree of consistency in different countries. We close by briefly considering the directions in which the news media in the Arab world might develop in the future.

Overview and summary

The chapter by Al-Jaber and Gunter offers a wide-ranging overview of the media systems of the six Arab states of the Persian Gulf – Bahrain, Kuwait, Oman, Qatar, Saudi Arabia and the United Arab Emirates (UAE) – and shows how, despite their many similarities in terms of religion, language, culture and their economies' common dependence on oil and gas reserves, there are important variations between them that have significant impacts on the nature of their media, the regulatory frameworks in which they operate, and their news output.

By global standards and in comparison to other countries in the Arab world, press history in these countries is generally relatively brief, in some cases (e.g. Oman), extremely so, but their media systems are characterized by a steady expansion of indigenous news outlets, their numbers increasing significantly in the last decade or so. This period has also seen greater freedom for the distribution of foreign newspapers in some countries (e.g. Qatar).

The development of satellite television (TV) and its availability across the Arab world at large has been an important driver of change and Al-Jaber and Gunter note its particular significance in the Gulf. This and other developing media technologies and the multiple platforms they have created for the delivery of news services have been part of a challenge to the dominance of state-financed and controlled news services in the Gulf States. These changes have been joined by calls for the liberalization of media markets and increased consumer choice. The resulting shifts in media policies and regulation have led to signs of a slow, uneven, but gradual relaxation of controls over news and greater freedom of expression across the Gulf region.

The Gulf States dominate satellite television across the Arab world in terms of ownership and control. Although individual states no longer have monopoly ownership over these channels they remain powerful in regulating content in each country. Historically, the centres of journalism and news production have shifted across the region with the changing policies of governments, and Al-Jaber and Gunter note how certain states, notably Bahrain, Kuwait and the UAE, have at different times in their histories represented the more liberal end of the political spectrum in the Gulf with regard to the media. The Emirate of Dubai, for example, is currently unique in the region in allowing in its 'Media City' a free trading zone for privately owned broadcasting organizations.

All the Gulf States own and run their own news agencies and these have traditionally been seen internationally as the mouthpieces of government and Islamic orthodoxy, but there appears to have been a gradual recognition by Gulf governments of the benefits of liberalization. Among these has been the increased potential to use the media to promote national interests regionally and internationally. Opportunities were identified at an early stage to work with private media enterprise in order to reap these benefits, the Qatari government's backing of *Al-Jazeera* being the most obvious example. Other countries in the wider Arab world have attempted to emulate Qatar's success with similar ventures.

Alongside these developments there has been a rise in the provision and popularity of entertainment channels, rapidly making ground on the traditional government information and propaganda channels that characterized broadcast services in the region hitherto. This in turn has supported an increase in the number of available news services, *CNN* and, again, *Al-Jazeera* being the most obvious, but by no means the only examples. *Al-Jazeera* is perhaps the most significant, Al-Jaber and Gunter note, because of the broad range of Arab opinion it promotes via its programmes and because of its influence on professional practice in the production and presentation of news in the Arab world. These authors note the implications for national and regional stability and speculate on the progressive influence of *Al-Jazeera* as a catalyst and support for cultural, political and economic advancement and for opening up the news agenda to encompass a range of topics previously taboo or unacknowledged. *Al-Jazeera* has helped to alter relations between the Arab world and the international community, Al-Jaber and Gunter argue, though these developments have been at times controversial (e.g. the coverage of international conflict) and the positions and perspectives transmitted by the channel sometimes hotly contested regionally and internationally.

While liberalizing tendencies have brought benefits of various sorts, they also present challenges for governments concerned about the erosion of tradition and authority and the potential influence of Western values and culture. Al-Jaber and Gunter conclude that there seems little doubt that the changes in the news media are not only accelerating the pace of social and political change within the region but are also having an impact internationally on the perception of the Arab world.

In their chapter on Iraq, Al-Rawi and Gunter trace developments in Iraq's news media, charting their history from their origins as tools of the monarchy but concentrating on their most recent evolution into plural news services serving diverse markets during the period after the war in 2003. These authors report on some ground-breaking empirical research on the nature of TV news in a rapidly changing context in which political parties, sectarian and emergent political movements struggle to exert their influence.

Under Ba'ath party rule in Iraq there was a history of overt and overarching party political control which bred uniformity across all media – a state of affairs not uncommon across the Arab world. Unusually, however, in Iraq there was a clear policy outlawing any reference to religious factionalism. This began to break down after the Gulf War of 1990 when the Kurdish region of the country in the north saw a rise in the number of media outlets affiliated with political parties promoting Kurdish interests. In the political and administrative chaos following the war of 2003 the Iraqi media as a whole became similarly divided along political, sectarian and ethnic lines. The United States had intended to promote free and independent media by instigating a mixed media economy (government-financed 'public service' radio and TV services alongside privately owned newspapers and broadcast news services) but the steps towards this have been faltering. The challenges posed by low levels of professionalism and lack of training among media personnel coupled with political, religious and ethnic pressures have all arrested the development of Iraq's news media. At the same time, government control over the distribution of and access to foreign news services has continued.

In recent years attempts by members of the news media to call their leaders to account and encourage wider political debate have been harshly suppressed. The tactics of coercion and repression by the Iraqi and Kurdish authorities against journalists, political activists and protestors continue to limit freedom of expression in Iraq. Radio services have been shut down and public protesters are frequently arrested, journalists have been subjected to physical assault and arrests by security forces, and have been kidnapped and murdered. According to the Committee to Protect Journalists (2012), Iraq is now regarded as one of the most dangerous places in the world to report the news. Even experienced journalists who find themselves employed by politically sponsored media find it almost impossible to practice according to traditional journalistic principles and frequently find themselves with little choice but to follow the strict and politically narrow editorial policies of their newspapers and TV stations.

Against this background Al-Rawi and Gunter present the findings of a detailed study of TV coverage of the 2010 Iraqi general election by four of that country's television channels. They show that the TV services were divided clearly along party and sectarian lines in their coverage, and show that there were extreme contrasts in coverage between different channels reflecting these contrasting allegiances. In the main the TV services linked to these movements end up speaking only to themselves and their supporters with the result, Al-Rawi and Gunter suggest, that social, political, religious and ethnic divisions are being gradually deepened. Plurality in the Iraqi television system of a sort has been achieved following the 2003 war, but this is evident only across television channels, not within them. The traditional principles of balance and impartiality in broadcast journalism appear to be absent, despite the commitment to them in Iraq's US-inspired regulatory framework for the media.

In Chapter 4, Nuseibeh and Dickinson describe the long history of Palestinian media and their role in documenting and contributing to the struggle towards the establishment of a Palestinian state. The authors identify seven phases of Palestinian press history reflecting the changing fortunes of the Palestinian people politically and territorially. In every phase of this history, Palestinians have been served by news media that have been tightly regulated and frequently subjected to repressive laws. Freedom of expression has been limited, first by the occupying powers, second by those governments and 'host' countries in whose lands Palestinians were forced to settle, and latterly by occupying forces and those political factions seeking influence over their people and support for their political ambitions. Often, Palestinian news organizations have been forced to relocate to neighbouring countries in order to continue to publish for their Palestinian readership, but over time, though new newspapers and periodicals have frequently come and gone, there has been a burgeoning of titles reflecting the many shades of Palestinian opinion and political affiliation. It is a story that demonstrates how important the news media can be in contributing to a sense of nationhood and shows that, in an increasingly media-saturated world, the availability of media from other countries in a region serves to attenuate the effectiveness of repressive media controls. Here, as elsewhere in the Arab world, satellite TV and the internet have brought contrasting perspectives into play, their reach and scope being harder to keep under control.

However, the current Palestinian division between the Hamas-controlled Gaza and the Fatah-controlled West Bank has divided the press firmly along factional lines. This polarization has led to a narrowing in the scope of news coverage in each case and an increased cautiousness among journalists and editors over which stories to cover and how to cover them. The consequent abandonment of professional standards by some journalists – a result of intimidation as much as personal affiliation in many cases – and increasing self-censorship have diminished the level of public trust in the traditional news media. Their recent performance is seen by some to have helped to deepen the internal divisions between Fatah and Hamas.

Accordingly, the internet and social media have become more important as platforms for independent journalism, but in line with these developments attacks on journalists by Israeli, Fatah and Hamas authorities have increased and several critical news websites and blogs have been blocked, and journalists associated with them threatened and intimidated. The picture here, again as elsewhere in the Arab world, shows that journalists face ever greater threats to their security. To some extent, however, the story of Palestinian news media is one that depicts journalists and journalism as irrepressible forces in the Palestinian struggle.

Mohammed and Gunter offer a historical account of the news media in Egypt in Chapter 5 describing how, throughout its history, the country has cast its media in central roles in the political system as mobilizing forces and as instruments of government. Although in some respects Egypt has led the Arab world in the adoption new media technologies and investment in them – it was first, for example, to establish satellite broadcasting in the region in the 1990s which led to a rapid growth in the number of TV channels available – the Egyptian electronic media are either owned and controlled by the state or by individuals loyal to the ruling party. Though political parties may own newspapers (several indeed owe their existence to newspaper companies) they may not own TV stations. The history of Egypt's printed press is thus key to understanding its contemporary news media and their political role and significance.

Under the Nasser regime following the 1952 revolution several of Egypt's newspapers were closed and a policy to coerce journalists into following the official government line was established. Nationalization of the press in 1960 placed it squarely in the service of the government to unite the mass of the Egyptian population. The political reforms of the Sadat era which saw the return of political parties began to ease the restrictions on media and create the conditions for a more free and independent press, albeit within limits which remained rigid and enforced powerfully enough to stifle significant political development.

The reform slowly continued during the Mubarak era when a more relaxed attitude began to prevail allowing private ownership of newspapers and – within limits – open criticism of the government. One effect of these developments was to contribute to the reform of journalistic practice in Egypt which began to show similarities with the journalism of political partisanship and open debate that had flourished prior to 1952.

During the 1990s more newspaper titles emerged to serve a widening spectrum of political opinion. This more competitive environment led to greater boldness editorially to the point where newspapers could be critical not only of the government but also of the President – a state of affairs almost without historical precedent. However, while comparatively rare, overt controls in the form of enforced closures and the arrest of journalists did take place and several journalists were jailed for their criticisms during the final years of Mubarak's rule.

Perhaps more pervasive, however, were the less direct means of slowing the progress of the independent media. A wide range of measures were employed systematically to disadvantage journalists who worked for them and they practised their trade in a culture of censorship and limited freedom of expression that permeated the whole of Egyptian society. There were also mundane practical restrictions on what journalists could do, limiting access to official sources, for example, and denying them membership of the journalists' union.

As is the case in most other countries of the Arab world, Egypt's electronic media under Mubarak were subject to even greater levels of government control than the printed press. All electronic media services were government-owned, their operations government-supervised and their staff government-appointed. The pattern in Egypt, as elsewhere, was for the tight structures of control over broadcasting established by the colonial powers to be taken over and strengthened by the independent state in order to use the broadcast media as tools of government.

Under Mubarak, the result was a divided news media system – the government press regarded as a 'national' news service whose chief editors were government appointees and an 'opposition' press that took its chances against the weight of a complex of media codes, libel laws and licensing regulations and the occasional intimidation of its journalists. Following the Arab Spring, the situation looks remarkably similar, though, if anything, worsened by the introduction of emergency laws by Egypt's Military Council (SCAF) that provide increased powers of arrest for the publication of open criticism of the SCAF and its officers and the suspension of former freedoms in the interests of state security.

However, it seems likely nevertheless, Mohammed and Gunter suggest, that the forces of liberalization will continue to assert themselves in Egypt, albeit slowly. The increasingly widespread use of the internet and the rise in social media, despite the frequent attempts by the SCAF to disrupt their progress and shut down those websites that provide a platform for dissent and criticism, are adding greater impetus to the forces for change. Mubarak's regime had recognized the dangers of the internet and social media and clamped down hard in the years leading to the uprising, arresting bloggers and shutting down websites. Bloggers, at first regarded as rivals by journalists working for opposition newspapers, became affiliated with them in a coalition of protest and political dissent that utilized the internet's connective power to link to non-media websites representing the human rights movement to attack government corruption and abuse of power and to call for political reform. Instrumental in the Arab Spring and the 25 January uprising, internet activism in Egypt is now widespread.

Mokhtar Elareshi and Julian Matthews's chapter begins with an overview of Libya's changing news landscape. They place their initial discussion in the broader context of change experienced across the global news industry, emphasizing the significance of pan-Arab satellite services in particular. They go on to offer an understanding of the consumption of Libyan news media from a vantage point that makes for an unusually well-grounded analysis, drawing on some original data on the television news viewing preferences of younger news consumers.

Initially satellite TV was the preserve of the Libyan elite but by the end of the 1990s costs of dish and decoder ownership had fallen to levels that made it accessible to ever larger audiences. One result has been to reduce viewing of local, government-run Libyan TV channels. With this picture of technological change and increasing competition in the delivery of TV news services as their backdrop Elareshi and Matthews report on some detailed findings from a study of young adult members of the Libyan TV news audience. Their main concern is with the impact of non-Libyan news sources on this audience, their preferences and their perceptions of quality. Although the research Elareshi and Matthews report on was conducted in 2009 – before the overthrow of the Gadhafi regime – this research focus remains highly relevant not only to the Libyan context but also to the wider Arab world and beyond, for it helps to reveal the precise nature of the challenges facing indigenous news providers: where do the attractions of foreign news services lie for younger adult viewers?

Elareshi and Matthews present some interesting findings on patterns of viewing across this audience, with clustered preferences for certain channels and programme types and differing motivations for viewing. The study shows that young adult Libyan viewers are attracted to pan-Arab TV channels particularly by their high production values, and by perceptions of high journalistic quality, credibility, comprehensiveness, reputation and 'usefulness'. Non-local channels outperform their local counterparts in all these respects. *Al-Jazeera* is a particular favourite, but interestingly, the data show that the knowledge that *Al-Jazeera*'s output is uncensored is not an important indicator of viewing-likelihood for the majority of young Libyans. Nor is it simply the case that local services are rejected as such; the qualities that attract viewers to non-local services also help to explain differences in the levels of appeal found between different local services. These audiences have learned to mistrust the longer-established Libyan news channels but are more positive about a recently introduced satellite-delivered local service whose production and presentation values are perceived to be higher. Additionally, the findings reinforce the important point that the success of satellite services lies partly in their capacity to differentiate between and offer specific outputs (often entire channels) dedicated to different sections of the viewing audience.

As in other parts of the Arab world, satellite TV channels present significant challenges to the Libyan government and its TV services. They compete with it as news providers but, importantly, offer diversity in terms of news values, perspective and commentary. Satellite broadcasting has presented Libya, as it has many other countries in the Arab world, with not only competitive but also ideological and cultural challenges.

Al-Jaber and Gunter in their second contribution to this volume share these authors' concerns with the satellite news audience but take a wider perspective that encompasses the Gulf States. They adopt a similar 'uses and gratifications' approach to the study of audience behaviour and ask a number of questions about changing viewing habits and viewers' perceptions of local and non-local news providers in an attempt to assess the likely impact these will have for local news services. Can the two sorts of news service coexist? Are there parallel or overlapping audiences for local and non-local news channels?

As Elareshi and Matthews show in their discussion of the young Libyan news audience, Al-Jaber and Gunter find that there are different motivations accounting for differences in preference for different news outlets, though they also note the importance attached by viewers across the Gulf to the quality of presentation in news services. Their data reveals a complex pattern of audience preferences and interests that varies markedly between states and between news services. The internet and pan-Arabic satellite services are the dominant sources of non-local news, and pan-Arabic news services are more widely used than local news services. Again *Al-Jazeera* appears to be a highly significant news source. Al-Jaber and Gunter note (cf. Elareshi and Matthews) that the keys to *Al-Jazeera*'s popularity in general are the perceived quality of its journalism and a style of presentation that has high viewer appeal but the more specific reasons for its popularity and other preferences vary from country to country. In Bahrain and Qatar, for example, viewing *Al-Jazeera* is associated with a liking for pan-Arab news services in general and an interest in news about Arab-world politics. In Saudi Arabia, *Al-Jazeera's* popularity is associated with an interest in news coverage of Arab-world conflict and the Israeli–Palestinian conflict in particular. As Al-Jaber and Gunter admit, underlying explanations for these variations in preferences and motivations are hard to come by but it seems highly likely that they are rooted in the nature of the political systems of each country and the part they play in shaping local news services.

In Chapter 8 Al-Shaikh and Campbell examine the role of the media in political socialization in Bahrain, a country that, like its neighbours, has seen continuous political and media change spanning at least a decade. The chapter draws upon data obtained from a survey of students aged 15 to 22 years from across Bahrain and across different sectarian groupings, comparing patterns of media consumption, political awareness and political engagement. Before doing so, these authors provide valuable contextual material on Bahraini history and its media system and a helpful review of the literature on political socialization in general and in the Arab world in particular.

Al-Shaikh and Campbell show that the period since 2002 has seen a late burgeoning of the printed press in Bahrain following political reform and an expansion in broadcast media services which is slowly creating a pluralist media system, with the state for the time being controlling radio and TV, and a rapidly growing appetite among the public for internet and social media services. Indigenous social media platforms such as internet discussion forums are increasingly popular, and are divided along regional sectarian lines. Al-Shaikh and Campbell suggest that these forums have become popular in Bahrain because of the relative lack of space for open and opinionated debate in the traditional media. Debate on internet forums is often centred on criticism of the other sect – whose members and beliefs are seen as threatening – and often entails the promotion of sectarian hatred. On occasion (e.g. when the government is perceived as having acted unfairly to one or another side of the sectarian divide) online debate has also been critical of the authorities and has advocated violent protest. From time to time the authorities have taken action to suspend some forums or have closed them down completely. Interestingly, however, the survey findings show that despite the importance of the internet in the lives of young Bahrainis and their commitment to online debate, they continued to express their confidence in the Bahraini government, its parliament, and its judiciary.

In contrast to findings from previous research on political socialization in the Arab world which has placed the greatest importance on religion as a source of influence, the research findings in this study showed that, despite the continuing importance of religion and the family for young Bahrainis, the media are significant sources of political information for them, that the internet runs ahead of television and newspapers in its importance in this respect, and that there are significant associations between internet usage and an interest and involvement in politics. Here, then, is more clear evidence that the internet has considerable and growing significance in the Arab context.

Conclusion

To a large extent the character of the news media in the Arab world has been shaped by two powerful forces – on one hand a colonial legacy of tight government control (felt to varying degrees across the region depending on the individual histories of their formation as independent states) and on the other specific national circumstances which encourage governments to initially experiment with media freedom before, often in the face of destabilizing internal political and sectarian divisions, reverting to pre-independence controls. The manner in which these are enforced varies widely; they can be crude and repressive or relatively subtle in their reliance on self-censorship, but the tensions between the media and the state are deep-seated and ever-present in every case. There are, however, signs of a generally slow-moving trend towards liberalization of the media across the Arab world. These signs have been apparent for some time and the evidence discussed in the contributions to the present volume suggests that the trend may even be acquiring some momentum.

Some countries – those of the Persian Gulf most notably – can be regarded as at the forefront of the changes. The movement in this direction has been boosted significantly over the past decade or so by the presence of *Al-Jazeera* (launched by the government of Qatar), but a longer term relaxation of the firm grip of government over the media has also been taking place in relation to the printed press across the region.

Al-Jazeera is a powerful symbol of this liberalizing process and its influence across the Arab world and beyond has been profound. It has undoubtedly been influential at an industry level, encouraging the launch in some countries of alternative channels that are modelled upon it. These represent attempts to win back national audiences by offering local news services terrestrially or via satellite with similar production and presentation values and a greater sense of professionalism, albeit with a less open news agenda. One effect of this has been that journalistic norms and practices in national news media services are beginning to be modified. This is an uneven process that clearly depends not only very much on the nature of the regulatory framework in place in a given country but also on the extent to which compliance with such frameworks is enforced. News audiences have responded to these developments by tuning-in to *Al-Jazeera* in increasing numbers but on the present evidence audience viewing preferences between countries vary depending on a) the availability of local news services and their ability to compete with Arabic and non-Arabic news channels, and b) the national/cultural climate, the appetite for non-local TV news varying according to national tastes and prevailing religious norms.

Pan-Arab world satellite TV news services are well-established across the region. *Al-Jazeera* competes for credibility, quality, audience interest and loyalty with Arabic and non-Arabic language services delivered by Western broadcasters (such as *BBC Arabic*, *BBC World News*, the US-government funded *Al-Hurra*, *CNN*, *France 24* and *Euro News*) as well as local services delivered by state-owned TV services. There are variations in the popularity of the many services between Arab countries, but it is unclear whether these variations reflect differing patterns of demand for news services across the Arab world that in turn reflect differing patterns of local news provision or whether local conditions are shaped primarily not by demand but by the nature of each national media system and its regulation. In other words, it is not clear whether *Al-Jazeera* succeeds consistently with the Arabic audience because of the contrast in the quality of its presentational style when compared with local news services, its apparent commitment to a certain standard of journalism, its Arab-world perspective on global news and current affairs, or its credibility as an observer and reporter on local/regional events. Context, as ever, is key: these factors play differently in different countries and are thus responded to in different ways. Some governments, for example, have financed local competition to reclaim local audiences lost to *Al-Jazeera* while others have not. The Saudi-financed *Al-Arabiya* – set up as *Al-Jazeera*'s direct competitor – appears to be seen in some countries as an acceptable balancing source of news that is welcome for following a more conservative moral and cultural outlook but does so with similar production values and local appeal, obviating, perhaps, the need for the creation of a new locally oriented satellite news service designed to compete with *Al-Jazeera*.

Printed newspapers continue to be an important feature of the Arab world's news landscape. In many countries of the Arab world the printed press has a very long and distinguished history and its relationship with governments has by turns been deeply conflicted, occasionally submissive and often oppositional. Typically, Arabic newspapers have been very closely aligned to political parties which are themselves linked with Islamic and other religious factions. This is both a necessity and an advantage in operational terms (e.g. news gathering, relatively stable and easily identifiable readerships) and for long-term survival (being under party-political protection), but it also means that, in comparison with the West, newspapers in the Arab world are sometimes precarious businesses, their fortunes rising and falling dramatically with those of their political affiliates.

The Arab newspaper industry as a whole reflects a degree of pluralism that is hard to find on a similar scale in the region's electronic media. The latter have typically been subject to the tightest regulation and have traditionally been simply extensions of, and the means of exerting, government authority. This of course is one of the reasons for *Al-Jazeera*'s appeal to Arab audiences across the Arab world, representing an alternative and more inclusive editorial stance and offering a wider perspective on regional and world affairs. Where a more plural local electronic media set-up exists (e.g. in post-invasion Iraq), it seems that expectations of an ideal Western-style free marketplace of ideas are unlikely to be fulfilled. Here the factionalism and political division of the printed press is mirrored in the electronic news media but with, perhaps, more profound consequences for the development and sustenance of democracy.

The internet and social media have presented profound difficulties for governments used to policing a tight framework of media regulation (Al-Saqaf, 2012). These platforms are being responded to in different ways across the Arab world but they are generally regarded as threats to stability (following the Arab Spring, perhaps for obvious reasons) and websites – be they commercial news providers, blogs or discussion forums – are often subject to blocking and removal. The indications are that even in those Arab states that can be regarded as more liberal in their approach to the media (e.g. Bahrain), activity on the internet that is regarded as offensive to political or religious sensibilities or incites violence and/or public protest can lead to personal harassment and/or arrest of those identified as perpetrators (e.g. bloggers, website owners) and the temporary closure or summary removal of user services.

Arab authorities are familiar with these tactics of media suppression – they are commonly used across the region to control and limit freedom of expression in the more traditional media. As the evidence offered by several of our contributors shows, whatever the platform, in the Arab world journalism can be regarded as among the most dangerous of occupations. The rise of digital media has created opportunities for disparate factions to organize themselves into more powerful collectives. These marginal groups are often oppressed communities with different cultural, religious and political leanings that cannot individually gain enough leverage to trigger political and social change. Internet tools including microblogging and social media sites have enabled them to communicate rapidly and repeatedly over large geographical distances to create integrated action communities able to orchestrate the scale of support that cannot easily be suppressed by ruling governments.

The widespread perception that the internet and social media platforms played a significant role in the Arab Spring runs alongside a sense of optimism that increasingly free and liberalized Arab news media are soon to arrive. This may be so, but it may also be the case that governments in the region will see these events as all the more reason to tighten their grip on the internet and step up their efforts to control the spread of news and information on these and other news platforms.

Second generation web tools such as Facebook and Twitter can be used equally by large institutions and individual citizens. Ultimately, though, social and political changes occur not because of the existence of digital communication technologies but because the people who populate societies seek them. Networked computers exist within specific social environments that are governed by social values and norms to which internet activists must adhere if they are to be widely accepted (Wilson and Peterson, 2002). Nation-states will decide on how much legislative freedom to give to these communications systems and restrictions will be expressed as laws. Laws however can only work if they correspond with social norms. For these laws to change and for media to be liberalized, the people at large must want to embrace these changes (Hydén, 2006; Hydén and Svensson, 2008).

Without further thorough and detailed empirical research that can deliver the kind of valuable insights offered by the contributors to this volume it is impossible to determine which outcome – greater liberalization or tighter control – is the most likely.

References

Al-Saqaf, W. (2012) Circumventing internet censorship in the Arab world. In L. Diamond and M. F. Plattner (eds), *Liberation Technology: Social Media and the Struggle for Democracy*. Baltimore: Johns Hopkins University Press, pp. 124–38.

Committee to Protect Journalists (2012) *Attacks on the Press in 2011: Iraq.* Available at: http://cpj.org/mideast/iraq/ (accessed 8 August 2012).

Diamond, L., and Plattner, M. F. (eds) (2012) *Liberation Technology: Social Media and the Struggle for Democracy*. Baltimore: Johns Hopkins University Press.

Goldsmith, J., and Wu, T. (2006) *Who Controls the Internet? Illusions of a Borderless World*. Oxford, UK: Oxford University Press.

Howard, P. N., and Hussain, M. M. (2012) Egypt and Tunisia: The role of digital media. In L. Diamond and M. F. Plattner (eds), *Liberation Technology: Social Media and the Struggle for Democracy*. Baltimore: Johns Hopkins University Press, pp. 110–23.

Hydén, H. (2006) Implementation of international conventions as a socio-legal enterprise: Examples from the Convention on the Rights of the Child. In J. Grimheden and R. Ring (eds) *Human Rights Law: From Dissemination to Application, Essays in Honour of Goran Melander.* Leiden: Martinius Nijhoff Publishers, pp. 375–92.

Hydén, H., and Svensson, M. (2008) The concept of norms in sociology of law. *Scandinavian Studies in Law,* 53, 15–32.

Lagerkvist, J. (2010) *After the Internet, Before Democracy.* Bern, Switzerland: Peter Lang.

Meier, P. (2012) Ushahidi as a liberation technology. In L. Diamond and M. F. Plattner (eds), *Liberation Technology: Social Media and the Struggle for Democracy.* Baltimore: Johns Hopkins University Press, pp. 95–109.

Wilson, S. M., and Peterson, L. C. (2002) The anthropology of online communities. *Annual Review of Anthropology,* 31, 449–67.

Index

Voice Radio 60
Vyas, R. S. 109

Wadi an-Neel, (Nile Valley) (Egypt) 85
WAFA 71
Walker, D. C. 34
Wall Street Journal 78
Wanta, W. 113, 130n. 14
The Washington Post 27
Weber, L. M. 159
Wicks, R. H. 34
Williams, D. 44
Wilson, S. M. 187
Windahl, S. 137, 140
Wohl, R. R. 138

women journalists 9
Wright, C. R. 136
Wright, L. 9
Wu, T. 174

Yang, S. 161
Yelsma, P. 115
Yousef, M. 138

Zalaf, M. A. 69, 80n. 2
Zamili, A. 46
Zanoun, A. 76
Zayani, M. 9, 11, 35, 36, 37, 38, 84, 110, 112, 113
Zuhoor Palace Radio 42